CW01424443

The Life of R.F. MacKenzie

A Prophet Without Honour

To Margaret, my wife

who encouraged me and
kept me going when the
going got tough

The Life of R.F. MacKenzie

A Prophet Without Honour

Peter A. Murphy

Foreword by Harry Reid

JOHN DONALD PUBLISHERS LTD
EDINBURGH

John Donald Publishers Limited,
73 Logie Green Road, Edinburgh, EH7 4HE.

ISBN 0 85976 506 7

British Library Cataloguing in Publication Data.

A catalogue record for this book is available
from the British Library.

Typesetting & origination by Brinnoven, Livingston.
Printed & bound in Great Britain by Bookcraft Ltd, Midsomer Norton.

Foreword

by Harry Reid

Much has been written about R.F. MacKenzie, most of it by journalists and educationists. In 1996 the distinguished historian Dr James Young chose MacKenzie as one of his radical heroes in his splendidly-titled study *The Very Bastards of Creation*. But until now there has not been a book wholly devoted to MacKenzie, an enigmatic but genuinely great Scotsman. I am delighted to welcome Peter Murphy's fine book, which fills a very obvious gap.

This book is not an orthodox biography. A great deal of it is about Scottish education, or at least how Scottish education was administered in the 1960s and 1970s. A sense of lost opportunity, approaching almost tragic proportions, pervades the book. An allegedly democratic and pragmatic and humanitarian education system simply spat MacKenzie out. Of course the man was difficult, cussed, and at times arrogant. But he had vision, he had compassion in abundance, he had courage, and he had a wonderful, zealous, engaging radicalism that was at times angry, but never truculent. Surely this extraordinary man, with his extraordinary gifts, should have been employed to better effect? Instead he was discarded, amid bitterness and recrimination.

At the heart of Murphy's book is a depressing catalogue of bureaucratic failures of nerve. We have here a detailed account of an administrative exclusion of vision. Because of this - correct - emphasis what we have is not, as I say, a biography in the normal sense. Certainly Murphy conveys much of MacKenzie's charisma, and as a biographer he has no false modesty: he is prepared to quote at considerable length from MacKenzie's own writing.

Indeed, MacKenzie will almost certainly be remembered as a prophet rather than a headteacher or an educationist. His books will live on. His masterpiece, *A Search for Scotland*, was, funnily enough, the book least concerned with education, although there is plenty of vintage R.F. on schools and schooling in it. Overall, it amounts to a devastating critique of modern Scotland, beautifully written, a warm and pungent personal analysis of where we have gone wrong.

Now, at a time when Scotland at last appears to be on the brink of a new, more hopeful, era, it would have been marvellous to have that soft but strong Aberdeenshire voice around, cajoling us, raising our eyes high to the sky, and teaching, always teaching us to reject the mendacious and the meretricious, to discard the conventional, to reject the divisive, and - above all - to be kind, and to think well and think big.

Harry Reid

Acknowledgements

This book would not have come about without the generous and unstinting co-operation of the MacKenzie family, particularly Mrs Diana MacKenzie, who gave me fulI access to R.F. MacKenzie's unpublished papers and manuscripts. I am also grateful to the late David Robertson, former Director of Education for Tayside and to John Nisbet, Emeritus Professor of Education at Aberdeen University, for the initial encouragement they gave me to go ahead – and, of course, the many people whom I interviewed while researching this book, both former staff of Braehead School and Summerhill Academy and former pupils of these schools. Finally, I would like to thank David Hartley and Angela Roger of the University of Dundee for their crucial support of the project in its later stages, and also The Carnegie Trust for the Universities in Scotland whose generous grant made certain the eventual publication of the work.

P.A.M.

Contents

In Rannoch I have seen the vision of Isaiah explode into reality. The mountains and the hills broke forth before them singing and all the trees of the fields clapped their hands...We began to get glimpses of how a Scottish cultural revolution might be set in motion. It would begin in country places.

– *A Search for Scotland*

CHAPTER ONE

Prologue

It was 1974. I was a Headteacher in Dundee. I had been thrown in at the deep end two-and-a-half years earlier to take over Logie School, a tough, four-year Secondary in the Blackness area of Dundee, after spending my formative years as a teacher of English at various Aberdeen schools.

I had been appointed Principal Teacher of English at Summerhill Academy in Aberdeen in 1966 after spells at Torry Junior Secondary and Aberdeen Grammar School. Five years later (in 1971) after abortive attempts to earn a bit more money to support a growing family by applying for the job of Lecturer in English at Moray House College in Edinburgh and the post of Director of Education for Orkney, I was, much to my own surprise (being still only a Principal Teacher) picked by the Education Staffing Committee of Dundee Town Council to be the new Headteacher of Logie School.

Logie School in the 1970s might just as well have been Logie School in the 1930s (it was founded in 1929) as it turned out to be a school caught in a time-warp. The regime that controlled the school was totally and unashamedly repressive and reactionary. The pupils were, to all intents and purposes, under complete subjugation. During the course of each day they were drilled and exercised like soldiers on a parade-ground before they were allowed into the school. The whole procedure was indeed known as 'Playground Parade'. The staffroom notice-board bore the following instructions as to how such a 'Parade' should be conducted:

Teachers to be in Playground	— 5 minutes by school clock ahead of time in the morning
	— All Intervals
East Duty Special	— Superintendent Milk Parade
	— Visit Lavatories regularly
	— Visit Dust-Bin Area
West Duty Special	— Control Glenagnes Playground and Shrubbery approaches

Parade Procedure	—	First whistle about 3 minutes in advance...not continuous whistling. The Monitor or first pupils in position falls in as marker. Others join ranks only from the left, placing right hand on left shoulder to take distance and dropping hand. Check by position of boy in front (West). Stand at ease without being told.

Attention! 'Right Turn!'
Silence during bell ringing.
'First Classes!' Forward March!'

They were marched to and fro along the corridors of the building which resembled a prison in its austere, institutional appearance; indeed, the building was openly referred to by its inmates as the 'pen' or the 'penitentiary', although in the post-war era it was occasionally called 'Colditz' as an alternative!

The teaching staff were in total control. Gowns were worn as a symbol of authority and academic superiority by the senior teachers. The belt or tawse was used indiscriminately to reinforce order and discipline, and physical abuse of pupils in 'confrontational situations' was not unknown. The less-able pupils, about 100 at least, were taught on a different site, approximately a mile away, in a building called 'Logie Annexe', not just on the principle that streaming of pupils was desirable, but on the assumption that the more troublesome and recalcitrant were inevitably also those who were the most backward and it suited the school establishment to have a 'divide and rule' policy to educate them in a separate building.

Playgrounds and classes were strictly segregated and there were also separate staffrooms for male and female teacher teachers. All classes were streamed according to ability and only the favoured few who aspired to doing 'O'-grades could look to continue their education beyond the age of 15 or 16 at the neighbouring Senior Secondary school in the West End of Dundee, Harris Academy.

At Assembly in the morning the pupils were marched in and made to stand to attention whilst the Headteacher addressed them from the platform and quite commonly a few youngsters would faint in the ranks as the lack of proper breakfast and the strain of standing to attention took their toll.

Looking back at this scenario over 20 years later, I cannot claim to have done all that I should have done to change this appalling state of affairs. As it was, the staff were very suspicious of me when I first arrived in 1974 – a totally unknown quantity, coming as I did from a school in Aberdeen whose Headteacher, R.F. MacKenzie, was a well-known radical and had no time for corporal punishment or exams. Besides, did the new man not boast an Irish name and therefore more than likely to be a Catholic (which I was not) and perhaps it was part of a wider conspiracy by the local Labour-led Council to amalgamate a Protestant Junior Secondary with one of the nearby Catholic Junior Secondaries to make way for Comprehensive schooling under the pretext of reorganisation!

By 1974, in the two-and-a-half years I had been at Logie, I had indeed brought change to the school. The old-fashioned timetable, the original of which was jealously guarded and kept locked in a special drawer in the Headmaster's room, which, among other things, did not allow for girls to study for 'O'-grade Maths (as Maths was not considered to be a 'female' subject) was replaced by an updated version that allowed for differentiation and a degree of pupil-choice where none had existed before.

The school building that had been largely neglected structurally and starved of new equipment and resources over many years was given a boost through the setting up of a Parent Teacher Association that campaigned successfully for building improvements. The curriculum was expanded to involve leisure and recreational activities and strong links were established with the countryside and the hills through the purchasing of a mini-bus and renting a cottage in Glen Isla for promoting outdoor education.

Ironically, all the changes that I had struggled to put into place (often against stiff opposition) in the hope that Logie might one day become an all-through Comprehensive school in its own right were largely in vain as the Education Authority in its wisdom decided late in 1972 (just a year after I had been appointed) to phase out Logie over the next four years as a separate school and, instead, to make it an annexe of Harris Academy that would largely replace it as the main Comprehensive school for the West End of Dundee. So it was a strange experience for me in 1976 that I should have to supervise, at one and the same time, the closing of a Secondary school at one end of the town and open a new one, Whitfield High School, at the other end, to which I had been appointed as Rector Designate in 1975, a school which had been newly built to serve the needs of a huge housing estate of 15,000 people.

Meanwhile, since the time I had left Summerhill in 1971, things had gone from bad to worse for Bob MacKenzie. I had been aware of the problems he was facing and had kept in touch with him during these intervening years, but the news of his suspension from duty in April 1974 still came as a shock. It certainly made the headlines in the local press, which in Aberdeen, in particular, did him no favours in the way it had so enthusiastically documented his troubles and by its predictably parochial attitude to education generally.

However, I do not suppose that MacKenzie's downfall made any great impact on the world at large in a 1974 climate dominated by such events as the Watergate Affair in America, Dr Barnard's first successful heart transplant operation in South Africa and, in the narrower confines of the UK, the disappearance of Lord Lucan, the sacking of Sir Alf Ramsey as England's Football Team Manager and four-star petrol rising to an astounding 50p per gallon.

But, in Scotland, among much of the educational establishment, there was a feeling of ill-concealed glee at MacKenzie's downfall. R.F. had got what he deserved! After all, the repressive regime characterised in such schools as Logie did not happen by chance. Although it may have been an extreme example of the genre, Logie School, as it was in the early 1970s, was no accident. It came about, as all such regimes come about, because of a strongly repressive and reactionary element in Scottish education and the Scottish psyche – a hardness and harshness bred of our Calvinist past with young people seen as innately evil and rebellious and in need of constant chastisement and physical correction. These characteristics manifested themselves in Scottish schools and took the form among teachers of an arrogant superiority that could be reinforced, as required, by recourse to corporal punishment and verbal haranguing and chastisement.

I felt at the time of his suspension a sense of dismay, but I also knew it was on the cards, given the way that such things develop; the whole affair had the inevitability of a tragedy played out in the somewhat incongrously douce surroundings of Aberdeen, a place not known in those far-off days for drama of this kind. I tried to put into words the sort of sentiments MacKenzie's sacking would arouse among the good folk in the town and the following verse-letter appeared in *The Times Educational Supplement* (Scottish Edition) in May 1974 under my name.

An Aberdonian's Farewell to R.F. MacKenzie (1974)

Whit's that? They've gi'en him the sack?
Nae afore time! Gi'es mair o'yer crack!
Nae man deserved better tae get the shuv...
Gangin' aboot sayin' skweels are places for luv!
Whit next? A' they young anes need nooadays

Is a gweed skelp...nane o' yer sympathy an' praise,
An' sic like trash. A'body kens whit skweels are for
Ye're there tae learn an' dae whit ye're telt,
Nane o' this speakin' back...that deserves the belt!
Teachers hae enough tae dae in the classroom.
Withoot fowk haverin' oan aboot the impendin' doom
O' Scottish education near deid frae a glut o' exams.
Whaur wid oor lads o' pairts, oor Jeanies an' Tams
Be, withoot their 'O'-grades an' Highers as weel?
Na, na, oor kids dinna want a holiday camp, they want a skweel.
Ach weel, maybe things 'll quieten doon noo in the Lang Stracht*
Noo that mannie wi' the daft notions been sacked!

Inevitably, when you think back, as I do now, in the late 1990s on the events of over 20 years ago, you are struck by the strength of passion and bitterness that surrounded the final years of MacKenzie's career at Summerhill. For there is no doubt that he was not the kind of man that people could feel unaffected by. As Elizabeth Garrett, his Depute Head during his last years at Summerhill, said, 'R.F. stirs deep feelings in the people who know him well: they love him, are empowered by him or they loathe him for the way he upsets their certainties and questions their truths; few are unaffected by him.'

Writing about R.F. MacKenzie in the late 1990s, one realises, painfully, after the capture of the education system by the Right, how different the system now is compared with 1974. A man like MacKenzie would never have stood any chance whatsoever under the present regime (in Scotland or in England) of becoming a Headteacher in the State system. He would have been unlikely to have got further than the rank of Principal Teacher. He would not have been able to come to terms with the vastly increased administrative chores and the esoteric mumbo-jumbo of 'buzz words' associated with the duties of upper management in schools nowadays. He would not have had any understanding of, nor would he have had any truck with, the cult of consumerism and customer-care that has developed like a cancer in recent years, linked to a crude obsession with accountability and 'value for money' that reduces schools to arid competition with each other for survival as business enterprises measured for their success by results that appear annually in Exam League Tables. Headteachers in such a system have had their individualism stifled in the frantic need to conform and assume more and more the mantle of chief executives running the schools via a computer screen and endless reams of computer print-outs.

Education in the 1980s and 90s has increasingly become more a

*where Summerhill was situated.

commodity than a right. Parents, more easily than before, have been able to 'buy' their way into living in the areas where the so-called 'best' schools are. Until recently* they have been able to exploit the Assisted Places scheme to send their children to Grant-Aided schools such as Dundee High in Dundee or Robert Gordon's in Aberdeen to acquire what is perceived to be a superior form of education that has served only to sharpen and perpetuate the present divisions in our already divided society by creaming off the children of comparatively well-off people into academic hothouses that smooth the way for such children to join the ranks of the élite. Meanwhile, the remainder of the school population has had to make do with the Comprehensive system that was put in place in the late 1960s and which has struggled in vain to put into practice the ideals that people like MacKenzie stood for – schools where all children from whatever background could mingle together and where the overriding principle that governed them would be (in the words of MacKenzie) 'to have an equal concern for every pupil'.

Things have gone from bad to worse in education, if one views the changes that have taken place in education in the way that MacKenzie would have done over the past 20 years. Whereas MacKenzie would have railed against the two-tier system that existed in his day which meant that three-quarters of our pupils went to Junior Secondaries and one-quarter to Senior Secondaries on the 'say-so' of the 11-Plus exam, a situation that led in the late 60s to the implementation of Comprehensive education, what has happened since in education has not fundamentally addressed the malaise which MacKenzie saw at the heart of Scottish education. Although he lived long enough to witness the removal of corporal punishment from the schools, he would still claim that the system we now have is more than ever thirled to the dictates of Central Government or, indeed, the Establishment epitomised by the Scottish Office in Edinburgh,

Now, more than ever, we have as parents and as teachers and as people living in Scotland at the end of the 20th century to look at what we are educating our young people for. The questions that MacKenzie in his books and during his lifetime asked about the way we educate our young people are as relevant now as they ever were. He encapsulates in his life and writings the humaner aspects of Scottish education and culture that have their most eloquent expression in the Advisory Report on Scottish Education in 1947 written largely by that other great Scottish educational

*The new Labour Government signalled its intention to end Assisted Places when it came to power in May 1997.

figure, Sir James J. Robertson, whose distinctive voice (which I still remember as a pupil of his at Aberdeen Grammar School some 50 years ago) can be heard in all its wisdom and compassion in this brief but memorable passage from one of the key sections of the Report:

> The urgent problem is to evolve a new type of schooling that will suit the many as well as the old fitted the few. In the light of these considerations it is evident how outmoded is any conception of secondary education as a luxury or a privilege, a social stamp or an aid to careerism. On the contrary, Secondary education emerges as one of society's most significant functions. and from the side of the individual, it is at once a right and a necessity. When this is recognised, the demand for equality of educational opportunity ceases to sound like the voice of envy; rather does it express the determination of an awakened community that no smallest part of its previous store of talent must be lost.

MacKenzie also personifies the Scottish tradition of dissenting from the norm because of a deep inner conviction and a need to serve others. In this sense, MacKenzie was a true advocate of the A.S. Neill school of thought in putting the child at the centre of the educational system and not the dictates of a curriculum conceived in terms of exam results only.

The other, most compelling reason why we should re-assess the place of MacKenzie in Scottish culture and his contribution to it is that he brought to our educational thinking and to our lives as people living in Scotland in the latter years of the 20th century a sense of vision associated only with those very few who have the gift of prophecy; indeed, when MacKenzie was suspended, the Education Convener, Roy Pirie, confessed to being astounded that when MacKenzie was given the chance to defend himself in public against the charges of incompetence being levelled against him, he did not answer in direct terms at all. In the words of Pirie, 'The man is at the most critical point in his career – yet he speaks in parables!'

In his preface to the book *The Unbowed Head* in which MacKenzie wrote about the events at Summerhill between 1968 and 1974, Harry Reid, who at that time was Education Correspondent of *The Scotsman* and is now Editor of the *Herald*, enlarged on Pirie's remarks:

> The term 'parables' had unavoidable Biblical connotations...it is pleasant to recall how that night [Reid was interviewing MacKenzie just after his suspension] I gradually realised for the first time in my life I was in the presence of someone of genuine vision: a prophet.

In the pages that follow in this book which tells the story of MacKenzie's life, Reid's conclusion that R.F. MacKenzie had the vision of a prophet 'explodes into reality'.

CHAPTER TWO

The World of Wartle Station

Throughout his life R.F. MacKenzie never lost the gentle lilt of the speech rhythms of his native Aberdeenshire. The distinctive cadence of these speech rhythms imparts a special 'flavour' to his writing, as he recalls his early days being brought up and cared for in the close-knit community of the Garioch where, on 27 April 1910, he was born into the family of Robert and Catherine MacKenzie at a little place called Lethenty where his father was stationmaster. Soon after, the family moved to a bigger station a few miles away at Wartle which was where the young Robert grew up.

> From the age of four to sixteen I delivered telegrams to an area within three and a half miles of Wartle station and knew every person and house and road and farm track and dog. Sometimes I got a jam piece or a sweetie or a drink of reamy milk. It was a friendly community, not censorious. The sociable postman was sometimes offered so many drams that he lay down at the road-side he news got to my father who was sub-postmaster and he cycled to the post-office and helped him home. Nobody complained...On a winter evening I remember a farm kitchen where I delivered a telegram. There was a good fire and the farmer and his family sat around in comfort, mending harness, knitting, reading the morning newspaper. It was a warm, benevolent scene. There was the same relaxed business at a midsummer noon where farm-workers sprawled at their ease round the foot of a straw rick and joked. Once a farm-worker said, 'Could I get that bicycle of yours to hang on my watch-chain?' A hand-written notice on a tree said that on a certain evening local people would gather at a local croft to hoe turnips of a crofter whose leg had been broken by the kick of his horse. The notice was headed 'Love Darg'; it means a task undertaken without payment. It was a sociable, amiable, self-contained world.

According to his younger sister, Alice, the MacKenzie home was strict and God-fearing, but no more than typically so. Alice sees her brother in her father, 'Big-hearted, slow to criticise. always reasoning why, and not interested in money' The mother did all the worrying about money, handling the family finances with housekeeping genius.

On his father's side the MacKenzie family had strong links with Speyside, the area in the North-East of Scotland associated with the rough, hilly country to the east of the Cairngorm Plateau, famed for its fast-flowing rivers and its whisky distilleries. MacKenzie, in later life, often expressed a hankering to have ended up as a Headteacher of a small, rural school in this area, but that never came about. He felt a strong kinship with the lives of those who, like himself, bore a clan name and had to contend with the harsh realities of ekeing a living out of the unproductive soils and bracing climate in the crofting areas of the Highlands. His mother's family, on the other hand, were fisher folk who lived in the villages strung out along the Buchan coast. These were close-knit communities whose lifestyle was strongly influenced by the strictures of the religious cult known as the Closed Brethren which demanded adherence to a narrow set of rules governing the way they lived their lives MacKenzie's mother, although brought up in such a community and playing the piano at their services, nevertheless eventually escaped the suffocating atmosphere surrounding such communities. In his memoir of this period in his family history, Mackenzie re-enacts the circumstances of that escape.

> It was a hard life digging for sand-eels, shelling mussels, putting out to sea in a small boat to earn enough to keep a large family from becoming hungry. When my mother left the school,, she got a job sewing at a tailor's in Port Errol and when she got home at night she had her supper and sat for hours sewing for the family, and for neighbours. Often she told me, 'I sat and sewed and sometimes looked out over the grey sea and thought is this all that I'll do all my life, just sew and look out over the grey sea?
>
> Later, to escape from this monotony of sea, sky and sewing, she got a job in Aberdeen, and then in London as a lady's maid and travelled abroad. Her father, whom she loved, said, 'Katie, there'll always be plenty for you here', seeking like a parent to hold on to his children. But she left the village and travelled as a lady's maid in France, Switzerland and Italy. This adventurous spirit later brought rewards to us, her family. Our Aberdeenshire village horizons were widened when we listened to tales of Bordighera and the boatmen on the Italian lakes.

The Mackenzie's house was a modest one, rented free from the Railway Company – a kitchen, a bedroom, and a room that was used for special occasions. When his parents felt that one bedroom was insufficient for five people – his parents; and three children (MacKenzie had two sisters, Catherine born in 1913 and Alice in 1917) – the Railway Company refused to add a bedroom unless his father paid an extra rent of ten per cent, which, in fact he eventually did. MacKenzie recalls:

> The house was damp and the wallpaper peeled off the bedroom. In some airts of the wind the kitchen chimney wouldn't draw and the reek was blown back into the kitchen, suffocating billows that dimmed the light of the paraffin lamp and covered the shining-white, newly-ironed clothes with a myriad of black smuts and my mother wept tears of frustration.

MacKenzie dwells on the image of his mother as a perfectionist, 'playing the piano or mandoline, singing, embroidery, fine needlework, cooking, drawing – her laundering bore the same mark of excellence.'

His father, however, had a more direct influence on him in the way he developed intellectually. His father was in the tradition among those from a working-class background who were filled with the spirit of enquiry who saw 'the Reformed Religion and a Reformed Politics as indivisible and alike accessible to the questioning of those who were making an independent search for a way of life and an attitude to the universe.' His father studied the Scriptures diligently and attended a local Prayer Meeting where they studied biblical texts. They developed a sort of scholarly insistence on getting biblical quotations meticulously right and there was also a determination not to accept the word of any human authority, but to enquire about the nature of things and find out for oneself. MacKenzie recalls the insistence his father had for finding the truth about something on its merits:

> One spring morning my father digging in the garden as I returned from University, stopped to ask me what I thought of something or other. I started to say 'Professor so and so thinks'...when he interrupted me. I still remember his hand moving in a slight gesture of impatience, 'Never, mind what that Professor thinks. What do you think? An incident like that put me into the way of asking questions...a casual exchange of views between the garden gate and the supper table in the kitchen– and its enduring memory.'

Another potent influence in MacKenzie's early thinking was an unnamed railway clerk who was brought up on a small farm at Kirkton of Rayne and had left school at the age of 14 to begin work on the railways. At the age of 17 he had suddenly woken up, having had in his own words 'been asleep for the preceding part of life. 'He read widely about history, politics, religion, philosophy and literature, submitting everything to a rigorously independent judgment. At Inveramsay, the junction where a branch line to Macduff left the main Aberdeen–Inverness line, he and a shunter shared a two-roomed shack which they called Utopia. One-half of it was partitioned off for sleeping. In the other half there were two chairs, a table, scores of books and a paraffin stove 'that went glug-glug as occasionally we sat into the night discussing everything in heaven and earth.'

It was this clerk that introduced MacKenzie to H.G. Wells's *Outline of History* which had a profound effect on MacKenzie's attitude to everything around him and further convinced him that the received wisdom of the schools and universities should be questioned.

> Wells astounded me by telling me that, half-way through, the book had only got as far as the decline of the Roman Empire. Scottish school education

> had not focused on the perspective of time. History before 55 BC was a gloom, like a November night and we weren't encouraged to peer into it. There were disconnected constellations in the night sky, the Pharaohs, the Hebrew prophets, the Greeks, the Romans, but they were out there free-floating, inaccessible...Wells, another disrespectful amateur, came and integrated all that and put it into focus. It was as if he gave us a map to tell us where we are and where we might want to go from here. I was amazed, and then delighted at the chapters on Caesar and Napoleon. Wells was saying, 'I'm a man. They were not more. Let's have a look at them.' These were words of emancipation. They were keys that fitted the locks with which any school and university education had enclosed me in a prison of ideas...Wells said about his own early days that he felt that Oliver Goldsmith held his hand. I felt the same indebtedness to Wells.

MacKenzie's sensitivity to the landscapes against which he lived his early life comes out strongly in his writing. He recalls. for instance, the days he spent at Whinnyfold on the Buchan coast where his mother's folk came from, going out to sea as a boy with his great uncle:

> My great uncle put up the single cinnamon-coloured sail and made for the open sea. The line of houses on the brae face receded until the land was only part of the framework of a picture. Then he took down the sail and threw out our baited line and waited. The mast like a pointer traced out a magnified record of our movements in the boat and the water slapped its sides like a playful whale. Far out a coaster moved south, leaving a thinning line of smoke, or an Aberdeen trawler bound for the fishing grounds...the clouds massed and disintegrated and reformed. The sun broke through and sparkled on the face of the water...But even ashore, life at Whinnyfold was richly different from life in rural Aberdeenshire. Tar and pieces of cork and basket lay here and there on the shore. The flotsam of the high-water line was cork and planks, an occasional fish-box washed off a trawler...a shallow cave undercut the rock, and the sound of our boots on the round stones and the clanking of the stones against one another produced low reverberations; a low moaning sound came intermittently from a horn, fixed on a reef not far off-shore which was covered over at high tide. It was strangely in tune with the gull's cries and the subdued roar of the sea and the sound of the returning wave roaring through the stones of the shore of the creek.

By contrast, the impact of the Aberdeenshire land and its farming rhythms made an even deeper and more indelible impact on MacKenzie's sensitivities. He perceives how the poet Charles Murray and the writer Lewis Grassic Gibbon imbued their work with the unique flavour of the North-East of Scotland, painfully shaped by farming practices over centuries into fields enclosed by rough dry-stane dykes, but still dominated by inclement weather and the humps and howes of the primeval landscape. MacKenzie quotes the ending of Gibbon's *Grey Granite* as an example of this strange blend of terrain and geology and climate:

> Over the Hill of Fare, new timbered, a little belt of rain was falling, a thin screen that blinded the going of the light; behind, as she turned she saw Skene Loch glimmer a burnished minute; then the rain caught it and swept it from sight and a little wind soughed up the Barmekin.

It is the drama of the annual ups and downs of the farming year that fascinates the young MacKenzie, as, indeed, it dominated the lives of the farming folk who formed the core of rural Aberdeenshire in the 1920s. The benign picture of spring and summer work in the fields is contrasted with the devastating effect on normal life of the snows of winter:

> In Spring and Summer the morning hill-side was dew-pearled and the sound of larks and peewits filled the air...the rough winter earth has been torn up, ploughed and grubbered and weeded to make a bed for oats and barley and turnip seed. The seeds have been bedded down and tucked in comfortably and the roller has evened out everything into a brown tidiness, ochre when it is dry and a rich, soft brown when it is wet. In April and in May there is a clear, sharp light that makes the newly budded trees vivid and sparkles on granite chippings on the road...In a blizzard in the twenties when the roads were blocked, local folk, their day's work over, put on luggit bonnets and gravits and greatcoats and puttees and foregathered in the railway station office where the tinkling morse needle was their only contact with the outside world. My father interpreted, 'The Alford line's blocked...the Buchan lines are blocked...the Deeside's blocked'...everybody looked grave, and, with a child's love of drama I hoped against hope that the shut-down would be total. After a long interval the news came through, 'The main line's blocked!' Now our community was on its own, as in pre-history. As the gathering prepared to scale, my father announced the final message that the Railway snow-plough would come through at ten o'clock. We were allowed to stay up to see the snow-plough. It was a magnificent sight...A blizzard was an act of God and here was Man beating the blizzard, forcing a line of communication against the worst that Nature could throw at us.

MacKenzie followed the tradition of many before him in doing well at school and progressing from the local Secondary school at Turriff when he had reached the age of 14 to Robert Gordon's College in Aberdeen. Looking back, however, although he appeared to his parents to flourish at the school and, indeed, was a dux, yet in his memoirs, he had deep reservations about the value of the education he was given there:

> Three years of schooling in Robert Gordon's College in Aberdeen were spent mostly on mental exercises for their own sake. We learned nothing of the past of the city or the country. We reached a stage of writing almost impeccable Latin but nobody mentioned that Roman soldiers had marched through our region. We learned details of treaties made by castle-defending armies but never visited any castles, I didn't know that the North-East of Scotland had a richer heritage of castles than most areas. I didn't know that

Aberdeen holds gems of 18th century architecture. We didn't see the city as a growing organism, spreading out during the centuries from marshy areas at the mouth of the Dee westwards, workmen digging granite out of the ground to build stylish houses. Anything done outwith the classroom was regarded as an unnecessary and unjustifiable break in the continuity of word-smithing, the manipulation of word-symbols or numbers for their own sake. Mathematics was a kind of higher chess for which we were acquiring the skill Physics made little reference to the physical world about us. History was not about us.

When I was asked, 'Do you like the school?' I gave the routine answer 'Yes' but it wasn't true. I tolerated the school; I didn't dislike it and several of my teachers were very good to me. A mathematics teacher taught me to eliminate everything except what was 'necessary and sufficient' to prove a proposition in geometry, and that was a useful lesson. Another maths teacher brought me a beaker of tea with sugar and without milk so that I could get on with mathematics in the school while waiting over an hour for the evening train and I enjoyed the stimulus of the tea and the strenuous mathematical thinking.. I enjoyed translating French because we were encouraged to take time to choose the right word to convey the feeling and nuance of the French, like connoisseurs. But most of the school-work was done uneasily, for prizes.

What emerges very strongly in all of the records that he kept of this period of his life is the unmistakable influence of MacKenzie's father in the shaping of his views of the world around him, coupled with a deep affection for the sort of man his father was as head of the family. MacKenzie admired, in particular, his father's independent spirit and his almost blind belief in the pursuit of knowledge as a virtue in itself. MacKenzie examines the impact upon him of his father's independent approach to life and the repercussions of his father's absolute determination to send all of his children to university in this extract from the memoirs he wrote about this period of his life.

Even in the friendliest gathering of farmers, waiting beside his office fire for the morning train, my father wouldn't hesitate to express an opinion or an unpalatable truth which was anathema to most of them. And he retained their goodwill and esteem, I think, because they knew that there was no sting, no will to hurt, in his statement, however much they disliked it. One of his heroes was John Knox because he 'neither feared nor flattered the face of man'.

This independence was the more surprising in one who had a Celtic sensitivity against giving hurt. My mother was a good mimic and her impersonations were sometimes so well observed that they verged on the hurtful, and I have seen my father admiring the talent but trying not to smile because that would have implied consent and complicity. Even when the unwashed Jock Stewart, the tink, came into our house and sat at the fireside while he consulted my father about his pension and the rest of the family sniggered at the smell, my father maintained a perfect courtesy and neither then, nor after he left, took any part in making fun of him. But neither did he reprove us for our amusement.

There was no calculation in his nature, no self-seeking or personal ambition. But neither was there any condemnation of the self-seekers, pursuing their careers. He felt that, if they wanted to spend their lives on a career, it was right that they should live that way. He sent all of his family to the local university. One of my sisters Catherine, got an Arts degree, and a Diploma in. Music. My other sister', Alice, got a degree in Medicine. He told me that it was the extra money that he was paid for being sub-postmaster that covered our fees. Our neighbour, a farmer, summed up the local attitude to the university when he counselled his friends, 'Gie your bairns education if they'll tak it.' My father accepted this view. It was an article of almost religious faith that in some inexplicable way, education was good for you; and everybody said that Scottish education was the best in the world. Village people were in no position to enquire into why education was good for you. It helped you to 'rise in the world', to have a better chance in life than your parents had, but that wasn't the main reason that my father and mother gave up the luxuries of life to subsidise our college days. My father quoted from the Book of Proverbs, 'With all thy getting get understanding.'

Even today I have difficulty in describing how I felt as a university student from a working class home. The educational landscape was indistinct as if I were seeing it through a fogged-up railway carriage window. An admission of the naiveté of what I then felt may help to clean the window. I was aware of my father's qualities; but then I thought, if he is as I believe, why is he content to remain a village stationmaster? The current cultural belief was that such people rose like the cream, to the top...the university never repudiated that view. In the Mitchell Hall of Marischal College we heard its Rector, Lord Birkenhead, telling us that there were still 'glittering prizes for those with sharp swords.' I don't remember that anybody pointed out the similarity between Birkenhead's advice and the devil's as described in St Matthew's story: 'The devil taketh him into an exceeding high mountain, and showeth him all the kingdoms of the world, and the glory of them; and saith unto him, "All these things will I give thee if thou wilt fall down and worship me." '

But I've a soft side for Birkenhead and the devil. Their advice was clear. The university wasn't. It wanted all this, and heaven too. I wanted to know what the university was for but it wouldn't say. I had a feeling that things ought to make sense if only we could get to grips with them but the university wasn't accessible to that kind of enquiry. We weren't living in that kind of society. Everything was different from what I thought.. The evasion was deliberate.

At that time I was reading Hardy's novels. He gave me the impression that he really did believe that a Wessex countryman like Gabriel Oak was as worthy as a professor or a prime minister. Robert Burns certainly meant his declaration that a man's a man for a' that to be taken literally. I was not alone in my puzzlement and later disillusion with Scottish university culture. Many years later, a contemporary of mine, Hunter Diack, said, 'Sometimes I wish I'd spent my life on the land and done real work instead of being a pseudo-intellectual.' Another North-East writer, John R. Allan, returned to the land. 'My natural inclination was to follow the ways of my fathers, to be that for which my first years had formed me, a peasant; but the training of my later years made me aspire to be the shadow of a gentleman. The unhappy

> years at school and university, those years in which I had worshipped so many idols stuffed with straw, became tiresome memories of futility, compared to the new ease I had discovered...I did not pretend to be anything more than I was...I lay back on my heritage, as a tired man lies down on a grassy bank, in thankfulness for the solid earth and the green shade.'
>
> He added, 'That is all I have to say about Scottish education – that it isn't real education at all...There may be real education when a young man from the joiner's bench returns to his bench after three years at a university, and when the community is wise enough to leave him there.'
>
> John Allan, probing the folklore, put his finger on the sore bit. Is the university about giving glittering prizes to those with sharp swords or giving wisdom to the joiner? But there was no voice, nor any that answered. It was all left vague, so that working class folk in Aberdeenshire should continue to believe that the university offered the bread of life to any of the people in its hinterland that sought it. All that the university offered, however, was the cultural galshichs of an acquisitive society.
>
> But little of that was clear to us the day that we graduated.. The usual greeting was sometimes followed by the query, 'What does it feel like to be an MA?' It was partly humorous but there was in it a hankering after magic. We replied, 'It's no different.' What wisdom the university failed to give us we would have to seek for ourselves.'

What emerges out of MacKenzie's early life, therefore, is his growing realisation of his own powers as a thinker in his own right. The strong and abiding influence of his father had taught him to be wary of the value of the received wisdoms and to test out for himself the validity of the knowledge he had been given at school and at university. H.G. Wells had opened up for him in historical terms an acute awareness of how the past shapes the present and profoundly affects our view of the future. And with that came a realisation on MacKenzie's part of the power of the individual intellect to circumscribe the mysteries of civilisation and see everything in a perspective that comes out of one's own sense of vision MacKenzie's early life follows a path towards such realisation. It is a path that tackles the deeper issues of history, religion and politics. For MacKenzie saw increasingly in his early years how far short his own preparations for life fell in terms of opening up his mind to get to the real meaning of truth. It leads him, even at an early stage in his career, to adopting a non-conformist view of life, particularly in his growing suspicions of what is known as the Establishment – the educational, religious, political, and social agencies that largely shape and dictate the sum and substance of our lives. These suspicions helped him to acquire his own sense of identity as someone who felt an urge to write with insight and integrity about what he saw and what he felt about the world around him. He is fascinated by the Bible as his father was before him and looks long and hard in it for truths and inspiration –

though disinclined to believe its more conventional messages about Heaven and Hell and everlasting life. The Christian dogma he has really no time for, but he is at one with Christianity in its reverence for Humanity and its preoccupation with the truth and reaching after a state of 'grace'.

> My religious forebears believed that we reach a state of grace, and I'm reckoning to wonder if there may not be a deep psychological truth in that statement.

For MacKenzie, then, the developing years up to the time he left university in the early 1930s were years that shaped and moulded the way he would go in the future. It also prepared him to respond as an artist and as an observer to the world of humanity around him. His sensitivity to the countryside of his native Aberdeenshire and its influence on the character of those who are brought up in it established in him an enduring touchstone for his future career as a writer and as an educationist. Allied to that were his vivid recollections of childhood experiences that he so often uses to transmute his opinions into graphic pictures that gel with Scottish life and landscape as in these moving reflections on the nature of patriotism:

> When we were children, we went for holidays to my father's mother who lived in Speyside. Somewhere about the No Man's Land of Keith we passed from the prose of the North-East Lowlands into the poetry of the Highlands. The hills were higher, the burns fast and frothy, the delicate tracery of the birches and their silver bark more fairy-like. The smell of the larches was richer, the speech of the people softer. The train snaked past a long loch and the ravine of the Fiddoch and emerged in Strathspey, a new world...It was the land of the salmon. Beside the river was a notice about smolts and parr, strange new words. My uncle, until he joined the Gordon Highlanders, was a water ghillie on the Spey. He was killed near Arras and there was a military funeral at Aberlour. Shots were fired over the grave and the piper played 'Lochaber No More'. It was the most beautiful music of sorrow I have heard. This is a strange thing, that human beings, forcing breath through the holes of a chanter as my uncle's body was returned to the Highland earth, could soften the limp, empty sense of irreparable loss by channelling it into haunting abiding music...On the day that my uncle announced that he had decided to enlist, his elder brother, a tailor in the Scottish industrial belt, was visiting his parents, 'What have you to fight for?' he demanded, 'Six feet by two?' It was the first searching question I heard, the first jarring note in the symphony of patriotism.

CHAPTER THREE

Travels in Europe in the 1930s

It is hard for us now to appreciate and come to terms with the boldness of what MacKenzie and his friend Hunter Diack did in the early 1930s in deciding to undertake a six-months' cycle tour of Europe shortly after they had both graduated from Aberdeen University. Coming as they both did from similar backgrounds rooted in the slow-changing, rural rhythms of the North-East of Scotland, their education had, they felt, equipped them to do little more than simply take for granted 'the way things were'. The North-East of Scotland, during the early life of both men, was still very much a community that was feudal in structure. Its rural hinterland was still dominated by the triumvirate of the Laird, the Minister and the Dominie, and its farming economy was heavily dependent for survival on the hiring of cheap labour – the hiring of vast numbers of 'feed' farm-servants whose appalling working conditions on the 'fairm toun' and in the fields throughout the seasons of the year as well as the primitive conditions that they endured in the farm bothies that were their living quarters made them little better off than the serfs of the Middle Ages. Even by the early 1930s, the area was still relatively unaffected by the internal combustion engine and the telephone – the ordinary folk still used bicycles to get about, and gossip or 'claik' was the main source of finding out what was happening in the world around them.

Why then did MacKenzie and Diack decide to undertake this adventure? Clearly, they had already decided to challenge the conventional wisdoms that had dominated their education up to now. As they say in the opening page of the book that they wrote about their travels – *Road Fortune* (published by Macmillan in 1935):

> A variety of motives lay behind the taking of this journey, and not the least of these was curiosity about a way of life...we had both taken what is known as the Honours course in a Scottish university which means that for four years of developing life we played with words and imagined we were handling realities. It seemed to us then that a definite break with our old lives for a life stripped of softness might enable us to learn what are the realities that a man will pursue if he is to live a full life. That proved to be a naive optimism; the only reality we met was hunger.

At university MacKenzie had begun what was to become a life-long friendship with Hunter Diack who was born in Kemnay, Aberdeenshire, in 1908. He was eighth in a family of nine, his father being the local tailor and clothier. At Aberdeen University the two young men were known to be outgoing and outspoken as well as full of life. In an article for the *Leopard* magazine (June 1989) Vivienne Forrest, telling the story of Hunter Diack, says:

> Of all the richness of anecdote from that time perhaps the most picturesque is that of the pair of young socialists refusing to stand for the National Anthem...and nobody noticing; but later in a letter to MacKenzie, Diack tells how he did the same in Toronto and got the angry reaction, 'You can do that in Aberdeen but you can't do it here!'

MacKenzie and Diack also shared an early interest in writing. During their European cycle tour, they sent back occasional articles for *The Press and Journal* under pen-names – Hunter Diack was Clay Davie the country name for a clay pipe, while MacKenzie was Picky Say, the farmer's hat. Besides that, they both contributed to the *North East Review* which was produced by a group of 'left-wing' intellectuals, including John Foster and John Mackintosh who, in those days, would meet in the back room of the Cults Hotel, just outside Aberdeen. The *Review* was published at 10 Belmont Street in Aberdeen where Garnet Fraser printed it. The *North East Review* was (in the words of Vivienne Forrest in her article in the *Leopard*): 'A presentation of North East country and people and wit, with hard-hitting comment – and also a resident genius named Jamie Fleeman, (late of Udny), funny, disrespectful, right 'on the nail.'

So it was in December 1932 that MacKenzie and Diack set off with high hopes for the continent. Each had a sturdy touring bicycle equipped with acetylene lamps and were burdened with panniers, a heavy canvas tent, and an old Remington typewriter on which they planned to record their adventures. As their staple diet, they carried with them a 30-pound bag of oatmeal that was nearly stolen from them before they set off from London. Despite the excitement of going to the continent where everything was in a ferment (there was rumour of war, the Polish corridor anti-Semitism, the Spanish revolution, and, of course, the Balkans), it was the physical stress of hard cycling and living under canvas that dominated their early progress through France.

> The cold seemed to have inspired my companion to a frenzy of violent action. As I pumped up the stove and warmed my hands to the accompaniment of its welcome roar, I would hear him lugging huge boulders from the stream bed and crashing them down near the head of the tent so that the tent

> trembled. The canvas would tighten here, and gradually all chills and draughts ceased to be. The bestowal of the luggage was always a prolonged ceremony. Here they came tumbling on top of one another…brown bag, typewriter, knapsack, haversack, box of books…and I was, as usual, amazed that all these things were carried on a couple of bicycles.

During the course of their journey through France, they learned from a newspaper that H.G. Wells had gone to spend the winter at Grasse in the south of France, and, since that was on their route, they wrote a letter to him saying that they expected to reach Grasse in January and might they come and have a talk with him. Much to their surprise and delight, they found when they reached the Post Office at Grasse that he had left them an invitation there to visit him and because it was difficult to find the way to the house outside Grasse, he would send his chauffeur to meet them and take them to his house for a meal. The chauffeur was there on time. They had to explain to him that they had to take their bicycles with them, and so he told them he would lead the way saying 'J'irai doucement.' 'Often afterwards', MacKenzie recalls, 'in the intervening years we recalled these words.'

> Out of the town, at high speed downhill he went, and suddenly his rear lights disappeared at the bottom as he turned sharply, and our brakes screeched as we turned after him, determined not to lose this tenuous connection with the fulfilment of a dream. In the moonlight we raced through the shadows of myrtles and perfume factories and we were relieved when the car slowed down. 'Monsieur would be waiting to receive us', said the chauffeur.

Wells is described as a smiling, short, energetic figure who poured the two lads generous whiskies before serving them a meal. In the course of conversation he exhibited his fundamental optimism for the future of mankind, declaring, 'What a wonderful time to be young! Students and young people from all over the world will be travelling, as these Scotsmen are, and inquiring and discussing world problems and putting their minds to the question of how to organise things better.' He then persuaded them to stay the night in a guest-house in the garden. MacKenzie then vividly recalls the later part of their stay at Grasse:

> Outside the moon shone on a sparkling Mediterranean night. I remember Wells dancing with happiness on the terrace of his house. It was the same exhilarating gaiety as bubbled through his conversation over dinner. 'Do you know who your immediate predecessors in the guest-house were?' he asked, and supplied the answer, 'Charlie Chaplin and Grenfell of Labrador'. Under his arm he brought us bedside reading. One was an inscribed copy of a recently published book, Bernard Shaw's *Adventures of the Black Girl in her Search of God*.

> Next morning we got a message that 'Monsieur Ouelle' said we were to go and collect our baggage and return and spend another evening with him and sleep in the guest-house. We had several hours of talk that evening.
>
> I think now that he was almost as interested in us as we were in him. There we were, graduates of a Scottish university, just beginning to ask the questions about the tradition which the university hadn't encouraged us to ask, beginning to emerge from a belief in the infallibility of professors, seeing our whole upbringing and background from outside in a new light.
>
> He was then at work on *The Shape of Things to Come*. One of the characters, we discovered later when the book appeared, was a student who cycled through France and Italy observing as he went and from whose note-books the book quoted. We like to think that this character owed something to our stay with the author.

When MacKenzie and Diack made their way into Italy, they encountered severe weather conditions that at one stage, in Tuscany, confined them to their tent for a week. The countryside and the way of life of this part of Italy was unremittingly harsh and still medieval in character having at its core a hardy, but vibrant, peasant culture:

> So rather drearily we noted a farm steading with the dwelling part above the stables, a pig with a chain round its neck grubbing under a solitary myrtle tree, cattle in a pound at mid-day, eight huge oxen drawing a plough, their horns sticking out two feet on either side, daisies, dandelions, a kind of furze with blue blossoms upon it, and all that was enlivened by the sight of two women over fifty, hoe upon shoulder, riding men's bicycles, and a still older woman coming home from the fields on the handlebars of a man's bicycle.

During their stay in Rome where they had the good fortune to get lodgings at a Catholic Seminary, they encountered the strong influence that Fascism was exerting on the education system at that time. The sort of propaganda that was being used by the Fascist government to influence university education is blatantly illustrated in this editorial from one of the local newspapers at the time, 'In revolutionary Italy, university professors must bring into their teaching a spirit actively Fascist. There must be unceasing vigilance lest they give seditious and destructive knowledge under the cloak of erudition.' And MacKenzie and Diack conclude, 'There is no doubt that there is being raised in Italy today, to a greater extent than is at first apparent, the most war-hungry, imperialist and presumptuous generation of the Europe of tomorrow.'

Beneath the surface, however, there lurked in the Seminary where the travellers were staying, certainly among the more discerning students, a keen sense of ironic humour at the lengths to which Italians had allowed themselves to be carried away by the triumphalism of the Fascist bandwagon, 'You should have seen Rome in the old days at carnival time (one of the students remarked to MacKenzie and Diack) especially on the last day before Lent. It was some sight! These Italians can fairly let themselves go. Mussolini, however, put a stop to all that. He's a very abstemious chap...has cabbage for his dinner, and never drinks anything but water and milk.'

Travelling south from Rome the two cyclists again encounter difficult conditions on the roads connecting mountain villages near Monte Cassino.

> Progress that day was a series of jolts, for we merely dragged our way up hills to high-set villages, then swooped down to the plains again. Most inland villages in Italy are fortresses. The brigands are gone, the malaria of the low-lying marshes is rapidly disappearing but the Italian villagers still spend most of their energies carrying food and fuel skywards. It is a curious way of spending a life. One would think that the carrying of necessities uphill had become a reflex action...Instead of calmly reasoning that in a few weeks they could build houses near the fields that supply them with food, they will unthinkingly spend half a century carrying beans, onions. spaghetti, faggots and water five hundred feet up a rock-face in order to carry on their existence at the height, at which their forebears ate and slept.

After reaching Naples and Pompeii, MacKenzie and Diack parted, Diack taking the Appenine road through Abruzzi, and MacKenzie crossing Italy to Bari and so on to Albania and Yugoslavia and finally Austria where they planned to meet up again.

MacKenzie found much to admire in the rough, mountainous regions he passes through on his way to Bari. Here he discovered an Italy that still knew of Fascism only from the increase in taxes, whilst the countryside remained largely unchanged and reminiscent of Scotland in its Spartan beauty.

> At 2,000 feet the air is cool and quiet and when you pause for your lunch of bread and cheese and water, there is not a sound but the singing of the lark and the droning of a beetle. You sleep under an olive tree and in the morning you have to brush away dew from your tent. Having risen with the sun, a boy of twelve with a little hat and long trousers patched at the knees crossed the road in front of a herd of sheep and pipes tunes as he leads them to new pastures. An Appenine summit with snow on it rises above a misty cloud, and in the mist there is a long bar that might be blue smoke rising into the still air or a shaft of sun-light. The river valley below is very like Strathspey. Women carrying pailfuls of cement on their heads helping the men at their road-repairing and great buxom women they are. Then for kilometre after kilometre nothing much to see except an unusually blue poppy in the grass...

He sailed third class from Bari in the SS Monti Gargano to the little port of Durazzio in Albania. Here he found a country that was still recovering from being the victim of aggression at the hands of its neighbours, Yugoslavia in the north and Greece in the south, which was going through a surge of nationalism epitomised by the cry of 'Albania for the Albanians'. He then travelled with difficulty in a mountainous under-developed country with few good roads, many of them under construction, and after visiting the capital, Tirana, he made for Elbasan which he describes in raw, graphic terms:

> Elbasan is a squalid town of mosques and a bazaar; there is nothing else remarkable about it. You cross a bridge over a burn to it, past an olive-oil factory, and up a narrow street which has dirty water running down the sides in narrow channels...you think it is just a. huddled village, and it is a surprise to learn that there are 15,000 people in Elbasan...There is, of course, no water circulation. Malaria, I learned later, is very rife and shortly before I was there, many had died of meningitis...Meanwhile, civilisation from the north and the west does not penetrate very quickly; it is just struggling south at Elbasan. There is indeed a telephone system, but it is woefully insulated, supported by rude sticks and nails, and sometimes the wires are only three feet above the ground.

From Albania, MacKenzie made his way somewhat painfully through the mountainous country of Montenegro which had become part of Yugoslavia some 15 years earlier. The pain came not just from the mountainous terrain he had to cross, but from the difficult roads he had to make his way along.

> Round the next corner, however, I was disillusioned, for the road descended almost to the lake, and then could be seen like a piece of narrow tape laid insecurely along the side of the next mountain...it looked as if a strong wind would blow it into the water. There was more climbing, more dust, there were more punctures. These roads of Montenegro threw away the advantages of height one had so laboriously earned. They were so steep and rough that one had either to walk down the hill or hang on to the brakes until arms ached, wheels buckled and the spokes snapped with the jerking...these were the times of inward cursing.

Eventually, 'tired of this uneven struggle', he capitulated and took a bus for part of the journey, from Cetinje to Kotor on the Adriatic coast.. From there he made his way to Dubrovnik before boarding a steamer to take him further up the Dalmatian coast to Sidernik and then to Fiume. His voyage on the steamer turned out to be a memorable one:

> When the mountains towered higher into the sky and half their extent was covered with permanent snow and the ship had called at two bare, wind-swept villages late in the afternoon, Split hove into sight. From the sea it too seemed as lovely and small as a Hebridean fishing village, and two bare roads winding on the hills away from it...gave it a background that suddenly

> recalled Mallaig. One expected to see Skye in the mist over the Sound of Sleat, and wondered if the Dalmatian islanders had a Prince Charlie they sang songs about.

Part of the remaining journey through Croatia took MacKenzie by train from Fiume to Zagreb. On board the train he shared a large compartment with a number of students on their way to the university at Zagreb after vacation, who entertained their travelling companions with impressive community singing.

> The voices blended perfectly in the different parts, and, as the song rose to its climax, the market women, who had been gossiping, fell silent, and the ticket collector paused at the end of the carriage to listen. The singers seemed to be putting their very best into the song, and there is always a gripping fascination about effort on the stretch...the cadence fell away quietly, and then ceased. One of the singers made a joke, and all laughed open-heartedly as if to pass off lightly the seriouness into which they had been betrayed...

His journey continued by train from Zagreb to Ljubljana which he regarded as a dream city because it was a popular radio station in those days. He was disillusioned to discover, however, that the radio station emanated from a little room above a cramped shop that sold gramophones on an ordinary street. Even worse, he met the Director of the radio station with four days' growth of beard! Getting over his sense of disappointment, he resumes cycling and makes rapid progress to the Austrian border, enjoying a downhill exhilarating ride once again on good roads:

> It was now dark, and the bulb of my lamp was broken. I came off to tighten the strap of the carriers and flew into the tunnel of a thick wood with a fine feeling of security......When I emerged from the great wood, the stars were out and the new moon was risen above the west horizon...down another three kilometres was a village where in the street men walked, tall, upstanding fellows in green hats, each with a cock's feather stuck on it...by and by I turned into a grass field which was white with hoar frost, rigged up the tent, crawled into my sleeping bag, and thanked the stars for that glorious five thousand feet of Alp between me and Yugoslavia.

He then comes to Klagenfurr, 40 kilometres from Villach where he is to meet up with Hunter Diack once again. The reunion, when it eventually takes place, turns out to be a bit of an anti-climax. One greets the other:

> 'Indeed! Where did you come from?'
> 'The main Naples-Hamburg road. What did you expect? And you?'
> MacKenzie replies, 'Durazzo, Sibernik...Fiume...Ljubljana.'
> 'Ljubljana? You used to rave about that name in World Radio. Was it up to

> expectations?'
> He shook his head sadly.
> No, the wireless Director had a few days' growth of beard and the studio is a wee room over a shop!'

The reunion has about it the sense of understatement and droll humour associated with the North-East of Scotland. The feeling of relief at joining up together again from their separate paths is masked by the job of picking up the pieces and resuming their cycle tour through Austria. and Germany.

It was now the month of May and the time of year seemed to coincide with local celebrations going on in Austria.

> As the morning wore on more and more people seemed to be converging on the bigger villages, and Obergau was crowded with men and women in holiday attire lags were flying everywhere and occasionally came the words in giant lettering, 'Ein Volk, Ein Reich!'
>
> There were brown shirts in full rig-out...we reached Salsburg at noon and found it en fête. The windows of every book-seller and photographer and of many other shops...were full of pictures of Hitler and Hindenburg but there were a dozen pictures of Hitler to one of Hindenburg.

Soon they reached Bavaria which still bore the signs of May Day celebrations. Flags, mostly red with big swastikas, flew on every village flag-staff.

> House fronts were decorated with a swastika in fir branches and the words 'Heil Hitler'...Hitlerism covered the country like a rash. Every village had at least one of its streets renamed 'Adolf Hitler Street'...shop windows were full of pictures of Der Führer, taken addressing meetings his long lock of hair brushed back, Hitler in uniform, Hitler in mufti, Hitler with his troops...became tiresome. We met a man who had found work, and remunerative work too, hawking Hitler photographs. He carried them in a letter-case, a large selection – big and little, coloured and plain, framed and unframed. Children raised their arms in salute to us as we passed and said, 'Heil Hitler'. Every other car and bicycle had a pennant flying with a swastika upon it.
>
> Beyond Augsburg near Blenheim we crossed the Danube and continued towards Nuremberg. Alas! The old town of watches and toys and dormer windows seemed to be wholly given over to the making of toy Nazis in uniform, and every window was full of toy Hitlers, startlingly like a photograph of him.

After parting at Jena, MacKenzie and Diack go their separate ways, MacKenzie went to visit Goethe's Gartenhaus, then Weimar and Magdeburg and Diack went straight to Hamburg. Thus their cycle tour had come to an end after six months on the road. The route that MacKenzie himself took to get back home was via Munich, Frankfurt and the Rhine. He crossed from the Hook of Holland to Harwich and went by train from there to Aberdeen.. He remarks in the memoir that he wrote later recollecting this period of his life, 'The last thirty miles to our Aberdeenshire village of Insch I covered by bicycle, and in so doing linked the highways of Europe to the Aberdeenshire road which went past our own back door.'

Soon afterwards he and Hunter Diack began the task of collaborating in the writing of their book about the cycle tour, *Road Fortune*, which earned a brief preview in *The Press and Journal* just before its publication in 1935. The article reminds readers that both authors are better known to them as 'Clay Davie' and 'Picky Say' in that they had both contributed regular accounts of their European cycle tour to the newspaper in 1932–33. Indeed, MacKenzie continued to supply articles to the newspaper under the name of 'Picky Say' from 1934 to 1936, when he did a lot of travelling in Europe, sending back, for example, his own impressions of Hitler's rise to power as the newspaper's 'Correspondent travelling on the Continent' under such headings as this one which appeared on Tuesday 26 March 1935 – 'Hitler's Appeal is to Domestic Instincts'.

In many ways *Road Fortune* was a remarkable achievement. The book has value not just as a travelogue but as a historical document, incorporating, as it does, the views and observations of two young and gifted graduates on the political, social and economic changes that were affecting Italy, the Balkans, Austria and Germany in the early 1930s.

As a personal document, it does not tell us a lot about the character and personality of either of the travellers. It does, however, reflect their eagerness to discover the truth of things for themselves and the discipline they had already acquired as writers in making detailed and exhaustive notes on what they were doing and what they were seeing as they toured the countryside and the towns.

They purposely let events speak for themselves and submerge their own personalities in faithfully recording what they see and hear. The episode with H.G. Wells typifies the flavour of the book at its best in that it shows the extent to which they were willing to go to find out the truth of things for themselves (just as their mentor Wells had done himself). Their exhilaration at meeting with and talking to one of the cult figures of the time lends an excitement to the narrative that is not always sustained.

Above all, the book reflects the powerful impact that events in Europe were having on the two young men as they cycle through the towns, villages and countryside. They capture, for instance, the curious unreality of fascism as it insidiously takes a hold in Italy. They capture the deep suspicion and antipathy of the Yugoslavs towards the Italians and the feeling of instability in the Balkans generally. And they capture most memorably of all the air of gathering doom and foreboding that lurks behind the triumphalist atmosphere in Germany and Austria with the emergence in these countries of Nazi-ism as an all-embracing and pervasive force.

MacKenzie had further opportunities to explore the nature of Nazi-ism when he stayed on in Germany in 1933 after his cycle tour and later in 1938–39 when he went back to Germany and did regular English teaching and tutoring. His thoughts on the subject, and on the country of Germany as a whole, were set down in a memoir of those times that he put together much later from the diaries he kept of his travels abroad.

> I spent one of the best mornings of my life in May 1933 strolling through the woods above Heidelberg. The buds were bursting, there was sunshine, and if there had been music to hear beside the birds' song, it should have been the music of Schubert. A big, red, white and black swastika fluttered over the students' inn 'Zum Roten Ochzen' where I was spending the. weekend.
>
> It was when I was on my way home from the cycling tour. A French student whom I met in a little cafe beside the Neckar, took me to the inn because he thought I'd like to see a German students' rendezvous, and he introduced me to the proprietor's son. They showed me trophies, drinking horns, lidded mugs, student flags, names carved on the tables (some illustrious like Bismark's son). I was introduced to the proprietor's wife and she said, 'I want you to stay here for a day or two as our guest. You will see the town and the palace of the Winter King at Schwtzingen, and these things I, think, would give you much pleasure. So I stayed.
>
> 'It was comfortable and pleasant there. The Germans have a word for it it, 'Gemütlich' which means cosy and friendly and homely. My hostess told me about Nazi-ism. It was a simple thing to her.
>
> 'During the 1914–18 War it was awful at home. There was no food. The armistice came and we thought, 'Now it will be all right. But it was no better. And then came the inflation when we discovered that the small fortune which the family had saved was enough to buy one loaf of bread. And there was fighting in the streets...'
>
> She paused, as if in memory, and then added with a child-like confidence, 'But now Hitler has the answer. It will be all right now.'
>
> At the beginning of the following year I was in South-Eastern Germany, near the Polish frontier. I came to the town of Hindenburg shortly before ten at night and asked a young storm-trooper in uniform the way to the Youth Hostel. He said it was rather difficult to find and that he would show me the way. But, when we reached it, no lights were showing and repeated knocking brought no answer. 'Come with me', said the storm-trooper. He looked about twenty. I accompanied him, expecting that he would be going to show me some other place where I could 'overnight', as they say, cheaply. He took me to a house, left me for a bit and then led the way into a kitchen-livingroom where people were sitting around a coal stove.

'This is my family', he said, 'and they will be glad if you stay the night with us. We can sit and talk about our countries.'

However, a very different picture of storm-troopers emerges when the Jewish family that MacKenzie is staying with in Wuppertal, Germany, four years later, in 1938, is paid a visit by storm-troopers at the height of the Nazi pogrom. This is how he describes the scene in the memoir he wrote of the event.

When I opened the door, I saw that the storm-trooopers had paid their call. My room was off the surgery on the first floor and I had to cross the surgery to reach it. Outside in the street everything was silent and deserted, and the front door and the windows had not been disturbed.

There was a bright moon, and, in the moonlight streaming through the wide-open surgery windows, I saw destruction. The room reeked of chloroform. The operating table was smashed. A large cupboard of chemicals had been smashed and a thick oily mess of liquids lay on the floor. Surgical instruments lay about in it and the glass-front case, in which they had lain neatly, was broken in two as if by a single blow from a hammer and it was hanging by its fittings from the wall. The telephone lay broken on the floor.

I picked my way through the broken glass and the acids and oils on the floor and I opened the door of my own room. The wardrobe was overturned and its door-hinges were twisted. The bedding had been ripped and feathers were scattered on the carpet. The chairs and table were overturned. Two letters which I had left on the table in the morning were swimming in the oil which was seeping through from the surgery. None of my belongings had been damaged.

The house was silent, outside there were footsteps of somebody down the street, but usually at that hour, shortly after eleven, the street had more people moving along its pavements. I crept out of the surgery and tried the doors of the rooms on the ground-floor but they were locked and when I said once or twice in a low voice, 'Is anybody there?, there was no answer. Outside in the street, as I walked to a hotel for the night, the quietness emphasised the fury of the destruction that had come to the house since I had left it in the morning.

On my way to work I had seen splinters of smashed plate-glass windows being swept up, but thinking there had been a motor accident I did not join the crowd round the window. But near the Markt-platz there were more broken windows and in the afternoon we had seen the synagogue burning. In the evening there was wore traffic than usual in the streets. The people I was living with were German Jews, the husband being a veterinary surgeon but I hadn't imagined that the day's destruction would extend beyond shop-windows and the synagogue.

On the following morning I returned to the house to try and find out what had happened to my hosts. Two non-Jewish women were there and one of them was the housekeeper, who had a flat with her husband on the second floor. I asked them if they knew where the Herr Doktor and Frau Doktor were, but they shook their heads and said that they knew nothing, and went away.

Halfway down the street somebody touched my shoulder softly and I saw it was one of the women, not the house-keeper. She whispered that the Herr Dokter and his wife had left their house and that she was giving them shelter and refuge in her house. She added quickly that if I wanted to see them, they were returning to the house for a short time in the afternoon.

They were already there when I returned. They told me that, although they had not mentioned it at breakfast-time on the previous day, they feared that the reports pointed to the rising storm of a pogrom. Events in the town-centre during the day had increased their anxiety and when a non-Jewish friend had invited them to leave their own house for that day and night and stay with her and her husband, they had accepted. Thus they had escaped the fury that had descended upon their house. My host added, 'I'm sorry that this has happened while you were staying with us. But we didn't guess that things would become so bad; otherwise we should never have invited you. I think you had better leave.'

I tried to find out if he were merely being considerate, or if he really wanted me to leave, and I decided to stay. This was the time when the Gestapo were picking up Jews right and left where they came across them and taking them to concentration camps. Those who evaded them during those ten days or so, until the fury of the pogrom died down were all right, but it was a desperately anxious time. Hearing that most Jews were lifted from their house at night, my hosts decided to accept the hospitality of their gentile protectors during the succeeding nights and to spend the day-time in the ground-floor rooms of their own house, which hadn't been damaged. Every evening about nine o' clock husband and wife would steal out of the house, and I would let them out and lock the door carefully behind them and put my British passport under my pillow before I fell asleep. In the morning before breakfast-time they would return.

The Sunday (of that same week) had a nightmare quality about it. Every time the front door-bell rang, the vet descended quickly and furtively to the cellar while his wife reconnoitred the caller through a small, iron-barred glass panel in the front door. Most of the callers were Jews bearing news of other friends in Essen or elsewhere in the Ruhr. It was a day of anxiety and increasing gloom and tears, as they heard of this and that friend who had been 'taken'.

After a month, Jews began to reappear from the concentration camps, most of them with bad colds and all of them with close-cropped heads. You could easily tell if a Jew had been imprisoned or not. Then began a busy time amongst the Jews of trying to get passports and visas, visits to the British consul at Stuttgart, letters to friends in Britain and America and Australia asking them to guarantee them the time after immigration until they found work and their feet in a new country.

After the Jewish family with whom I had been staying had left because of the persecution that they had been subjected to by the Nazis, I found lodgings with an elderly couple who were not Jews. It was usually after ten thirty at night before I finished evening class work, and often my landlady would sit up so that I could have a hot supper instead of the usual bread and cold sausage slice. While I ate, she would sit and tell me the story of Goethe's Faust. Sometimes she quoted, although my German was not equal to following the quotations very well. But there was the bit about Faust looking at the setting sun and saying, 'Welle nur! Du bist so schön.' That stays in the memory. Often she spoke about the chances of war and often she said anxiously, 'I do hope there'll be no war.'

And there was the middle-class and fairly well-off family who lived in an old, rambling, comfortable house a few miles outside Wuppertal. They used to invite a colleague and me out there on Sunday afternoons and on free days, and we had a glimpse into German middle-class life, its friendly politeness and family pride. There were paintings of the last two generations on the walls of the living room. The only daughter of the family was a very attractive and intelligent girl of seventeen. She spoke English well and told us that her parents weren't very keen supporters of the Nazi regime. 'We are called the "Backwoodsmen" ', she said, 'because they think that politically my parents have not kept up with the times but live in an out-of -date world of their own.'

It was in the living room where the paintings of the previous generations of Germans looked down upon us that we toasted one another while we listened in to the German radio welcoming in the New Year of 1939. An hour later, because of the difference in times, we listened to the welcome that was given to 1939 by the BBC. We wondered not very hopefully what the year would bring.

Just before the war broke out, I sent a note to them saying that the Nazis had brought on the war but that we should not forget their kindness and hospitality. The day before the war began, I received a reply from their daughter. She said that Czech workmen had been drafted up to that valley where they lived, and they had been surprised to find how human and normal these Czechs were; German propaganda about the Czechs had led them to expect something different.

The writer of the letter tried to look into the future, 'we do not know how this war will end for us', she said, 'but probably with Russian boots.'

That was forty years ago. When, from the other side of the war, I think of these German people that I knew, the puzzle that remains uppermost in my mind is how it comes about that in a world that contains a large and widespread amount of excellence – goodwill, kindness, enthusiasm for a cause – there should be so much confusion and trouble and fear...When we try to say simply why we are making such a hash of our world, we never reach a full and clear answer.

But we do get baffling glimpses of what the answer might be. 'When our grandchildren and great-grandchildren describe the period through which we are passing', said the *Manchester Guardian*, 'they will be interested not only in political events but in the events that are happening in the minds of men and women.'

'That is why', MacKenzie concludes, in his reminiscences of this eventful part of his life, 'I want to set down something of this, something about the men and women I have known and the events, known or guessed at, that were going on at the back of their minds.'

CHAPTER FOUR

The War Diaries 1939–45

It must have been a source of concern for his parents that for a number of years after he had graduated, MacKenzie showed a complete reluctance to capitalise on the good Honours Degree he had obtained at Aberdeen University in 1931 by using it to train for a profession such as teaching. His close friend, Hunter Diack, had, for instance, done just that and was appointed to Robert Gordon's College, Aberdeen, as an Assistant Master not long after he returned to Scotland from the European cycle tour. However that may be, MacKenzie plainly felt unwilling to settle down to any form of regular employment, apart from his brief spell as an uncertificated teacher at the experimental Forest School in England from 1934 to 1936.

It seems that at one stage, MacKenzie had thought of making a career in journalism, and to this end briefly took up a post with the *Mearns Leader*.His sister, Alice, recalls that he also at one point embarked on medical training in London with the intention of paying his way with his writing. His state of mind, however, was such that he felt an overwhelming urge to travel and find out for himself what was going on in the world, especially in Europe. And so he found it practicable when he visited Germany, as he did, in the late 1930s to combine his insatiable appetite for news, particularly in relation to the rise of Nazi-ism, with a curiosity as to how such events affected the lives of ordinary people. Had it not been for the advent of the Second World War and a change in family circumstances back home in 1940, it is hard to imagine what career MacKenzie might have eventually followed.

It was in 1940 that MacKenzie's father died. He had been ill for some time and his death had a deep effect upon MacKenzie. He loved and revered his father, not just as a man, but for his intellectual powers as an independent thinker. MacKenzie felt eternally grateful for the gift of intellectual curiosity that his father had bestowed upon him, which remained with him for the rest of his life both as a teacher and as a writer. His father was also widely respected and well liked by all who came in contact with him – a fact which MacKenzie readily acknowledged in his memoirs. Since the house the MacKenzies lived in was a tied house, belonging to the Railway Company, the family moved to Aberdeen in 1944, where, for a time, before he was called up to serve in the forces, MacKenzie had a job working in the Censor's Office.

MacKenzie served in the RAF during the war from 1941 to 1945, having been called up at the age of 31 nearly two years after the war had begun. His diaries of the war date from August 1941 to April 1945 by which time he was on flying missions with Bomber Command over Occupied Europe. He spent much of the time prior to 1945 training as a navigator, first in Canada and the USA in 1941 and then in South Africa during the period October 1942 to October 1943 He was then stationed for much of the rest of the war at various locations in the Midlands and South of England before being 'demobbed' in January 1946 with the rank of Sergeant Navigator.

The book *Road Fortune* that he and Hunter Diack had written in 1935 had, to a large extent, been based on diaries and notes that they had kept, recording the daily events of their cycle tour through Europe in the early 1930s; so that MacKenzie had already got into the habit of writing down on a daily basis his observations and impressions of the world around him. Hence the war diaries do not come as a surprise. They encapsulate, nonetheless a unique record of what it felt like to be involved in training to be a combatant in the Second World War; for it is clear that much of the time that servicemen had at their disposal was not directly connected with the war itself but with 'putting in time' and coming to terms with the war's impact on their personal life and with the changes it would make to the shape of their lives, and indeed, on the world, after the war was over. And this is, in fact, where the war diaries contribute richly to our perceptions of what life was like for people like MacKenzie caught up in the uncertainties and dangers that a World War imposed upon them, as well as the effects it would have on their views on life generally.

The strength of MacKenzie's diaries lies in his relaxed and informed approach to the business of recording what catches his interest from day to day. There is always an acute awareness of the weather and the seasons of the year which reflects his natural concern as a native of the countryside for what was growing in the fields and the gardens and the effects it had on his senses. Besides that, there is in his diaries a keen sense of what is going on around him, ranging from the almost incidental nature of the training he has to go through to the implications for this country in the future of the daily events of the war as heard on the wireless or read about in the newspapers. As befits someone who had grown to admire, in the inter-war years, many aspects of Germany and its people as individuals, we find no special hatred of the Germans expressed in the diaries – rather a regret that they have allowed themselves to be duped and misled by the Nazi regime; and there is, from time to time a candid commentary on the performance of the Allies and their leaders as their relative merits are discussed by the servicemen in their barracks of an evening. Predictably, however, barrack-room conversation on most occasions had an earthier preoccupation (as MacKenzie readily admits) with sex and *News of the World* news.

The parts of the war diaries that I intend to use for illustrative purposes for this period in his life are largely taken from the last two years of the war when he openly considers the historical significance of diaries such as his in recording what it felt like to be in a major conflict such as the Second World War – much as in the same way a diary kept by a Roman legionary in the time of Julius Caesar would have given future generations a similarly unique insight into what it was like to be involved in the Gallic Wars or in the invasion of Britain in 55 BC.

The 'flavour' that he wanted to convey in his diaries is summed up in this extract taken from his memoir of the time:

> The history I had read at school and university was unreal. We got Caesar's pep-talks to his troops but not the reactions in the centurions' mess. We were never told what Agricola's Cretan archers talked about in the evenings overlooking the Tweed at Trimontium. We didn't know what the Highlanders really thought of Montrose when they were making those hurried journeys through the mountain passes. The history of wars presented to us was a generals' eye view – how it appeared to Marlborough or Nelson. Now, for the first time, and at first hand, we were getting the soldiers' eye-view. Reality was bursting in on hundreds of thousands of us. The clerk of the Gas Light and Coke Company found he was making as many marks in meteorology as the university graduate. Traditional drills were universally described as 'bullshit'. Questions half-formulated themselves in drilled minds.'

The earliest diary entry that I have come across in MacKenzie's papers is dated 1 August 1941 which is written just before he is about to be shipped from Britain to Canada and the USA for training. This conveys the mixture of drama and the mundane associated with events as they unfold and brings the atmosphere of the war years close to us in the directness and immediacy of presentation.

> 1 August 1941
>
> Parading in flying kit. Air Commodore with specs and microphone asking everybody what they would do after war. Then a speech in a quay shed, 'Where you are going you will be meeting many Americans. Don't be critical there. Try and see their point of view. Give them yours, but not aggressively. As you know, we want them badly.'

Another speech from an Air Commodore from Air Ministry on arrival here today, 'The most pleasant two years of my life were spent in America. Try and see as much of the country and their customs as you can. Don't criticise, you're the guests there. One thing, in interviews with neutral journalists, don't give any secret convoy information. Refer them to your CO for that.' He had wings, DFC and bar and other decorations, two rows of them.

Night train special for airmen, from Torquay. Left about 10.30 pm. Padres seeing trains off. One padre said his Group Captain from Air Ministry expected the war to be over by Christmas. Dozed to Bristol. Drank a pint of water there without a stop. Men asleep, two on a rack, four below. Wakened after six; green country...a barge on a river or a canal. Then Crewe station...Then march to PD (Personnel Disposal) Camp and breakfast...'

In this next extract MacKenzie is now in Florida, USA, and is giving an account of his first training flight.

2 September 1941

Left the ground 9.37 am and returned 10.18 am – 41 minutes flight, dual, my first.

Got difficulty in getting leg straps of parachute tight. Got an idea from instructor about what he was meaning to do. Got safety belt fastened. We were taxied out and left ground...you looked over and saw, rather than felt, that you were in the air.

Rush of air; vague feeling of wanting to jump out; earth getting further away; blue sky above; bright; and bright yellow, steady wings; look at instruments; at surroundings; uncertainty...sitting during turns at upper side of seat until instructor turned round and told me to let myself go with the plane...which I did; after that with great comfort. When I did this, not the slightest feeling of being on one's side at a banked turn...also I thought to myself, 'Well, this aeroplane is a good reliable plane, I'm pretty secure here', and relaxed further and enjoyed the run. We got above the white, soft, gauzy clouds and they later disappeared. Flying over Florida there were thin white tapes of roads, green country, beautiful little trees, as simple to draw from there as a child's picture of a tree; muddy round pools that looked slimy and stagnant; the village of Nicotee...just two or three short strings of houses and Arcadia which looked bigger. The mounting altimeter, even when you felt unaware of climbing; when asked to keep straight forward rusing the rudders, I kept my eye on a point of cloud and although there was a noise of engine and a rush of air, I felt that we weren't moving anywhere, except the slight movement when the 'ship' deviated from the point of the cloud I had in view.

A question about direction of the aerodrome; difficulty in hearing clearly through the speaking tubes; the aerodrome like a few, light-grey corrugated sheds in the distance; the earth from a few hundred feet looking like an enlargement of a photograph compared to its appearance from three thousand feet. Landing...didn't know when front wheels touched, but felt one slight bump when rear wheel touched.

In this next extract MacKenzie graphically chronicles the intense interest at that time among servicemen (and also among the civilian population as a whole) in issues of civil liberty, particularly in a wartime situation. The meeting which he describes took place at Central Hall, Westminster, and had been called by The Campaign for Civil Liberties.

Saturday 11 April 1942

Michael Foot and Aneurin Bevan made stirring speeches in the Campaign for Civil Liberties meeting in Central Hall, Westminster, this afternoon. Rose Macaulay, who spoke too, watched them. I wondered if it may not be that the initiative has passed to these men, that they are no longer regarded as irresponsible, agitating critics, but responsible men who carry on the great tradition of freedom in Britain and represent this country's people and traditions more truly than the men they attack. They spoke with outspokenness and with deep sincerity. 'It's the old men who are irresponsible', said Bevan, 'youth which is responsible.'

There was a lighter tone in the speeches of the older people Joad, Pritt, Rose Macaulay, than in the burning sincerity of the younger ones. Frank Owen, Evening Standard editor, now called up, was in the audience. He was called up although other men of similar age in journalism and status have not been called up. Why? Someone said that for the same reason as the Mirror was threatened with suppression, that he and the Mirror did much in the criticism of the generalship of the army.

Owen (and somebody near him) offered to go to the platform if fifty pounds were given to the collection. Near me a man of young middle age stood up and said, 'I'll give fifty pounds to shake hands with Frank Owen! He went down and walked to the platform and they shook hands and spoke into the microphone, 'I'm a merchant sea-man', and spoke of fair play for everybody and every race out of God's earth.

The newsreel cameras snapped them and also much of the speeches. Interesting to see what gets past and what gets cut out...Floodlights, half a dozen of them or so shone on the platform. From where I sat I could see another big shaft of light coming perpendicularly from a roof window. Several flashes took place when camera-men took close-up stills of speeches.

The place was full. Several people left after Joad spoke. H.G. Wells was absent on account of illness. There were many service-men present in uniform. All the speeches were of a very high standard, holding the audience. I wondered if there was something historical about this meeting...it was a non-party political demonstration for freedom. I thought of the Peasants' Revolt and Milton; and of the many (but little publicised in history books) fights for freedom fought not by servicemen but by civilians in the story of Britain. 'The price of liberty is eternal vigilance', a speaker quoted. And in a minute speech at the end Owen spoke of making this country the great commonwealth of freedom...this being an issue on which honest men, could, without reservation, join hands.

I wondered if this meeting, eloquence for liberty in the midst of the war, were significant, a common feeling rising through to an expression of something important and 'in the British tradition' and something that is too significant to be omitted in the history of this country now.

This next extract written in Eastbourne not long before he went for further training, this time in South Africa, shows how the awareness that MacKenzie has of the changing seasons of the year creates a colourful distraction from the incidental dramas of the war.

21 June 1942

White flowers on the acacias here in Eastbourne. I've seen a laburnum still in bright flowers and another with its flowers wan-yellow and with soft, dead petals lying thick in a small heap under them, a summer's carpet. Last night I noticed swallows in large numbers flying about at eleven pm (double summertime) and twittering fairly loud. Flower beds look good; poppy leaves are falling off; there is at Crosby House that grey and white flower I remember in our own garden at Wartle and haven't seen since; there's an olive-green-stalked, leaved plant from which a red flower like a pink emerged at the top; and Canterbury Bells. Last night I was awakened at 12.45 by gun-fire, of different kinds, rat-tat-tat of machine-gun fire but still quick fire, and, dull, bomb-sort-of sounds; shore searchlights were searching the surface of the sea; soldiers moving at the double and joking loudly; sound of motor engines in background. I didn't know what it was. We wondered if it was action or practice. I noticed the rim edge, curved lip of the waves, shallow as they came up the sand, bright, yellow-brown edge under the bright light of the searchlights. Tonight at 6.30 pm there is again much noise of firing; I've seen Canadian and Home Guard busy on the streets near the sea-front. It's been a day of bright sunshine, very warm. A year ago I remember at Torquay that Germany had invaded Russia. Today I heard that it was announced in the one o' clock news that the Axis had taken a large part of Tobruk.

Conversations in our room overlooking the sea is often on army strategy about a Second Front; and various things concerning the practical waging of the war. There is much argument. On politics there isn't much argument because there is agreement on a Left, progressive point of view. There seems to be agreement in the opinion that Rommel is a pretty good general.

At this moment (6.45 pm) the moon is south, well up in the sky. Now at 11 pm the moon has moved round to the west from the south. Round the building are valerian and lavender. Round the outskirts of the garden are white campions. From the roof one can see Eastbourne and the sea and the outline of houses in the gloaming; green blurred, rounded shapes of trees; the moon getting more colour now; small uprights mark the shore-line. There are white chalk scrapes and places where the vegetation doesn't cover the white. There's a bit of Beachy Head to be seen, rounded cliff tops, and a dark green with chalk showing through.

There are irises, blue with the pouting lip a deeper, richer blue...the roses are out and smell good. There's a fine straight cut of a tree-lined avenue

> from the sea right out past here. There are churches and church spires to see from the roof. The air is balmy with a slight ruffling wind. There is a hazy fog seawards and the visibility is about eight miles.

It was during this time when he was stationed in Eastbourne and staying in a room that five of them shared at the Grand Hotel, overlooking the sea, that MacKenzie was seeing Diana Lister whom he had met the year before when she and he had been in London. She had joined up with the Women's Royal Navy Service (the Wrens) and because of the exigencies of being on war-service, they had scarcely been able to see each other. However, in the middle of the course he was doing at Eastbourne, he was lucky enough to get a long week-end free and the exhilaration that he felt at meeting up with her again amidst the uncertainties of the war, comes out very strongly in his memoir of the time.

> For these precious hours I escaped from my own RAF associates. There was a sense of luxury in meeting a girl (Diana) out of uniform and strolling through the outskirts of Dorking, looking at the delphiniums and phlox and roses and evening primroses. No hotel accommodation was available, but a smiling housewife gave us a room and in bed we forgot the war and the RAF and the Wrens.

MacKenzie, after a spell of embarkation leave in Aberdeen, where the family had moved two years earlier, was shipped out from Liverpool at the end of September 1942 to South Africa for further navigator training. It took six weeks of what he describes as 'evasive courses in convoy' to reach South Africa.

Once there he took an obvious delight in discovering the country for himself in the course of going to East London where the training would take place. Some aspects of what he sees on the train journey from Durban reminds him of home, according to his recollections of the event.

> The train journey north-east from Durban to Kroonstadt and south to East London showed us a South Africa which was all I had hoped it would be – the High Veldt, its koppjes and kraals and sunshine. When we passed through the 'Valley of a Thousand Hills' and climbed beyond Pietermaritzburg – looking back on it from the climbing train I thought it was as beautiful a town as ever I had seen – the evening light and the clear hill air gave to the countryside a startling clarity. We passed a little railway station with a narrow old road leading up to it, and a cattle loading-bank, and a house with a garden where vegetables were growing, close to the line-side. It was surprisingly like the little branch-line station in Aberdeenshire where I was brought up. When the engine reached the platform, and the driver of our train and the stationmaster exchanged pouches containing the key, which, placed in the signal-locking frame, made it possible for the stationmaster to

open the line ahead, I remembered that that was also the Aberdeenshire practice. It was oddly pleasant to see in a mythical land the details of my own recollections of everyday life at home. The postman of my childhood, who used to get drunk on his rounds, had been a railwayman in South Africa.

Mackenzie then goes on to describe the train journey from Durban to East London with the eye of someone totally enraptured by the scale and scope of what for him was a wondrous new land.

All that day the train went slowly south, but that pleased us since everything we saw was new to us. Even in the flat country of the Orange Free State the railway continued to make twists and curves. South Africa jogged past our window like a news-reel with always something new to offer – sixteen oxen drawing a plough; flowering cactus; waterholes; windmills for charging electric batteries; rolling grassy country rising to conical hills and rocky outcrops; sand blowing through the grass like a threadbare garment; a fine new goods station at Springfontein; flowers red, yellow and blue; the Orange River, very muddy; an immense figure of a man on horseback carved on the hillside at Burghersdorp to commemorate the Great Trek of 1836; hillier country now, and dried-up stream beds.

The following morning we reached the Indian Ocean again, at East London. The work at Queenstown Air School, a hundred miles inland from East London, was hard. In the summer we got up early on flying days and flew three hundred miles before breakfast and lunch. Our aircraft were the reliable Ansons, coloured yellow. Our instructor pointed out that a good navigator uses every available method of checking his position lines; he crossed bearings on the sun, moon, planets and stars with wireless bearings; he used neat little pieces of geometry like 'doubling the angle on the bow'.

On lecture days we did chart work, tried to master the intricacies of radio-navigation and the theory of astro-navigation, the theory of bombing; we studied weather, aerial photography and dead-reckoning navigation, and looked into the constructions of the bubble sextant...We studied the variety of ways in which ingenious people have tried to overcome the difficulty of putting on a flat map the outlines of a spherical world. We studied the trick that the earth's magnetism plays on the aircraft's magnetic compass.

And there were the fringe benefits of travel and meeting new people and talking to them. One of my instructors at Queenstown Air School, Whose name was Pinfold, had been an architect in civilian life. He was keen on navigation and keener on architecture and he always was busy on some ploy. Sometimes he would be making a table with an engraved top to illustrate the lines of poetry on which Debussy based his 'Prelude'; sometimes he would be making a harpsichord; another time he would be reading Schweitzer's monumental life of Bach. We'd go along to his room and listen to gramophone records and he'd read aloud a passage from Van Loon's short book on Bach. Then we'd go to the airman's canteen for beer or to the YMCA for tea and sandwiches. One conversation started from a paragraph in Van Loon's book which says that it was poverty and the loss of trade consequent upon the Mediterranean's diminished importance, that caused the flow of culture of those years in the Palatinate and Thuringia. We argued about whether real, culture was a product of poverty and hardy living or of relaxed, easy living and plenty.

We were both of the opinion that the best political philosophy was that of anarchism; that is, as we understood it, the policy of leaving people to live freely without enmeshing them in a hampering network of laws, rules and discipline. But as we walked back to the aerodrome in the darkness we wondered if the idea of discipline shared by Nazis, Communists, Puritans and army officers mightn't have something in it. We wondered if it were true that insistence on effort was the only thing that kept human life from slipping back into the kind of ease and the inactivity and comfort that has robbed the adult parasitic fluke of its sense organs.

Through the story of mankind upon the earth runs this attempt to weigh two ways of life against one another. There were the Epicureans and Stoics, Cavaliers and Roundheads, the Southern States and the Northern States in the American Civil War.

There wasn't much time in our navigation course at Queenstown however, for the discussion of politics and philosophy and the post-war world. On the days we weren't flying we had seven hours of lectures, and study to do after that, in the evenings. We slogged away at navigation and bombing in lecture-rooms and in the air, but the infrequent breaks from our work were doubly refreshing. Occasionally, under the excellent Toc H hospitality scheme we would spend a weekend at a farm. The hospitality was always extraordinarily generous during these visits. A black girl would bring us morning coffee; we got up for breakfast, and, by the time we had strolled round in the morning sunshine watching the fourteen-oxen teams ploughing, the forenoon tea was ready. Then lunch. After lunch we sat in the stoep talking, or reading the Bloemfontein farming paper, or dozing, until a cup of afternoon tea was brought. And once, after supper-time I remember the farmer asking me to go with him to his orange grove, and there, lighting matches to examine the oranges before we pulled them, we filled a pail with fruit. Then we sat round the fire in the living room and peeled and ate them.

Once we got horses and spent several hours riding over the veldt at high speed. There were odd encounters with black people. One very old man, smoking a pipe, stopped me in the street one day and said, 'You are an Englishman?' I said, 'Yes.' He said, 'Is Lord Roberts dead?' And without waiting for an answer he went on, 'I saw him in Johannesburg. The English attacked the Dutch. Ha! Ha! And he laughed to remember seeing the Dutch getting the worse of it.

One day a black man at the Air School, who made tea and swept out rooms stopped me near our lecture block and said, 'I see you are enjoying an afternoon smoke.'

'Yes', I replied.

'I also enjoy a smoke', he informed me.

I said, 'Oh, indeed.'

'Yes', he replied in a cultured polite tone, 'but to tell the truth my tobacco is finished at the moment.'

So I said, 'Well, if you go into that room you'll find a pouch of tobacco on the table. Help yourself to a fill.'

'Thank you, sir', he replied.

Later in the afternoon I met him and asked him, 'Did you get the tobacco?'

His answer, nearly word for word as he spoke it was, 'It is indeed true that you instructed me to partake of the tobacco in your pouch. But in the circumstances, and on reflection, I considered it unwise to do so, sir, during your absence.'

A friend of mine asked a black lorry-driver in the South African Air Force, 'If your child were ill, would you consult a witch doctor or a white doctor?'

He replied, 'I'd consult both.'

It didn't take us long to disengage ourselves from the simple view of black people propagated by missionaries and British government officials. British airmen went out of their way to ignore the official order not to fraternise with them. There wasn't much defiance in the attitude, merely an unsentimental curiosity and sympathy and an intuitive awareness that there is a time to pay heed to an order and a time to disregard an order. I was surprised at the intelligent mastery of detail with which an Xhoso, working in the Air Force kitchen, summarised some of the articles he'd read in the magazines I'd lent him. And all of us flying over the small towns of the Karoo could not fail to see the black man's crowded shanty locations situated outside the white man's ampler townships. Our horizons were widening. We were seeing things for ourselves.

One evening I saw a tall black man some distance behind me as I was returning to the camp. He was singing trails of song and then would lumber on in silence and break into song again. He was slightly drunk. I waited for him to catch up and said, 'Good evening.'

'Good evening, Bass', he said.

We walked together in the semi-darkness.. He told me he was a Zulu from Natal; he had a different appearance from the Xhosa who lived in these parts of the Cape. He said that he had always hoped that something would be done to improve the conditions of the black people of South Africa. 'I always thought, "Jesus will make it all right." But it is too late now. I don't hope anymore.'

By the time that MacKenzie returned to this country from his training in South Africa (October 1943) the war was beginning to move in favour of the Allied cause. Nevertheless, his own personal involvement in flying operations over enemy territory had now become only a matter of time. So when he writes his first diary entry for January 1944, he openly declares his intention to use his diary entries as a way of recording his personal testimony of a great event in human history that can be read by future generations looking for an insight into what actually took place.

23 January 1944

Here in Lancashire between Preston and Blackpool the country, very green because of the heavy rainfall, is slightly undulating and there are white windmills. In Preston there are army and RAF fellows in the YMCA canteen and in the pubs. On the roads are Yank jeeps. It rains nearly every day and the camp paths are raised above the surrounding level. There are twenty in a hut and we have a coal stove in the centre of the hut. There's over half-a-mile to walk to the cook-house for meals. Planes of all kinds circle overhead...There's a camp cinema, large and comfortable, where I saw Mission to Moscow. We do field training and get lectures on administration and get a 36-hour pass every fortnight. We're waiting for openings in the Advanced Flying Units and Operational Training Units and every good flying day helps us nearer that and every bad day means a day back. There's a meal twice a day. Food is generally good. We get Sunday papers to read at breakfast on Sunday morning. For the first time since I arrived back in this country there was a NAFFI issue of oranges – one each; there was half a bar of chocolate each and a cylinder packet of sweets.

I'm writing this down for two reasons. I haven't kept a diary since I arrived back in this country in November, but in the Daily Mail, Ann Temple suggests keeping a diary of this year as an excellent idea since everybody's diary of a crucial period in human history is just about bound to be interesting and maybe valuable. I've wondered what Caesar's legionaries thought about and their day-to-day life was like when Julius was marching about in Europe and Britain. I've wondered what the Elizabethan soldiers and sailors and crowds thought about at the time of the Armada. So I would like to put something down here of what RAF sergeants are doing and what they are saying and thinking. Secondly, writing down these things clears up the mass of incidents, memories, impressions and ideas in one's mind.

The conversation in our hut is preponderantly about sex: the increase in VD, the Americans and VD rates, types of WAFS (Women in the Royal Air Force), News of the World news which seems to be on the increase so that it has to be reported in other papers, all sorts of sex court-cases; other subjects are 'also rans' (except grousing about restrictions in the camp). Other subjects are Second Front, Russia, Germans; but there is little of such conversation, only at the time when some news in the papers momentarily draws the subject to the focus of attention. Things spoken about are those of immediate interest: first and foremost – sex; then air-crew conditions, regulations, pay, weekends, sleeping out passes, pubs (which I should have given an earlier place), letters, aircraft seen flying overhead, news just heard over the wireless or in the NAFFI, food, films seen, dances, antipathy to Americans (even in officers' talk, a Flight Lieutenant here said this week, 'Having won the last was for us (pause) they lost the peace for us), football pools, occasionally something about where the 94 per cent of NAFFI profits go after the 6 per cent NAFFI rebate is taken off to provide armchairs, etc. for airmen. places where you can get whisky...

Against all this there are some things to be set. This morning one bloke returned to bed after breakfast to read the Sunday papers and one of them is now reading Rupert Brooke's poems in New Writing. Another chap went to Preston yesterday to get a sketching block and pastels but couldn't get pastels, so he got six sheets of ordinary paper and spent the evening making a good copy in pencil of a large photograph of a film star, Alexis Smith...

9 February 1944

Today we saw number 4, concerning the Battle of Britain (number 3 was the Fall of France) of a series of films prepared by America on some such title as 'What we fight for'. The two I've seen here are excellent. I thought this afternoon that it would be a good idea to write down as much as I can remember of the war from a personal point of view.

There was Dad speaking about the first of the evacuees' trains going north and the first troop trains. There were the evacuees and the first welcome they received decreased when their hosts discovered that some people who had plenty room had no evacuees; it's not the load people have to bear that breaks their backs so much as the feeling that other people are getting out of bearing their share. John Macpherson's evacuees got the best of food but couldn't eat it, on account, I suppose, of not having been accustomed to such good food. There was news of leaflet raids and from Eric Morrison I saw some of the leaflets and they were as dull as a dull sermon. There was news from the Maginot Line region, patrols and mopping-up operations. There was news of the daring exploit of a German submarine in Scapa Flow and the news of an attack on shipping on the Forth...

After we came to Aberdeen we could still get the phone put in during the summer of 1940. They were taking down sign-posts, hotel signs which gave away a village name-place, names on vans, railway station names. There were road-blocks that first struck me, bringing the war suddenly much nearer and making it more real. There were the LDVs (Local Defence Volunteers, later the Home Guard) and the Fire Service. I remember the summer mid-day in which I heard on the wireless of the fall of France; not long before that, Mother had heard on the wireless a pathetic appeal from Prime Minister Reynard to America, ('Come quickly! It is now that we need help, now, now...' There were Churchill's speeches and Priestly's post-scripts. And then I remember one morning getting up early and cycling down a valley to Tillyfourie and hearing there of the high scores of German planes downed in the previous day's Battle of Britain. Then I went on to Alford and had an excellent breakfast in the hotel and then went slowly through the village and sat at the bridge at Keig and then to Insch and in the afternoon cycled back to Aberdeen...

27 April 1944

In a lecture on bombing the lecturer spoke of the refinement by which a German, dealing with a delayed explosion bomb, thinking he would make it harmless, would set it off. And there have been many, many, clever dodges, like that of an explosive charge in an incendiary bomb, to make for more efficient killing. Yet the extraordinary amount of busy ingenuity in making bigger and bigger bombs, in counteracting the German attempts to deal with our bombs...all this lethal activity is not different in nature from the ingenuity expressed in clever navigational equipment. The wizard bomb-sight is a product of mental energy of the same nature exactly as the wizard navigational equipment. Same with deadlier and deadlier poison gas, if such is being produced, as I expect is likely. It's not a refinement of cruelty at all, it's not sadistic like medieval torture. It's impersonal, a mental problem to solve.

I'm still unconvinced about the wickedness of Germans as a nation. I think they are too representative a cross-section of white humanity for the Allies to say so with impunity.

7 May 1944

Left the camp at 3.15 pm and at 4.30 pm arrived by American fast lorry in Northampton. Met my sister Alice. Her stories of life as a Medical Officer are good. She played at a camp church service this morning and at the end of the service, the ATS C.O. suddenly said, 'The King!' She looked round in surprise (almost expecting the King to walk in) and turned over the hymn book hurriedly to find the music for 'The King' but couldn't find it. All the people were now standing to attention. She didn't want to do it improvised so she decided to let them wait and she turned up the index deliberately at the end of the hymn book and found the number and got the hymn and played the music. I think that's a good example of not flapping in an emergency...

We walked out the Bedford road, watched two boys throwing (with some skill) a boomerang; she had a lemonade and I a beer at a pub; we saw limes, willows, sycamores or planes, elms in leaf, ashes coming into leaf, lilac out, hawthorn out; the warm red-brick of the town against the fresh green; the Spring; Dakotas flying in striking formation; Wellingtons altering course; a mallard; cow-parsley out; poplars reflected in still water; fruit trees in blossom. It was quite cold. When we came back, we searched for a cafe and at last found a little transport cafe but they wouldn't have Alice in it (if we allow one woman in, we'll be getting all the disreputables along) so I took out two mugs of tea and sausage rolls and cake and when I came out Alice said, 'I've found a window', and in the light of the full moon we had a picnic, sitting our tea and plate of food on the ledge and standing on the street while we drank our tea.

It's pleasant to get away from the discipline and restrictions of the camp, even for a '48' and feel free.

17 July 1944

Sunday's lectures brought the following additions of information. To kill a hedgehog, you tickle it on the underside and when the head emerges, hit the head. Then cover it up all in clay and bake in a fire for ten minutes; then the skin and spikes peel off. For rats and mice you cut off the head, skin like a rabbit, take out the entrails, and boil. Many continental plants are poisonous apparently. Don't hide in woods on the continent because they are taken up with dumps, depots, etc. Get thirty miles away from your landing point on the first night; then you can lie up for two days rest and make your plans. On landing use a benzidrene tablet because you might be less well than you think you are. You can easily go nine or ten days without food but water is different. If you are going into hiding and see some water, fill your water-bag and put one or two purifying tablets into it and shake it up for ten minutes and drink it all, then refill, put in more tablets and take into hiding with you. You can use the British Government's credit up to several hundred pounds to pay a guide to take you over the Pyrenees, a boat-man to take you over the Channel...and the Government will honour the bargain. You must be fit before taking on a job like crossing the Pyrenees; so lie up for a day or two to gather your strength for it...While you are in full uniform (like the Wing Commander who landed on a German drome and shot two soldiers who came up before he'd burned his kit) you are free to kill or use violence and still be treated as a prisoner of war after capture, but if you have the

> slightest disguise at all and are not in full uniform, you forfeit the right to use violence and be treated as a prisoner of war; if in disguise and found with papers about troop numbers and positions you may be shot as a spy; therefore, anything valuable you see must be committed to memory...
>
> 22 August 1944
>
> Tonight during the nine o' clock news they played the Marseillaise after announcing that Paris had been taken by the people of Paris armed and unarmed together, after four days battle. It must have been great, after the tension of four years and two months of captivity for the Parisiens to hear Roget de Lisle's battle-song of freedom again. The news everywhere is good and according to the papers the Normandy victory is a complete one and a rout. The Russians have taken Jassy and are standing on the outskirts of Warsaw. The army in the South of France is advancing. The Maquis are in command of several districts and towns of France. Only the Flying Bombs still land in London.

MacKenzie's preoccupation with the impending Allied victory in Europe did not mean, as he implies himself, the end of the war for civilians living in the London area who were in constant danger from V1 and V2 rocket attacks. His own concern for the plight of such people was sharpened to some extent by his personal anxiety for the safety of his fiancée, Diana. She was still serving in the Wrens and was stationed in the London area. She and MacKenzie had kept in touch by letter while he had been training in South Africa and after his return had eventually got engaged on 8 July 1944.

Their wedding day was Monday 5 February 1945, the marriage taking place at All Saints Church, Kingston on Thames. Their honeymoon was spent in the Westward-Ho Hotel at Bideford in Devon where Charles Kingsley had written his novels. As MacKenzie remarks in his journal, 'It was a respite from the war, an interval of escape and quiet. We strolled round Clovelly and watched the new amphibious vehicles called "ducks" floating into the shore of Bideford Bay and coming up the beach.' Not long afterwards (only a week in fact) Diana had to return to the Wrens depot in London where, because of the Flying Bombs, she was arguably in as much danger from enemy action as MacKenzie was in Lincolnshire where he was now stationed. 'It was a time', MacKenzie ruefully observes in his memoir. 'of hurried journeys and brief meetings.'

It was also a time when MacKenzie began inwardly to reflect on the passage of the war and what impact it might have on the kind of society that would come into being when it was over. This comes out in his memoir as he considers the effects upon himself and others of the strange experience of trying to make compatible long stretches of boredom and inaction with the stress of going on bombing missions over enemy territory. That and the way in which men from different ranks reacted to each other in the interpretation of military discipline continually exercises his thoughts:

> Stretches of boredom and discomfort were relieved by unexpected and sometimes heart-warming incidents. Once when our squadron moved to another station I was among the navigators sent to clean out the navigation rooms. A squadron leader set us on the job of pinning up maps while he went down on his knees and scrubbed the floor. His braces were repaired with bits of string. On another occasion the wing commander addressed us. 'Well, fellows, it appears we have got to have a weekly parade. What the hell for, I don't know. Bloody silly, these parades, it seems to me. But we've got to have them. That's all I wanted to say to you. Good morning.' Once a notice from very high up indeed was pinned on the notice-board. The saluting on many RAF stations was slack, not up to standard. Disciplinary action...Thereafter for two or three days there was a rash of saluting and then everybody forgot about it. In a citizens' army, the military priesthood were out-voted. It was a glimpse of a society in transition. I admired the wisdom of the station commander who did his duty in posting the notice and went to no great length to enforce it.'
>
> The war-time RAF was a catalyst, speeding up reactions in society. Ideas and attitudes that otherwise would have remained inert were changing. Communication replaced isolation. Prejudices were diluted. Many of us found that there was much that was different from what we had been brought up to believe. People were different. The gunnery leader was a slight figure and he had an extreme Oxford accent. When others would have given an order, he asked a gunner to go out to an aircraft and check the guns, and in such a friendly manner that the gunner felt that he was conferring a favour on the gunnery leader by complying. He had been on ninety operational trips. For a brief period, while ideas were in flux, a new society could have come into being, of which many different people would have been proud to be a member. It had the makings of an open society, without pretence. There was little of the before-Agincourt rhetoric of Henry V. To be scared before a flight was regarded as a natural reaction, described in the RAF's own vocabulary as 'having the twitch'. Old values were in suspension, and there was a generosity of outlook which made us more accessible to new ideas. It was ironical that these potential generations of a new society were too busy dropping bombs to apply this generosity to a wider purpose.
>
> It was probably the tension over the target that concentrated our minds wonderfully, the bursting flak, the probing searchlights, black planes silhouetted against a blaze on the ground. A shiver went down my back when I heard the voice of the bombing leader say, 'Come right in and bomb.' It was high-pitched because that way it was heard more clearly on the intercom, and the high pitch accentuated the tension. The moment that our own bomb-aimer said 'Bombs gone', the pilot swung the plane on to the new course for the short leg out of the target, losing height rapidly to increase speed. Even back across the Rhine there was the danger of night-fighters. The French coast came up ahead; then the English coast. Then the aerodrome

perimeter lights, illuminating the Midlands like a fairground. After the debriefing there was a meal of bacon and eggs. I remember particularly one frosty night when there was a full moon high in the sky. It was half a mile back to the billets and, although the rest of the crew had clambered on to a transport, I decided to walk. It was a relief to put one foot past the other after all these hours cramped at the navigator's table. It was a peaceful night in the heart of the English countryside. There were dark ploughed fields and meadows and trees, and barely a sound. If you hadn't been there, you would have found it difficult to believe that only a few hours ago there was a fury of exploding bombs and bursting shells and destructive energy and angry flashes of light over a German marshalling yard.

You would have thought that after all that it would never be the same again. We would really get down to it and begin a major overhaul of our society. But we didn't. We forgot so soon.

Although the war in Europe was clearly drawing to a close by the spring of 1945, and thoughts of what sort of future lay beyond the war did, to some extent, exercise people's minds, nonetheless the war still laid its claim on those like MacKenzie who were engaged in the final stages. He was now part of an aircrew of a Lancaster squadron that was on regular bombing missions over Germany and Occupied Europe. By the time of the following entry in his diary he had flown on nine missions.

22 February 1945

The Spring is here and Fulbeck looks a pleasant village of red brick and the fields look a pleasant green and birds sing in the mornings as we go to breakfast.

We've now put in nine trips (ten if you count in the skipper's second 'dicky' trip). Trondgem was the first and at eleven and a half hours, the longest. Compass trouble after a hasty take-off. Circling the target at a big radius. 'Do not bomb', code-word came through; then the long trip home. Heimback dams twice and on the second trip looking out of the aircraft and seeing other aircraft and bombs bursting and feeling safe for knowing that our fighters were about. At Giessen I didn't look out, but the reargunner's reports of seeing a fighter, which wasn't after us, weren't too pleasant. Royen was a better trip. I had a good look out when we'd dropped our bombs and saw the angry, stormy glare and the bursts of light. After the trip I remember walking back to the hut, comparing the peace of the country scene in the middle of the night with the glare and confusion of the target area. Brux in Czechoslovakia was a long trip. Where I didn't look out or didn't have time to look out, little stays in the mind except being busy all the time getting fixes, checking up ground speed and the short, pleasant relaxation of thermos tea and chocolate on the way back. Of Merseburg I remember little. At Rositz we were attacked by a fighter JU 188, after it had been under us and the mid-upper had opened up at it and we had been corkscrewing. As it came up behind, the reargunner's guns had a stoppage and jammed and the skipper went into a starboard corkscrew so that we were hit on the starboard wing...After that hit, the rest of the shells went past our port side and we got into cloud about the same time and got away okay. Bill said he was scared but his voice sounded firm. There was two to three minutes of that.

25 April 1945

This morning at 9 am exactly we bombed the SS barracks at Berchtesgaden. Last night there was a three-quarter growing moon and we had a meal at 11 pm and briefing at 12. We then went out to the aircraft, the navigators last, after having got the turning-point times. Each got off the truck as he came to his aircraft, B Baker, etc. We were Q Queenie, which was in a nice rural, secluded sort of dispersal point near the Newark road. I walked about a little as there was some time before take-off. We thought it might be a very easy or else a really sticky target.I ate a spam sandwich and had a drink of tea from a flask. I feel I could have done with another good meal. I took my bar of chocolate and poke of barley-sugar sweets up to my cabin beside me. At 4.22 we were airborne and about 4.30 we went down the Thames estuary and then to Cape Gris Nez and turned there to cross France to reach our squadron's rendezvous point. Before we got there, the light had come and I drew back my black-out curtains. The skipper saw an aircraft ahead showing green vereys and fell in behind and ended with a crowd of aircraft and we all made for the main rendezvous. We were near enough to see the squadron letters on the aircraft and I had a list of which squadrons we went along with for a bit. I looked and saw that we were with the stream.. Below France. An air-field pockmarked with bomb-craters; some aircraft on it. Bomb craters on fields for no apparent reason unless there were attempts to hit the roads when all France was on the road in the refugee tragedy of 1940. Some of the craters healed over, green at the edges like the scar round a wound or the roundness of the bark round a tree where a limb has been sawn off. Verdun down on the starboard beam and I told the gunmen that that was where Pétain made a name for himself in the last war…Below us a region like a limitless plain, beginning to lose its shadows in the morning light: scene of two wars within my life-time. But this morning, apart from the bomb craters, which looked like the dimples in hottering porridge or like the depressions in telescopic pictures of the moon, it looked a peaceful scene of accord. Then mountains began to come up and we crossed the northern end of the Vosges, a counter line on the Mercator marking their outline. Then down on the port side, Strasbourg. Just in these mountains where there was occasionally a hamlet and an isolated steading, I wondered if in the last four years every one of these French houses had known German soldiers. Did a girl from that house walk out with a German soldier and what did the people think about it? Were the people collaborators or was there sabotage and resistance there and were the Germans afraid to walk that little, lonely, hilly road alone? But there was no hate at fifteen thousand feet; nothing to be seen but peaceful countryside. I thought of the Maginot Line and of the truffles that Bernard Newman in his spy story of that title mentions that you can get there. Then the icy-white mountains of Switzerland came into view and as we came nearer Lake Constance, I could see that the average line of the mountains was slightly above us, or so it seemed; they had a general level with no outstanding peak visible. Over there, I told the crew, on the starboard bow was the Schaffhausen salient. I asked the bomb-aimer for a pin-point, giving him our approximate position...there was little wind, certainly under 20 knots, so navigation was easy. Then rougher country and we were among the mountains and that green-yellow river was the upper reaches of the Iser on which Munich stands and that next one was the Inn on which Innsbruck stands; we turned to port before reaching the Salzach on which Salzburg stands. The mountains here in Bavaria, I think, look impressive from our height, but the valleys were narrow. The target landmark was a lake but because it was between high mountains and the sun was still low on the horizon, it wasn't easy to find and the bomb-aimer, when he did see it, said it looked like a river.

It was nearly 9 am – 'zero hour'. Some aircraft were ahead of us. 'Bomb-doors open!' The aircraft ahead didn't seem to be opening theirs. 'Twenty degrees left correction.' 'Steady!' Ahead I saw an aircraft that had completed its bombing run and was turning to port on to the first leg of the homeward journey and I wished that we had reached that stage...maybe two mountains ahead. There was flak at our height...'Steady!'...then in a quick tone, 'Bombs gone!' I noted, '0.900:bombs gone', and my pencil broke and I inwardly smiled at myself for that happening. I had been marking down the heading course, air-speed, height and API reading and now made the target readings and checked them. We looked out to see what the other aircraft were doing. I wondered if in the absence of the Controller's instructions those which hadn't bombed were going to orbit the target and come in again, and we were orbiting and waiting till he gave instruction. But we were moving on to the course out. Behind, I looked at the brown-black, angry and thickening group of flak bursts and was relieved when next time I looked we were out of that area. There was smoke rising from the ground. There was a feeling 'Have we come through that?' I was too late to see Salzburg. One aircraft that hadn't bombed, dropped his bomb on a bridge after asking permission and being told by the Controller to hurry up and join the gaggle like a small boy on a school walk being told not to loiter behind looking at a bird's nest or a ditch. 'Hurry up', said the Controller. 'But what shall I do with my bomb?' Somebody told him what to do with the bomb over the UHF, and the Controller curtly cut in with, 'Less talking, please!'

We had a 1,000 pound bomb hung up. Bill saw a village and wanted it to be dropped there. Macintyre said, 'Oh hell no!' Finally, it was just jettisoned anywhere. Munich was visible down on the starboard beam, maybe 15 miles away. Then later there was wooded country with little clearings and with a house in it and some space round the house. There were sharply twisting roads whose sharp turns showed that the slope must be steep. There was what looked like a quarry; and later, near the town, a factory whose camouflaged roof demonstrated that it must be important. Then we saw Strasbourg again and saw how by letting the Rhine in to make docks on either side they make it a river port...Then there were French fields, more dotted with trees and the colour was less clear and bright than in Germany. Then the battle zone of the last war – Cambrai and the coal-mining area. Then England. We got back at 12.50 pm. There was a briefing and tea and questions about the route in. Then a meal and then I went to bed at 3 pm and got up at 7.30 pm.

The war diaries, naturally enough, tail off with the conclusion of the war in Europe in May 1945. Fortunately for MacKenzie the dropping of the atomic bombs on Hiroshima and Nagasaki in August 1945 brought a swift end to the war in the Far East as well and prevented his having to be posted there for active service which would have been the case if the war with Japan had not ended when it did.

For MacKenzie, like so many others, the war had been a formative experience. Like his travels in Europe before the war, it had taken him away once more from the narrow confines of the North-East of Scotland and had on this occasion exposed him to the different cultures of North America and South Africa. South Africa, in particular, made a lasting impression on his mind, not just in relation to the obvious delight he experienced in getting to know the physical characteristics of the land, but in its political and social structure, and in the parallels he drew between the culture of the Boers of South Africa and that of the Presbyterian Scots.

He also had in the course of his war service to come to terms with the extremes of tedium and crisis that characterised modern warfare. The keeping of his unique diary of what these extremes meant on a day-to-day basis helped him to resolve this problem personally and provides us with a rare insight into the climate of the war years as seen through the eyes of a shrewd observer.

For him, as for many others, particularly in the RAF, the enemy was largely unseen and disembodied in that warfare for them largely consisted of flying to targets in enemy territory and unloading bombs on these targets with little thought given to the resultant suffering of the people (mostly civilians) upon whom the bombs were dropped. For MacKenzie as an individual this was a strange and haunting experience as he had grown to admire many aspects of German life and culture and to like the Germans as a people in his pre-war visits to their country; and his fundamental regard for them as a people never left him, despite his having to participate in their destruction as a member of the armed forces.

Lastly, as a Sergeant Navigator,* he saw the war through mostly in the company of 'ordinary' servicemen which, in a way, suited his native suspicion of the Establishment represented by the 'officer class'. If anything, the war reinforced his belief that society, as it was, needed changing. A war-time situation had created a climate that had helped to break down class barriers and prejudice but MacKenzie was fearful

*MacKenzie was promoted, nevertheless, to the rank of Flight-Lieutenant, shortly before the end of his war service (see plate 1).

that the restoration of peace would inevitably bring about a reversion to the way things had been in the past, despite the social and economic reforms that the newly elected Labour government had promised to put in place during their term of office.

The war, then, had matured Mackenzie both emotionally and intellectually, and had enriched his experience of human nature. Now, of course, as a married man, he had to give immediate thought as to how he would earn a living. Inwardly, he still had a great desire to investigate the truth of things and to develop his powers as a writer. That it was to teaching that he was to turn his talents was perhaps not a surprise, given his early attempts at it in the 1920s and his abiding concern with the role of education as a key function of the state.

CHAPTER FIVE

'Shadows of the Prison House': MacKenzie in the Borders and Fife 1946–67

Between the time that he finished his cycle tour of Europe in 1932 with Hunter Diack and the outbreak of the Second World War in 1939, MacKenzie seldom had regular employment. Mostly, he had to rely on payments he received from incidental work he did for the local press and on such payments (often in the form of free board and lodging) he got for doing tutoring work, as in Germany just before the war broke out, to pay his way. He had always been in the habit of living frugally and this stood him in good stead during the pre-war years when he did his extensive travels in Europe, virtually on a shoe-string.

His first formal experience of teaching as such occurred in 1934, when, unemployed in London, he answered an advertisement for a vacancy for a teacher of English and Biology in a Pioneer school at the edge of the New Forest. The salary was nominal – £30 a year with full board and lodgings.

He got the job and found himself in a small independent school called Forest School. It was run by a society called the Order of Woodcraft Chivalry. Its Head was Cuthbert Rutter who came from a West Country Quaker family. The keynote of the school was its informality. Rutter would read stories of an evening to those of the pupils who were interested in listening and would try to carry out in practice the sort of advice the Pupils' Council advocated to help run the school better.

The school did not go to the extremes of freedom which A.S. Neill, with considerable courage, had adopted for his school at Summerhill in Suffolk, but on occasions the Headteacher allowed to be carried into effect resolutions of the pupils' meetings which made some eyebrows rise. A girl of ten complained to the school meeting that a boy of 12 was always following her around. The Headteacher asked the boy why he followed this girl all the time and the boy replied that he wanted to know what the girl looked like when she was not wearing any clothes. The girl was asked if she would object to sitting in the nude on the table in the common room while this boy made a plasticine model of her. The girl did mot mind at all, the plasticine model was made and the boy, having satisfied his curiosity about what the girl looked like, ceased to pester her.

At the primary stage, pupils had complete freedom to stay away from classes. At the secondary stage 'shadows of the prison house' began to close in on them. Rutter said to them, 'Now here are some outside exams that you will have to pass if you are going to be an engineer, biologist, etc., but I think that most of the knowledge you'll have to get is useless knowledge, but there it is. As a result of this laisser-faire attitude, many of the parents chose to take away their children to an 'orthodox' school at the age of 13.

MacKenzie had no knowledge of botany, though he had to teach it and told the pupils so. In that situation learning became for both teacher and pupil a process of discovery. In a memoir of this period of his life he recalls, 'I remember the satisfaction of discovering black bryony and sharing the discovery. I became a child again, finding delight in the delicate colour of mallows...I can never look on red campions now without entering into that excitement, the feeling of emergent life.'

In those botany lessons which largely took place in the New Forest he and his pupils 'came nearer', he remembers, 'to integrating education into a full enjoyment of life' than he had ever been able to since. The enjoyment of the natural world, he reckoned, owed much to the vitality of children whose parents cared more for education than for examination certificates.

He concludes in his memoir of this formative period of his life:

> I was at Forest School from the age of 24 until I was 26. It was as if the school had taken me to a high place and let me see the kingdoms of the world, broadening my horizons. They were practical people like the 6th-century monks of Monte Cassino, working away quietly converting dreams into solid reality. These two years stand out in my memory. Since then, former pupils have written that for them, too, their years at Forest School were among the best in their lives. There was freedom and partly because of that, there was what Goethe (in a letter to Schiller) called 'tranquil activity'. I'd been into the educational future and it worked.

Although there is no doubt about how critical in the formulation of his own ultimate views on education the experience at the Forest School was, ten years were to pass before MacKenzie decided to take up teaching as a career. Tutoring jobs in Germany before the war and service in the RAF delayed that entry as well as other interests he had, such as developing his talents as a writer. Indeed, there was a stage in 1946, when, had the opportunity been made available to him, he might well have joined the BBC as a writer and broadcaster. Such a post had been advertised at a time when MacKenzie had not fully committed himself to a teaching career; but, although he applied for it, he was not invited for interview and so that particular career route got no further. But the experience did not diminish his interest in broadcasting as he contributed numerous scripts to the BBC for school broadcasting during his stay in the Borders from 1946 to 1951.

As things turned out, however, he had already enrolled at Aberdeen Teacher Training College in 1946 to train as a teacher, not long after 'demob' from the RAF, and, having completed the six months' emergency course that was open to returning servicemen at that time, he was offered a post, which he accepted, at Galashiels Academy as a teacher of English and History and began his teaching career there in August of that same year.

Despite the fact that he had not been inside a Scottish school since the time he had been a pupil at Robert Gordon's in Aberdeen 20 years before, he found, to his disappointment, that nothing had changed – 'there they were again, the Tudors and the Stuarts as large as life, the notes on The Merchant of Venice and exercises on subordinate adverbial clauses'. In the staffroom education was not mentioned except at the time of the external examinations and the discussion was restricted to whether the exam questions were fair or unfair. MacKenzie felt a great sense of disillusionment at what he saw as a period of retrenchment setting in after the liberating atmosphere in society associated with the war years. This he saw being borne out in a particular incident involving the RAF that he had just recently been serving in during the war years.

> We set up a squadron of the Air Training Corps at the school and took the youngsters flying. One of them, who did exceptionally well in the ATC examinations, was taken on a flight to Iraq. On his return he was asked to write an essay describing his trip. He included a reference to what he saw as the waste of petrol in washing down aircraft at Habbaniyah on the Euphrates. The RAF took a dim view of this comment and asked me to ask him if he'd remove the comment from his essay. He refused, saying that it was true. A row started between the Royal Air Force and a boy of fifteen. The boy left the Air Training Corps.

And he goes on in his memoir to comment on the implications of this incident.

> This was not the war-time RAF that I knew. The war was over and a chapter of our lives was closed. The peace-time Headteachers and air-marshals were moving in to restore the shape of the pre-war world they knew. The

> examinations our pupils had to sit in 1949 were little changed from those of 1939. The Scottish Education Department were bringing down the curtain on the intervening drama and on the events that had been happening in the minds of men and women. They were against change.

Despite this, he and Diana enjoyed life in the Borders. For him, especially, the Borders was attractive because of its dramatic scenery and its deep-rooted connections with the way Scotland had developed historically as a nation over the centuries. Its special character as a place to live in is fondly dwelt on by MacKenzie in this extract from his chapter on the Borders in *A Search for Scotland*:

> The region has a unity of place; it is a kingdom on its own, inducing a tough local patriotism in its subjects. We lived on the Melrose Road outside Galashiels, looking across to Galafoot and the Tweed at Abbotsford. Near our home was a plaque in a wall recording that here Walter Scott, ill on his journey home from Italy, sprang up with a cry of delight on seeing the Eildons. The inscription gave a special poignancy to his generalised poem on patriotism:
>
> Breathes there the man with soul so dead
> Who never to himself hath said.
> This is my own, my native land.
>
> You don't venture outside the weel-kent territory unless you have to and then you get back as quickly as possible. 'A day out of Hawick is a day lost.' When James Hogg, the Ettrick Shepherd, was trying to make writing pay for his farming, Scott planned to help him, explaining that to gain patronage, he would have to go to London to attend the coronation of George the Fourth, but Hogg refused because, if he went, he would miss St Boswell's Fair.

Happy though he was to live in the Borders, MacKenzie was nonetheless continually frustrated by the narrowness of the curriculum in English and History at the Academy. On occasion, however, when the pupils were acting scenes from Shakespeare, some of them could bring to their parts, (as one girl did who played Shylock) the real drama of the original. He remarks in his journal:

> The whole performance leapt out of the school stage and clutched us who were watching...the fourteen year old actress discovered an ability to speak out fearlessly in a large school hall. She had escaped from the Scottish working class preoccupation with keeping your voice down in public...she had become aware of her worth.

Looking back at his teaching of history at the school, he regrets not making greater use of the Borders setting to illustrate to his pupils the different stages of history that the area had gone through. He would have gone for more human detail, 'visiting the site of the Roman camp at Trimontium and the Edinburgh museum to put us wise about Agricola, we'd have given to our pupils the feeling of what it was like to be living in that area of marshes and wild boars.'

Diana had already grown to enjoy life in Scotland and to adapt to Scottish life and customs. In a broadcast she did for the BBC programme, a 'Women's Hour' in January 1950, she talks about the changes moving to Scotland has made in the way she speaks and her husband's peculiarly Scottish eating habits and his perception of English as opposed to Scottish weather:

> When my mother visits us from Warwickshire, she tells me that I am picking up the lilt of the Scottish Borders speech and that my voice rises at the end of each sentence. She tells me I use the word 'wee' (little), far too often. And that I never used to say, 'I'll away and make the tea.'
>
> For some time now I've been writing down some of these little differences I notice between Scotland and England. The most obvious difference is, of course, in speech. We lived in Aberdeen before we came to the Borders and in the two regions I have learned new words and idioms. 'Is it raining?' I asked in Aberdeen, and the answer was,'Oh, it's only sparking!' And I heard my mother-in-law asking a relative who had been ill, 'What like are ye the day?' I soon became accustomed to use the word 'forenoon'when I would previously have said,'morning', and I have added to my permanent vocabulary the typically Aberdeenshire word, 'scutter'; anything that gives you trouble to do, anything that is finicky and hardly worth the bother anyway, is a 'scutter' But my Scottish relatives found my Southern pronunciation of the word amusing.
>
> For some reason or other, porridge and soup are plural in Scotland. 'Sup them up; they're affa fine' a child is told when he isn't too keen on his porridge. And speaking of porridge reminds me of my husband's insistence on having porridge and milk separately. The milk has to be in a small bowl beside his porridge plate and he takes a spoonful of milk alternately. I found it difficult to remember all the different things with which Aberdeenshire people eat oat-cakes instead of bread when they have high tea. It is not done to eat bread with boiled eggs, cheese, fish, or sausages. Oat-cakes and butter are served in its place.
>
> Another thing, the weather. When our neighbour in a Warwickshire village heard I was to live in Scotland, he told me, 'It's cold up there!' My husband is most impatient with this idea, and is never tired of saying how cold Lincolnshire was in winter when he was there in the RAF during the war. Every time Edinburgh has an hour's more sunshine than Cheltenham, he points it out to me triumphantly in the paper. 'There seems to be a general impression', he says, 'that England is a warm country; one almost expects to see sarongs in Warwickshire!' But he admits that Hampshire, at any rate, is warmer than Aberdeenshire.

And she concludes her impressions of how Scotland compares with England with these words:

> But I know that all of Scotland isn't the 'stern and wild' country that many people imagine. At midsummer Donside has the richness of colour and foliage of Hampshire almost. And from my front door now I look across the lovely Tweed to the trees behind Scott's house at Abbotsford and I realise how sorry I should be if I had to leave my Scottish home.

The delights associated with his stay in the Borders are also very apparent in the diaries that MacKenzie kept at this time, recording walks and rambles that he and Diana made at week-ends and half-term holidays as well as in the notes he kept constantly of the changing seasons. On Monday 3 June 1951 he writes memorably in his diary about a picnic he and Diana enjoyed that summer.

> Half-term holiday. Di and I walked from Ashkirk up the Air valley to Alemoor Loch and then the road to Hawick. Excellent warm weather and bright sunshine. We heard a wren singing; much better singer than we thought with a throaty twirl in the middle of the song. We made a fire of last year's dust-dry bracken and the very dry stems of burnt heather and some wood and boiled water and made tea and had a meal and relaxed to the sound of a streamlet. We supported the pan on stones and cooled the milk in the burn. Several new buds...One the colour of the weathered grey and lichened grey of dry-stane dykes. Much sheep wool on fences...in the valley dippers with persil-white shirt-fronts keeping up a continual dipping movement. Nearly as big as thrushes these dippers...I thought helicopters, when commom, could make these inaccessible and remote valleys worth making a house in and alter the economy of the Ettrick Forest. I bathed in the Ale and without a towel dried out in the hot sun in a minute or two. Then when we climbed out of the valley of Alemoor Loch and were going downhill toward Hawick (eight miles) a new ecology and a chaffinch singing. We watched at the edge of a wood two red squirrels standing on hind-legs and running playfully about and an old bearded man smoking a pipe and moving little; an ample shaded beech hedge with the new red-brown still on its leaves; ash trees not yet out; narcissi; rhododendrons in a sheltered valley. The Borthwick Water and Teviot and from near the Alemoor Loch, the three Eildons.

When in 1952 MacKenzie was appointed Principal Teacher of English at Templehall Junior Secondary School, Kirkcaldy, the MacKenzie family moved from their beloved Borders cottage to a council house in the new town of Glenrothes in Fife. The contrast between the two places was striking; yet for MacKenzie, it represented another challenge – another place to get to know and to 'make sense of'. In an article for *The Glasgow Herald* (for which he became a regular feature writer over the next decade) he describes what it felt like to live in Glenrothes at that time.

> It is in a New Town like ours where all the changes have come at once and everything is new that we realise how fast Scotland is changing. Gardens

> unenclosed by high wall or hedge bring a kind of Canadian openness into the town. There is a Dutch-like variety of architecture and we are perhaps indebted to Sweden for light pastel shades and open balconies. The school looks Utopian. It is surrounded by playing fields and has immense windows and the pupils dry their hands in hot air currents and do their PT bare-footed on a floor that doesn't splinter ...Most people are thoroughly delighted with their houses. It is an event in anybody's life to come into a newly built, airy house with big windows, warm-pipe airing cupboards, built-in wardrobes and plenty of cupboard space...It is a unique opportunity...the town has a long way to go before it is completed and by that time some of the faults may be amended...A teacher in the school told me she had 53 pupils in her class. There is an avenue lined with elm and beeches leading down to the river, but the river is one day full of factory refuse the colour of tomato soup and another day looks as if it had been thickened with dirty porridge...We are told that it is going to be very difficult to bring light industries here to supplement the main industry, coal-mining. Families depending on work other than mining find the rent difficult to meet...None of those difficulties should be insuperable. Optimistically, I think a sense of civic responsibility is growing, and there is already plenty of another quality that is necessary if we are going to smooth out these snags – goodwill. And we have interests beyond bus services and blue-prints...

One senses in MacKenzie's writing at this time (the mid-1950s) a genuine optimism, not just about his own personal life with the birth of his three children, Neil in 1952, Alasdair in 1955, and Diana in 1958, but in the way some of the newer schools were beginning to adapt to what he saw as the real needs of the youngsters in them. This growing optimism coincided with his appointment to Templehall Junior Secondary in Kirkcaldy, an inexpensive, single-storey building catering for the needs of Kirkcaldy children aged between 12 and 15 who had been allocated to a Junior Secondary course as opposed to a Senior Secondary course at a 'Grammar' school on account of 'failing' their '11-Plus' exam. Jack Stewart, the Headteacher, was a go-ahead man who believed in the benefits of outdoor education.

In an article in the *Evening Dispatch* of June 1957 headed 'School for Adventure' an interesting description is given of the activities that the school had become well-known for at a time when outdoor education was still in its infancy. The system used was for the children to save up for an adventure week by making weekly deposits in a school savings account and then draw lots to go mountaineering, flying in an aircraft over their home county (as a unique form of geography lesson) or go pony-trekking in the Highlands. For instance, a company of 26 boys and girls with two teachers spent seven days at Kingussie Youth Hostel where they made friends with a stable-full of hardy Highland ponies, reaching 1500 feet above sea-level, achieving lessons of self-reliance, of community spirit, endurance and resourcefulness. Jack Stewart is quoted as saying:

> We wanted to get over lessons that could not be assessed or taught in the classroom. Saving to go on an adventure trip has proved to be a wonderfully popular idea...we have sent pupils flying in the past and we have sent them on a mountaineering course at Glenmore. This year we wanted something different, but it had to fulfil certain conditions in addition to being reasonably economical...It had to call on powers of physical endurance and courage without exceeding what was to be expected of children aged twelve to fifteen and it had to be in some part of the country where a town child could find new interest, a part rich in bird, plant and animal life with natural beauty and potential adventure.

Hence, swimming, fishing and general nature study figured in the week's course as well as pony-trekking and, in addition, visits were made to the local Folk Museum with its vivid reconstruction of Highland life and to nearby Ruthven Castle. Hostelling was also seen as a valuable educational adjunct in that children had to learn (perhaps for the first time) to cater, not just for their needs, but for others by dint of learning the value of cooperation.

More than most people, and perhaps because he was in his forties before it happened, MacKenzie was captivated by the birth of his own children. He seemed to see in them a reflection of his own hopes and aspirations for the future and took a constant delight in recording in special diaries their early adventures and learning experiences. He found in his own children, especially in their infancy and as they grew in awareness of the world around them, a source of inspiration for his educational philosophy. He delighted in their sense of curiosity and their lack of inhibition; he delighted in their comparative innocence about the world and their spirit of enjoyment in all activity. He says in his journal of that time, 'It's their openness to experience, a lack of perceived thought or feelings, the newness of everything that maybe reminds us adults of our own largely forgotten childhood, nostalgically.' He is also amazed by a child's memory for clearly perceived detail, taking the view that memory is deepened by emotional involvement, a sense of enjoyment, and cites as an example one of his own children's remembering many years later holding a bird's egg tenderly in his hand as an infant and recalling clearly even which hand he had held it in.

Thus MacKenzie came to believe more and more in the sanctity of the child and to glorify 'childlikeness' in the same way that Rousseau did. He saw it as a state of grace which we would do well as parents and as educators to take full account of and to nourish in the early years when children were at their most impressionable. 'The child was, indeed, the father of the man', the way that MacKenzie saw it. And, as if to confirm this, he writes in his journal:

> Wordsworth had a keener insight into the world of children than most educators. When he spoke of the visionary gleam, he wasn't playing with words, like Isaiah, he was trying to describe reality:
>
> The growing child
> Beheld the light, and whence it flows,
> He sees it in his joy.
> He is glorious in the light of Heaven-born freedom.'
>
> Wordsworth spoke of 'Those first affections, those shadowy recollections which are the fountain-light of all our days, a master light of all our seeing:
>
> Which neither listlessness nor mad adventure,
> Nor man nor boy,
> Nor all that is at enmity with joy,
> Can utterly abolish or destroy.'

MacKenzie was now at a stage in his career when he felt ready to undertake more responsibility and consequently to put into practice, as Head of a school, some of the radical ideas about education that had firmed up in his mind over the years. He had become convinced that the school curriculum needed to measure up to what was happening now in the world; and he was also convinced that effective learning needed to be child-centred and that this went along with a need to value children for their sanctity as individuals each of whom had an intrinsic goodness that challenged the efficacy of using corporal punishment as a sanction in schools. He had begun to apply for Headteacher posts and finally was the successful applicant for the post of Headteacher at Braehead Junior Secondary School in Buckhaven in Fife.

It was, then, with a sense of purpose and considerable optimism that Mackenzie came to Braehead School in 1957 as its first Headteacher. The opening of the school was conventional enough as recorded in the log-book that MacKenzie kept of the daily events of the running of the school:

> Councillor Thomson and Chairman of the local Education Sub-Committee present.
>
> Psalm 23 Crimond. Lord's Prayer.
>
> Surprised at fresh appearance, healthy, well-clad, of pupils. They sang well.
>
> Gave out time-tables. Flowers on platform...afterwards used for dining rooms.

> Dining went so well that at the Staff Meeting a member of staff said they'd agreed gladly to have meals with pupils. There were table-cloths. They washed their hands before eating...
>
> Staff Meeting 2.45 to 4 pm

Teaching at Templehall School had helped him, under the guidance of an enlightened and sympathetic Headteacher, to firm up his ideas as to how a school could be steered in a particular direction to embrace the kind of curriculum he now began to envisage for children seemingly trapped in the narrow confines of Junior Secondary education as it was then. Conversely, it was because such schools laid comparatively little emphasis on examination success that there appeared to be much greater opportunities for a break to be made from traditional approaches to education in favour of experimentation in a whole variety of subjects. Such an approach, he felt, might well lead on to the development of a whole range of activities, many of them out of school, that would engage the interest of teenage working-class youngsters and do something to awaken their minds to their own potential as individuals living in a run-down town in Fife in Scotland, half-way through the 20th century.

Buckhaven, known as the 'Coal Town' held its own fascination for MacKenzie. It had been a fishing village, but those days were long gone. Only a generation earlier, the fore-shore had been covered with golden sands and had been enclosed by picturesque houses that in MacKenzie's words 'clambered up the slope beyond'. Between the school and the edge of the slope down to the sea was a grassy patch called 'the verandah' from which earlier generations looked out on a clear day to the Lothian coast,12 miles away. But during the Industrial Revolution the mine-owners had been permitted by the local council to sink a coal shaft close to the sea. As the pit-bing grew, the tides of the Forth swept it out into the estuary and back towards the shore, distributing the black silt over the sands.

The building that MacKenzie inherited in 1957 for his new Junior Secondary school was an old Victorian building which the High School had vacated to take over a fine new building on the outskirts of the town set amidst extensive playing fields. Braehead was a depressing-looking building with perpetual heating problems in the winter when the temperature rarely rose above 57°F and teachers and pupils wore overcoats in the classrooms. As MacKenzie noted at the time, the building lent credibility to the parents' belief that in every way Junior Secondary education was an inferior education and therefore appropriate to the needs of those children who had failed academically to qualify for entry to the High School. Despite this, the staff at Braehead School were persuaded, after a cautious start, to go along with MacKenzie's assertion that a fresh approach to the business of educating children in such a school should be adopted. For one thing, it was decided, after discussion, that the distinction between B1 and B2 pupils should be ignored and pupils taught in 'mixed ability' classes instead of being streamed according to their IQs in the 11-Plus examination. The top~graded pupils (about 25 per cent of the age group) had already been creamed off into the High School, which left the remaining 75 per cent to be allocated to the Junior Secondary School where further labelling normally took place on the basis of their IQ scores. This inevitably led to pupils at the bottom of the scale being written off as 'failures' not just by the teachers, but by the pupils themselves and, of course, by their parents.

The other radical approach adopted by MacKenzie and his staff at a comparatively early stage in the school's development was to blur the divisions between subjects by pursuing activities which encouraged a cross-curricular approach to education. This happened in the early setting up of a school newspaper which usually came out every week. This consisted of class reports, reviews of books and music, pages on school sporting activities, letters to the editor, school council reports, a serial or a poem and, of course, a leading article. It involved pupils in typing the reports on to stencils, keeping accounts, selling the newspaper and getting advertising for it. Another activity that was started that had a spin-off across different departments was boat-building which involved 40 to 50 pupils turning up at the Technical Department after school on a Monday where two members of the department helped them unpaid. The eventual launching of the pupil-built boats, as well as an old skiff presented to the school and repaired in the school's woodwork shop, was a memorable occasion for MacKenzie:

> The February sun was shining on the smooth water of the harbour, the pupils were thoroughly enjoying themselves...because they were trying themselves out against a new medium, in boats made by their own hands It was like a surge of new eager life in a dead place. The old fishermen would have been glad to see it, and maybe the pupils themselves, sons of coal-miners though they were, felt vaguely some awareness that their grandfathers and great-grandfathers had lived on it and forced a living out of it.

Another interesting feature of the Braehead experiment was the way in which departments such as the Art and Music departments became focal points for activity that affected the ethos of the whole school. At the heart of this concept was a belief on the part of the Art Department, for instance, that Art was not just a subject but a 'way of life'. The beaches were combed for bits of sandstone and driftwood that could be used for shaping into objects that depended on the imagination and creative impulses of the children who fashioned them – and from the red clay that was found on the shore, the pupils learned to make human heads and figures that reflected not just their own ideas about human shape but explored themes such as poverty and deprivation.

Above all, it was in painting that the Art Department inspired creativity among pupils. For instance, the pupils would go down to the old sea-town and make sketches of the fishermen's old houses, soon due for demolition, and later make full-size pictures of them. Each year, about two months before Christmas, the head of department would concentrate the art classes on a massive programme of Christmas decorations for the school. He chose different themes each year to broaden the children's knowledge and interest. MacKenzie recalls one such occasion:

> One Christmas the theme of the decorations was the past of the Coal Town. The school hall was covered with murals of what the pupils imagined the 18th century town had been like...fish nets, lobster pots and figures of many kinds of fish hung from the ceiling, and a gigantic figure of Neptune, thirty feet high, bestrode the fire-place regarding the scene. A cheeress building had been transfigured, and in these homely surroundings the Christmas parties were held.

MacKenzie reckoned that the atmosphere of tranquillity associated with the sort of work pupils were doing in the Art Department epitomised the quality of educational experience he was looking for – a classroom climate that offered a 'respite from pressure' and that is what the Art Department achieved – a pupil-oriented approach that depended for its success on the personal involvement that pupils felt they had in what they were doing, and, accordingly did what they were doing well, and not under duress.

The crux of the educational revolution that MacKenzie gradually came to envisage, emerging out of his headmastership at Braehead School, lay in his growing conviction that a school as such could not engender the range or quality of experience that were needed to counteract the restrictive and inhibiting influence of the pupils' home background. Instead, he looked beyond the school – to the Scottish hills and countryside as a source of inspiration where learning could take place in a natural setting. Pupils would get to know their native land, its history, its geology, its character and its physical shape by a mixture of travel and adventure (much in the same way as he had done for himself in his frequent travels through Europe in the 1930s). They would learn also how to live together by using hostel accommodation for their visits and would forge relationships with each other by taking part in hill-walking expeditions where teamwork and cooperation made the difference between success and failure. They would learn things at first hand with the help of staff and so would be uniquely involved in a process which would make learning come alive for them in a way that reading about something in a book in a classroom could never do; and the whole experience of learning in this way would give them more confidence in themselves and more understanding of their own strengths and weaknesses as human beings.

The search for this new form of education began modestly enough with the school's sending small groups of pupils with one teacher for a week at a time to a two-roomed cottage situated in the Black Wood of Rannoch which they rented from the Navy for one pound a year. This system worked well enough for two years, but MacKenzie soon realised that, if his dream of a radical change to the curriculum was to be effected, a much more ambitious scheme would be needed, involving more pupils and more staff going to live at any one time in the countryside for three or four weeks and this meant looking for larger premises. Almost out of the blue, he was offered the use of Inverlair Lodge which belonged to British Aluminium. This was ideally situated in Lochaber near the head of Loch Treig but it needed a lot of repairs and renovation to bring it up to standard for use by a whole school and this meant they had to elicit the help of Fife County Council in financing the alterations which were estimated at over £20,000. Trustees were appointed by the school to pursue their interests in getting the Lodge into an operational state and to liaise with the County Council, but despite their best endeavours, progress in getting things done through the County Council was very slow.

Despite the delay in implementing the Inverlair scheme, Mackenzie remained optimistic and let his own and his staff's imagination dwell on the kind of ideas they could put into practice there.

> We could ourselves put in a new septic tank if required, teach pupils how to adapt a water-heating system to our plans for the house. We could keep ponies and bees and get the reeds out of the tennis court...we could section one of General Wade's roads to see how he made them, and would establish an observatory and also a wireless station in contact with the school...there would be forestry in cooperation with British Aluminium foresters who were prepared to work with us. We would ask the Crofters' Cooperative at Roy Bridge, four miles away, if we could come in with them in their experiments in soil reclamation. Inverlair would also be the base camp from which expeditions would set out across the west of Scotland using a chain of bothies

on treks as stepping stones, never being more than one day's march from a bothy and enabling pupils to travel light without tents.

Hamish Brown, who was to become the first full-time outdoor specialist teacher in Scotland, was the person to whom MacKenzie entrusted the launching of such expeditions. Brown, as well as being a qualified teacher of English, was an experienced mountaineer who had the qualities of leadership and rapport with teenagers that made him the ideal choice for taking the initiative in outdoor adventure. He shared MacKenzie's vision of the far-reaching potential that an ambitious scheme for outdoor education could have for the pupils of schools such as Braehead. In a book that he was to write 30 years later, *The Last Hundred*, Brown recalls some of the trips to the Scottish mountains that he made with pupils at Braehead over the years. He reflects sadly on the fact that 30 years further on (in the 1990s) much of the freedom for school parties to roam the hills summer and winter in a true spirit of adventure is no longer possible because of the imposition over the years of stringent Health and Safety rules. The 'red-tape' associated with such legislation, Brown feels, has killed off much of the freedom and sense of optimism that went along with such activities in the Braehead years, 'How disappointed our prophet Head would be to see the emasculated education of today, the grey sterility of it all sagging down from guardians who do not care for people or for the future. Outdoor education (nowadays) is a farce.'

Brown celebrates in his book the amazing spirit and endeavour that his many expeditions to the Scottish mountains with scores of Braehead pupils brought out in the youngsters who got involved in such pursuits. He himself was convinced that these pupils were receiving an education in the best sense of the word in that they were absorbing all manner of learning 'without pain or pressure'. And he goes on to relate how years later, after he and a Braehead party had done a traverse of the Cuillin Ridge in Skye, he got a tap on his shoulder in a Skye bookshop, 'Hello, Hamish? Bet you don't remember me.' In fact, I instantly recognised the lad who'd taken two others up to leave vital water on the ridge on the day of the heat wave. 'I'm married now and have two kids and every summer we come to Skye – all because of you.'

In the same way as such expeditions influenced profoundly the future lifestyle of many of the pupils who went on them, so also did the school's involvement in outdoor education have its own impact on other members of staff (MacKenzie included) who were often asked to assist with the programme. As Brown himself puts it:

> I persuaded as many other teachers as possible to come along too. It was the quickest way to silence the girns that my work was just one long holiday. The Head, R.F. MacKenzie, needed no persuading. He'd try anything and everything – once anyway – so we scared the shit out of him on the Buchaille, near drowned him canoeing across Rannoch Moor and had him spewing in David Haye's boat bouncing over the Dorus Mor to Scarba...As far as I know, my appointment was the first in a Scottish state school to do what would develop into outdoor education. My remit, 'To take the boys and girls of Braehead into the wilds and do what I liked with them' had teachers suggesting specific nasty things to do to some of them. But that worked both ways too. I once lay in a tent listening to a conversation in the next tent (kids seem to think tents are sound-proof) where they were making up 'ropes' of teachers they'd take up the Ben (Nevis) – then cut the rope!

The pioneering work that Hamish Brown had already embarked upon in exploring the tremendous possibilities for introducing town-based pupils to the Scottish mountains as a key part of their secondary education would have linked in with the wider vision that MacKenzie had developed, centred on the Inverlair project. It was a vision that, for as long as the Inverlair project remained a possibility, sustained the dreams and the optimism of MacKenzie and his staff:

> The Welfare State had produced the fittest generation of Scottish children who had ever lived and we wanted to resume where the Welfare State had stopped. It might, after all, be only a dream but the school had a distinguished staff capable of translating the dream into reality, and the goodwill and tenacity to overcome the obstacles. We decided to encourage the dreamers.

Unfortunately, for MacKenzie, his hopes were dashed when, two-and-a-half years after British Aluminium had made MacKenzie a gift of Inverlair Lodge, the County Council overturned a decision taken previously by the Education Committee to make the school a grant to pay the salaries of extra staff to be employed there and to subsidise the bed and board of pupils staying there over an experimental period of two years. Instead, the County Council took the view that the building was too old and would take too much money to renovate and was too remote. Although he tried hard to find an alternative site, which might still have attracted the financial help of the local authority, MacKenzie knew in his heart that the Inverlair project was dead and with it the expectations that had been invested in bringing his revolutionary educational experiment into being.

Sadly, the intervention of the local authority in the collapse of the Inverlair project foreshadowed the eventual fate of the school itself. It was mainly because of the perception by those in authority that the school's emphasis on outdoor activities and its casual attitude to exam results and streaming as well as corporal punishment was one of alarm and suspicion that began to turn public opinion against the school. The grumbling had grown when the parents saw the canoes out on the sea and heard from their children that they were very much left to themselves. Many parents saw the experimenting and the comparative lack of discipline as an added insult; further evidence that their children were not up to it. Had their children been taught in traditional ways, they might still have been failures, but at least they would, in the parents' view, have gone through the proper motions.

Conversely, news of the school and its activities, published as it was in MacKenzie's books such as *A Question of Living* and *Escape from the Classroom*, attracted to it young staff who were keen to move from conventionally-run schools to Braehead which was looked upon as 'progressive'. Such staff made a significant contribution to Braehead by their vigour and commitment and they fitted in well with those other staff who had gone along with MacKenzie's approach to education and had given to the school invaluable continuity and the benefit of their experience.

With hindsight, however, much of the responsibility for the parents' growing unease about the school must attach to the Braehead staff and particularly MacKenzie himself for failing to understand that their methods and approach to education could succeed only if they involved the cooperation of the entire community. The Braehead Parent-Teacher Association was energetic but unrepresentative, and far too little had been done to spread the importance of the Braehead experiment into the homes of the people of Buckhaven so that they could have given the school the public support it needed in times of crisis.

There was no such excuse for the attitude of the authorities. The justification for the principles behind the 1944 Butler Education Act and its parallel in Scotland was that Junior Secondaries would be allowed to experiment. Yet the authorities, local and national, grew suspicious and obstructive when experiments were attempted in the most difficult circumstances.

The Scottish Education Department press officers were all too keen to refer enquiring journalists, particularly English journalists, to the 'great work' being done at Braehead. But official enthusiasm vanished when it came to practical support. Worse still was to follow. Ater much deliberation as to the future provision for Secondary education in Buckhaven, the County Council decided in 1966 that Braehead would eventually close and that its pupils be absorbed into the new Buckhaven High School which was to be run as a very large Comprehensive school.

For MacKenzie and his staff, many of whom had identified with MacKenzie's idealism, the Education Committee's decision was a tragedy. It not only left MacKenzie without a job to go to in the new scheme of things (nothing as yet had been offered to him) it also spelt the break-up of the key staff who had worked with him over the years at Braehead and had built up its reputation as a pioneering institution. His enemies in the educational establishment – and he had many of them – used the argument for the implementation of comprehensive education as a legitimate ploy to close down Braehead and silence MacKenzie once and for all.

Mackenzie had, after all, argued publicly against the comprehensive system.

> The Comprehensive school in its present form is assuredly not the answer. The Comprehensive school is an administrative not an educational change. The same treadmill is in operation in Comprehensive as in Junior Secondary schools. The trouble goes much deeper than administrative change can effect. It needs reassessment of the whole content and method of school work.

The attack that MacKenzie felt justified in making against the decision to close Braehead was directed at two levels: against the élitist traditionalists who still believed in the Grammar Junior Secondary two-tier system that divided pupils into sheep and goats at an early stage, and against Labour bureaucrats who thought the education problem would be solved if pupils of all abilities were simply educated together within the same buildings. It was an attack that was also an affirmation of faith in a genuinely comprehensive system in which all education for all pupils would be geared, not to the rat-race of examination, but to the creation of a fuller life for all the pupils.

For MacKenzie, then, the great experiment at Braehead School was brought to an end under tragic circumstances. Both the school and what it stood for, and his plans for the outdoor centre at Inverlair had been brought to an end by what he saw as the reactionary forces of the Establishment,fearful as ever of change, of challenges to the accepted ways of doing things and infuriated, as officialdom always was, at the sheer doggedness and determination shown by MacKenzie in defence of what he believed in for the sake of the children. It was that unshakeable belief in what he was doing that inspired MacKenzie during his years at Braehead to record his experiences at the school, and what he had come to believe in, in a trilogy of books that took his message about education to a far wider audience than the good people of Fife.

CHAPTER SIX

The Mackenzie Trilogy Thirty Years On

It still seems remarkable that MacKenzie, in the space of five years, and as a practising Headteacher, could have found the time and the energy to write three books on his educational experiences at Braehead School. Numerous articles of his, of course, had already been published over the years in *The Scotsman* and *The Glasgow Herald* and largely because of this he had become widely recognised as a stimulating writer on a surprisingly broad range of subjects. Here, for instance, is an extract from an article he wrote for *The Glasgow Herald* in February 1954. This well illustrates MacKenzie's fondness for linking up his Aberdeenshire background with literary and historical parallels that help us to visualise in a modern setting what things were really like in the past in terms that we can understand and identify with.

> We were travelling in the train along the side of the Ury, and on the high ground to the east we saw the Harlaw monument. I told a Garioch man the ballad story about Forbes who discovered that there was a battle in progress and sent his servant home to Druminnor (the Forbes ancestral home) as fast as he could ride for his coat of mail. The servant was back with it in two hours and a quarter and Forbes entered the battle. 'Aye', said the local man, 'they liked to be in on a battle in the old days. That would just be the same as if a man from a farm-town today came in and said, "Oh, there's a football match on", and raced home on his bicycle for his football boots.'
>
> Is there in the North East a stronger inclination than in other parts of Scotland to enter into the spirit of the past and to understand it by translating the records of the past into the idiom and familiar background of the present?
>
> There are, for example, Charles Murray's translations of Horace into North East Scots. It was an obvious parallel, of course, Horace in his Sabine farm north east of Rome and Murray in the Vale of Alford north west of Aberdeen, but Murray makes the most of it, and it is sometimes amusing to find how apt the parallel is.
>
> Mount Soracte becomes Bennachie; cypresses and ash trees become larch and rodden. Horace counselled his wife to pay no attention to the 'Babylonian numbers' of the Chaldean astrologers and that is translated into the 'spaewife'. And even though at the foot of Bennachie there's nothing to compare with hunting wild boars (Murray's farmer goes out with dog and ferret to catch rabbits), the two ways of life had a lot in common, not only in a general

sense, but even in details, or both the Sabine and the Aberdeenshire farmers caught hares, and ate sorrel ('soorocks'). The literal translation of one sentence of an ode is something like this, 'Drive away the cold by piling the wood high on the hearth.' But Murray's translation is much better...'Haud on the peats an' fleg the cauld.'

Over twenty five years ago one summer afternoon a Sunday school teacher in Aberdeenshire was telling his class about the journey of Joseph's ten brothers from Canaan to Egypt to buy corn. It was hardly surprising, the teacher said, that for all these years his brothers didn't know Joseph. But how was it that Joseph knew his brothers?

It was a difficult question, but one pupil shot up his hand at once, with the eagerness of a child who has suddenly understood. He said, 'Joseph would have seen the name on the cairts!'

For that youngster, the gaps in the background of the story that the Bible does not give, had been filled in by his own imagination. Jacob and Joseph and Pharaoh were real people, as real as the Aberdeenshire farmers he knew. There was Jacob with a pretty big place down in Shechem; it must have been a big farm because he had all his sons working for him. Joseph had struck out for himself and was doing well as manager of an even bigger farm, owned by a man called Pharaoh. Jacob had told his sons that they would have to go to Pharaoh's farm; it was the only place in the countryside where you could get corn...when they got to Egypt they had been well done to. They had loused and stabled their horses and gone into supper. All this unbeknown to Joseph. Joseph, maybe, had been coming up the close in the gloaming when he saw the strange carts. He went across to see whose carts they might be, and there, on a bright plate on the front of each, he read:

Jacob and Sons,
Mains of Shechem,
Dothan.

Mackenzie's experiences at Braehead more than anything strengthened his resolve to do all he could to change the face of Scottish education. He knew, however, only too well, that in taking on such a task he would be acting almost in isolation against the conventions and received wisdoms of what was then current educational practice and that the forces of the Establishment would very quickly ally themselves against him. But this made him all the more determined to use Braehead both as a focal point and as a proving ground for the changes he felt had to be faced up to in education at that time.

He concluded that the most effective way to promote the case for change was to employ his talents as a writer and polemicist to escape the narrow confines of the Fife Coal Town and bring the issues he felt had to be addressed – the need for curriculum reform, the case for child-centred education, the rights and wrongs of corporal punishment, what schools are really for – to the attention of a much wider public. Increasingly, during his years at Braehead, he felt his was a voice crying out in the wilderness-he felt inwardly driven to take a stance which would inevitably concentrate public attention, not just on his educational beliefs, but on what he was struggling to put into practice at Braehead. The theory had always been there at the back of his mind since his early days at the Pioneer school in the New Forest. Now at Braehead...mainly through the efforts of certain very talented members of staff, he had begun to develop a much bolder vision of education culminating in the Inverlair project that took education out of the classroom all together and into the natural and almost idyllic setting of the Scottish hills and countryside.

What is also remarkable about these books as they have come down to us 30 years on is how strongly the underlying passion and conviction shines through. Although the educational system has changed out of all recognition since MacKenzie's day, yet the message that his books carry, still has a potency that is timeless in its search for an ideal way of educating our children.

A Question of Living, the first of the trilogy, published in 1963, sets the tone for all of the books in its radical agenda. The book is an attempt to persuade people to start out on their own and decide what education is about. For too long, in his view, education had been equated with literacy and that had undesirable consequences:

> This has contributed to excessive emphasis being placed upon the results of written examinations and has produced...a class of people who combine an astonishing verbal facility with a meagre equipment of wisdom and little understanding of the complicated human situation and values involved in the words they so glibly use.

And he goes on to say in a key passage:

> The exam system in Britain is both a result of an ineffectual cultural education and the cause of the continuation of this education...forming a vicious circle...and ultimately giving teenagers a distaste for schools.

The book is used as a vehicle to show how this crisis in education can be overcome. And it is here that he uses his own experience at Braehead to tackle this theme. The very existence of Junior Secondary schools, he argues, underlines the deep divisions in society that the present educational system has brought about: 'The neglect of Junior Secondary education is the price Britain pays for the English Public School.'

MacKenzie and his staff decided to try to bridge the gap by applying their own solutions to the situation as they found it at Braehead by doing away with streaming and involving the pupils in activities that they enjoyed and gave them confidence in themselves – running a school newspaper, boat-building and navigation, learning more effectively through the imaginative use of radio and television and experimenting in democracy through the medium of a school council that was consulted about dealing with pupil misdemeanours. A much more direct approach would be adopted towards teenage sex problems through a properly devised sex education programme (largely unheard of in the 1960s) and ultimately, as a counter to juvenile delinquency and as a way of channelling pupil energies into constructive activities, expeditions would be organised to the hills and mountains of Scotland where learning for living could take on a totally new dimension. 'I doubt', claims MacKenzie, 'if any country in the world has as good natural resources as Scotland for bringing up children.'

All this he saw as part of a radical change in direction in schools away from the past emphasis on 'incentives, pep-talks, warnings, demotions, promotions and punishments' to situations in school where children could have 'respite from pressure' such as the Art Department where, because of the dedication of the staff and an imaginative approach to the subject, children could relax and enjoy what they were doing in class.

The whole tenor of school life as traditionally envisaged in drab surroundings full of chalk and talk needed to be questioned and radically altered to encompass things that teenagers would want to do and get much more out of – whether helping in local community projects or in nurseries attached to their own local school, in hill-walking expeditions or in nature conservation. Schools would need to be re-designed to enable pupils to enjoy light and space in comfortable surroundings that afforded them common rooms for relaxation. The basic premise for this alternative approach to education would be to make sure that all subjects would be applicable to the needs of the pupils so that they could relate what they were doing to real life.

It is MacKenzie's awareness of wider issues and how they might be addressed that comes across on a re-reading of *A Question of Living* in a present-day context. The passionate conviction of his case still rings clearly in the prose as does the deeper sense of his growing awareness that his is a 'cause célèbre' and one that will inevitably bring him into conflict with the realities of his own job of running a school in the state sector, balancing the needs of the school and its community against what he sees as his own role as an innovator and advocate of change.

Judging by the reviews that appeared in educational journals such as *The Times Educational Supplement* and in both national and local newspapers, all three of MacKenzie's books on the Braehead experiment were well received by the critics. Radical journalists such as Paul Foot and Peter Preston applauded MacKenzie's vision and his evangelical spirit and his courage in adversity when he had to face up to the imminent closure of Braehead, which is the theme of the final book in the trilogy *The Sins of the Children.* John Grigg, *The Guardian* critic, in his appraisal of *A Question of Living* in November 1963 drew a significant parallel between the impact of the Newsom Report, *Half our Future*, and the appearance of MacKenzie's book on the educational scene:

> I have just been reading the Newsom Report which deals with the average and sub-average children who make up a large proportion of those now being educated at public expense. There is much to admire in Newsom...There is an implied recognition throughout that education is a difficult art and not an exact science, and that the mere expenditure of public money, or the setting up of good administrative machinery, will not alone achieve any of the desired results.
>
> Newsom insists upon the need for a flexible curriculum, for relative freedom from the tyranny of external examinations, for up-to-date accommodation and equipment, for a closer relationship between school work and occupational interests; but, above all, the central importance of the teacher is emphasised.
>
> The personal factor is vividly illustrated in a little book which should be read in conjunction with Newsom by all who care about the subject – *A Question of Living* by R.F. MacKenzie. The author describes his experiences of running the Scottish equivalent of a Secondary Modern school in an industrial area, and his subtle, idiosyncratic reflections corroborate at many points the more ponderous and generalised findings of Newsom.
>
> Mr MacKenzie is a muscular humanist who would rather put the intractable teenager on a cold mountain slope than keep him imprisoned in a stuffy classroom. He is, in a way, the poor man's Kurt Hahn. Imaginative almost to the point of being a visionary, he is impatient of academic standards, contemptuous of officialdom. He is looking in each pupil for the secret spring which will transform and justify his existence at school: 'One parent came to complain that for a fortnight her son had done no work in the school. I found that for the whole fortnight her boy had been in an art room turning out pictures and reading encyclopedias.. While he was finding out what an archaeopteryx was like, his imagination would be kindled by a score of other things...All this I told his mother. 'I know that', she said. 'He's been taking encyclopedias home and reading them to all hours. But he hasn't been doing any of the usual school work. I mean the kind of work that will help him to be transferred from here to the High School.'
>
> It is exciting to read MacKenzie. There is a lot of sense, and a touch of poetry in what he has to say. His individualism may at times border on anarchism but this is a good fault. Education is essentially a question of learning, not a question of living; but unless children feel that life is worthwhile, they will never learn.

An exception to the favourable reception of his second book, *Escape from the Classroom* was a review by Tam Dalyell. Labour MP for West

Lothian, who complains of MacKenzie's 'contempt for all around him in the teaching world, the Scottish Education Department, the local authorities, and the mass of the teaching fraternity.' What Dalyell failed to appreciate was the inner vision and sense of wonder that MacKenzie associated with the kind of educational experience that *Escape from the Classroom* is essentially about. The best of the book is to be found, not so much in the polemical undercurrent which is similar in style and content to that in *A Question of Living*, but in the accounts he gives of treks in the Scottish hills with his pupils, as in this extract from the chapter 'The Road to the Isles'.

> Further west, as the sun was setting over in the direction of Nevis, we lost the path…a sleet shower came on,darkening the landscape, and we were back squelching in bog and searching for brown tussocks to get better footing. We stayed in a tight group and kept going north because we knew that we were sure to hit Loch Ossian, which has a road around it. The pupils were weary and footsore and hungry and it's always depressing to see the light dwindle from the west before you know where you are going to sleep. We came to a gate in a deer fence and found that the lost path came to this gate too. The path brought us within welcome sight of the loch. At the end of the loch we lit our candles and started up the primus stoves in a disused bothy. The glass was out of the windows and the wind came through the holes in the door. Cold and wet and miserably uncomfortable we sat on the floor and supped our soup balancing the dixies uncertainly. One pupil spilt his soup. 'Never mind', he said, 'I'll just put on my sausages.' There was not a word of complaint. Then, by torchlight, we set up our tents on short grass and crawled into our sleeping bags.
>
> I slept fitfully until daylight and then got up and went to the hut and made tea. The world was flooded with light and the hard, shining snow on the mountains glowed with a pink shade. The birds were singing a spring song. Gradually there leaked into the morning the warmth that you would have expected such brightness of light would have held all the time, and we all took the road again. Right ahead of us the snow sparkled on the Nevis range. The discomforts of the previous evening were a small price to pay for the elation of taking the Road to the Isles on a glorious morning.
>
> I think that almost unconsciously the pupils were learning a lesson you can't learn in a classroom, that in a Highland journey…the discomforts, the depression, the wet clothing, the spilt soup and the cold, are indissolubly bound up with the top of the morning happiness. You can't have one without the other.

The other most revealing aspect of *Escape from the Classroom* that provides insight into the Braehead years is MacKenzie's account of how the controversy over his experimental banning of corporal punishment at the school came to a head as an increasingly divisive issue among the staff at the school. MacKenzie had the capacity on reflection to acknowledge his mistakes. He does as much in the chapter entitled 'St

Dominic in the Classroom'. At his suggestion the school embarked on a trial period of three months during which there would be no corporal punishment(except in exceptional circumstances). At the end of this time a staff meeting was held at which MacKenzie suggested an extension of the experiment as the previous timetable was too short to be worthwhile. But the teachers were unanimously in favour of retaining the belt and opposed any trial period. In vain did Mackenzie argue about how corporal punishment had been abolished in many European countries and how immoral in principle it was for teachers to be involved in actually chastising pupils on the assumption that dealing out violent action as a corrective to wrong-doing only perpetuates violence in society. The discussion became increasingly bitter. The plight of uncertificated teachers in the school was highlighted who were having the greatest difficulty in maintaining any kind of order. Teachers gave examples, many of them of gratuitous violence committed by pupils. In the end the teachers got together and sent a statement to the Director of Education saying that MacKenzie's refusal to allow them to use the belt had made it impossible for them to do their work and asking for his advice. MacKenzie recalls that the statement was signed by every full-time member of staff.

> A letter came to me from the Director of Education 'for the attention of all staff'. I called a staff meeting and read it to them. It said that the policy on corporal punishment should be one that was willingly adopted by the whole staff. It was the Education Committee's practice to consult teachers on matters of policy...and I shouldn't impose a policy with which many of the staff were in complete disagreement.

And MacKenzie then said to his staff:

> You've got what you wanted. From tomorrow the use of the belt will be restored. I had hoped that at the end of the session, eight months from now, when the no-belting rule had had a real try-out, there would have been a vote of the whole staff on the success or failure of the experiment. For me this is a major defeat. From the time the school opened over five years ago, we have worked out a policy together...I thought that the mountain experiment and the opposition to the use of the belt were integral parts of the same policy, based on a different attitude to children. It hasn't worked out that way.

The candid way that MacKenzie goes over the events in the school on the contentious debate about corporal punishment reflects his willingness to face up to the rather inept way he had set about the problem in the first instance – trying to impose a pattern of classroom management on all staff without properly considering the consequences and not building in ways of supporting staff, especially inexperienced staff, in dealing with disciplinary problems with the belt no longer available as a sanction. The incident underlines a dilemma that was to come back to haunt MacKenzie in his later years at Summerhill in Aberdeen – his insistence in his chosen role as a visionary that the short-term problems his staff were facing on a daily basis in the classroom were as nothing compared to the national crisis that society was facing in tackling juvenile delinquency. The ordinary classroom teacher in a MacKenzie school found it hard to reconcile the daily demands of teaching as a job with the sort of long-term strategy that MacKenzie had in mind. There was a basic conflict of interest.

Mackenzie saw the problem of school indiscipline and its treatment as symptomatic of a wider malaise in society which would require a much more dramatic cure than could be achieved in one single school by a single staff. Only a revolution in the way we respond and react to each other as human beings, MacKenzie argues, near the end of this book, can we overcome the inertia that prevents us appreciating and getting the best out of our young people. 'The Welfare State was an achievement for which no praise can be too great. But it wasn't the end of the road, only the beginning, a foundation, not a building. We need an educational revolution to give all pupils...the understanding and the skills and the confidence to help them to take over their own country and create a one-class society.' And he believes that this can only be done through a revival of the true spirit of Christianity as expressed in Arnold Wesker's play *I'm Talking About Jerusalem*. It means that education will emerge from the sidelines where the ruling minority shunted it...and will become a major power in society.'

Escape from the Classroom thus allows Mackenzie the opportunity to see in a proper context the size of the task he has set himself in what he started out, almost by accident to do, at Braehead. 'We started out on what was a minor experiment to alter some things in the school curriculum. We found that we were challenging not only a traditional education system but an ancient conception of society. And when you do that you find what you are up against.'

There is an elegiac mood throughout *The Sins of the Children*, the final book in the trilogy. This is largely because MacKenzie has come to realise, however grudgingly, by this time, that the Inverlair project was doomed and that a question mark hung over the future of Braehead School itself. As a result of these misfortunes MacKenzie's mood is largely sombre and increasingly bitter, hitting out at the pressures imposed upon people like himself by the establishment that ironically had much of its own potency in the ranks of the educational world itself. Teachers themselves, he argues, identifying, as many of them do, with middle-class values, 'disassociate themselves from lower class pupils, especially in Junior Secondary schools. The pupils' table manners, clothes, accent offend them. The result is that discrimination in education is a subtle and persuasive thing built into the very tools of education.'

The strengths of opposition to his ideas, not just in the teaching profession, but among local councillors took MacKenzie by surprise. He confesses in *The Sins of the Children* of how great the pressures upon him to conform had grown over the years, 'In the Coal Town we have been trying over the past ten years to introduce a new approach to education, pretty much in line with A.S. Neill's ideas. We expected difficulties and opposition. The secretary of the Glasgow Association for the Advancement of State Education wrote, 'You need to show to a much wider range of people how the education you offer would give the recognition, status and security which those who successfully pass exams at present get from traditional schooling.' MacKenzie remarks that such objections to his philosophy are based on a fear that 'children brought up as we propose would lose the severity of the Old Dispensation.'

And he goes on to argue that this preoccupation with educational rigour is characteristic of the majority of people in Scotland, and especially among the middle classes:

> who are eager to submit their children to this kind of school work, believing that our education system is a noble heritage broadening down from precedent to precedent...there is a feeling that everything has been wisely ordered...this is where pageantry, pomp and circumstance come in. How could we fail to be persuaded of the wisdom of those predecessors at a graduation ceremony in their brightly coloured caps and gowns moving in procession to the music of Gaudeamus Igitur on the pealing organ?

At the heart of the book is his preoccupation with the way in which we are bringing up our children, how best to prepare them for the kind of lives that lie ahead of them. Into that context comes the way in which we construe the rights and wrongs of dealing with child behaviour. He recalls the controversy surrounding the incident on the Isle of May bird sanctuary when some of his pupils on a nature excursion there were guilty of breaking over 500 gulls' eggs. The incident was widely reported in the local and national press and brought very unwelcome publicity to the school at a time when it could well have done without it. MacKenzie was reluctant to follow the reaction of staff that the pupils involved should be banned from other outdoor activities as a way of punishing them for what they had done, but gives way in the end to the wishes of his staff on this occasion. But later he regrets his actions because he reckons they were dealing with disturbed children, 'We should turn the other cheek and forgive until seventy times seven.' And he goes on:

> I'm not a Christian but I come more and more to believe that the New Testament has the rights of it, 'Except ye become as a little child, ye shall in no wise enter into the Kingdom of Heaven.'...if we are going to create a participant society, the Arts will have to be nourished in the school...it was a search for excellence, a love of doing things well, a self-forgetting absorption to putting every scrap of ability one possesses into a picture, a poem or a song.

The Inverlair project had grown to be the centre-piece of how all his radical approaches to education could be achieved. How tragic, therefore, that circumstances had dictated otherwise. Nevertheless, he feels that what Inverlair had stood for had a relevance that needed still to be reiterated, in the hope that others might continue where he had left off and pursue a similar objective. Of Inverlair, he says, near the end of the book:

> We want them (the pupils) to see at first hand the web of economic life, the interdependence of foresters, lock-keepers and railwaymen and paper-workers and printers and the people who provide them with entertainment, build houses for them. And what we are looking for, for our pupils is that being as they are, 'displaced persons', for the Coal Town pit is likely to close down shortly...we want to give them an education which will help them to understand and endure and survive the Industrial Revolution which is disrupting their lives and to choose wisely when they take their place in tomorrow's world.

He ends the book on cautionary note. His scarcely concealed anger and frustration at the setbacks he has suffered at Braehead spill over into a diatribe against the Establishment which seems to him to be setting its face against change and against the wish of pupils such as his from Junior Secondary schools to promote their own interests and their own stake in society – a situation, he is now convinced, they will openly resist:

> They refuse to be patronised any more. The lesson of history is clear enough. The intellectual élites...will have to go. That means we shall have to start treating all human beings with the same respect. And from there it will be easier to find and tap a new emotional dynamic to put life and purpose and community back into a society which is at odds with itself.

CHAPTER SEVEN

Memories of Mackenzie from the Braehead Years 1957–68

Perceptions of what Mackenzie was really like in real life can be greatly enriched by tapping into memories of him gleaned from those who worked with him professionally or were affected by, or associated with, the controversies surrounding the way he ran his schools.

Letters published by me in 1996 in *The Press and Journal* and *The Dundee Courier*, requesting memories of MacKenzie to be sent to me to assist with the biography, produced a wide and varied response, shedding light particularly on MacKenzie's days at Braehead. Ian Flett, who was the Director of Education for Fife from 1966 onwards, has a clear and unsentimental view of MacKenzie based on his observations as an educational official doing his job at the time.

> I found him a likeable man, and perhaps our contact was cordial, because we both came from the same part of Scotland.
>
> Very soon after my arrival in Fife I heard about him before I met him. This told me that he was an unusual man. It was obvious that he was an irritation to some, and, evidently, partly because, in my previous post of Kingston-upon-Hull, I had been largely responsible for appointing a man who, from what I heard of MacKenzie, was a kindred spirit, to the post of the first Headteacher of a large new comprehensive school.
>
> There followed, in due course, a number of meetings between Mackenzie and myself mainly in the school. Sometimes, I went as part of my normal visitation programme but more often I went because an irate councillor had, yet again, 'bent my ear'.
>
> MacKenzie's major mistake, which he had difficulty in recognising, was that he failed in the main, to carry the population with him. He was a man in a hurry, to whom administration was an irritating nuisance and he would never see that he was the Headteacher of a school provided by the local authority, whose members were rightly concerned that it should be contributing to their legal responsibility to provide efficient means of assisting parents to fulfil their duty to have their children educated.
>
> Braehead was housed in old premises. It was the previous High School and became a Junior Secondary when the new Buckhaven High School opened. Frankly, the interior was, generally, a mess. This MacKenzie could not choose to see. I recall going into an Art room where there was, I think, more paint on the ceiling than art work...I also had never seen so much graffiti on toilet walls...He was so absorbed in providing what he considered

an appropriate curriculum for his pupils that such mundane matters as the school fabric were of minor consequence.

The school was in quite a busy street, and there were reports of pupils hanging out of first-floor windows spitting at passers-by, and making uncomplimentary remarks. This, of course, infuriated Authority members, and I had quite often to calm them, and point out MacKenzie's undoubted very caring attitude to his pupils, many of whom obviously liked him, and responded to his methods. I recall attending a school concert at Christmas, when the hall had been attractively decorated, and some most unlikely pupils presented an enjoyable show. MacKenzie presided with his usual bonhomie,and elicited an enthusiastic response.

At one time he vowed that he was not going to constrain his pupils by presenting them for 'irrelevant' examinations. He wanted them to be free to explore what he considered 'real' educationr. He thought that their spirits would be killed by being thirled to an examination syllabus.

What happened, of course, was that parents, aware of what children at the High School were being offered, 'rebelled', and insisted that their children must have the same 'as the children next door'. The situation was exacerbated by the fact that the then Rector of the High School was an arch 'conservative'who viewed MacKenzie with disdain.

Whilst I did have sympathy with MacKenzie, I obviously had difficulty in applauding all his actions, and I never persuaded him to take the 'softly softly' approach.

His appointment to Summerhill came as a surprise. I first learned of it by reading the announcement in the local press. He had not asked me for a reference. Perhaps he had become frustrated by his feeling of lack of progress at Braehead, and thought that Summerhill would provide more scope.

His influence did continue at Braehead, and the spirit of his teaching was retained by staff whom he had attracted, but his Depute, who was made Acting Head pending the reorganisation to a fully comprehensive system, did not have the flair. In due course Braehead was discontinued and the High School became comprehensive.

I was sorry to know about MacKenzie's difficulties at Summerhill, but not surprised. He had a very strong will to 'go his own way'. I sometimes wonder if Aberdeen were well aware of his limitations, and were prepared to take the risk, in order to have his vision.

He was, in many ways, like A.S. Neill, but the Fifers who, in many ways, were so generous in the provision of a very good service, were simply not ready for him.

Another individual memory that emerged from the responses I received about Mackenzie years at Braehead was this contribution from Bert Johnston who was an Inspector of Schools for many years but, at the time of the incident he relates he was on the staff of Jordanhill College of Education. He was attached to Braehead for a half-term about 1962. His most vivid memory goes as follows.

The occasion was a pre-Christmas, evening social for pupils and staff. Maybe there was just a touch more formality, convention then on such occasions.

'Dance' rather than 'disco'. Dancing was a more strictly, boy-girl activity than nowadays.

MacKenzie was anxious that the occasion should be immediately cohesive and participative. But there they were; boys at one end of the gym, girls at the other. They knew what was expected. A band was playing. The length of the gym continued to separate them. And the minutes were passing; five, ten, fifteen. So Mackenzie decided something had to be done.

I recall his darting to one end, grabbing the arm of the first boy he met, tugging him the length of the gym, grabbing the arm of the first girl contacted at the other end, and endeavouring to get them going as the first pair in the middle.

I suppose, in retrospect, I remember this so clearly because not only was it real drama...the MacKenzie intervention was sudden, overt, individual; there was an audience, realising what was about to happen and wondering what was implied for them...but also the incident illustrated MacKenzie's intensity, single-mindedness, frustration – and, I suppose, in a way, his innocence. There was a sense of desperation too. The convention, the formality, were 'again him'. And there wasn't enough time.

The outcome, as I recall it, was that staff and pupils decided to get mutually active so that they wouldn't be publicly embarrassed...the methodology had the desired outcome, but not through its own rationale.

Thanks to the generosity of Robert Cooper, former teacher at Templehall Secondary School, Kirkcaldy, who latterly became Head of the Audio-Visual Aids Department at Aberdeen College of Education, I was able to obtain a copy of a radio broadcast that MacKenzie had made for the Open University about 1969 on the subject of the curriculum, not long after he had moved to Summerhill in Aberdeen, featuring his impressions of his days at Braehead. The value of the tape is that it reveals not just MacKenzie's own version of events as they developed at Braehead over the years, but the impressions of councillors, teachers and former pupils and, in that sense, it encapsulates a unique commentary on how things actually appeared at the time.

Bob Bell, a lecturer at the Open university devised the programme in such a way that MacKenzie was asked to respond to comments and criticisms of how he had run the school over the years at Braehead. Prominent among those who represented the teaching profession in the broadcast is James Carmichael, a well-known Fife Headteacher and a former President of the Educational Institue of Scotland (EIS), the main teachers union. Carmichael praises MacKenzie's humanitarian qualities but feels that his approach to education is out of step with the times. Carmichael foresaw, even then, the imminent introduction of business methods and 'time and motion' studies into the way the teaching profession is run that would put more emphasis on the teaching 'process' than on the 'child' resulting in more control from the top and towards uniformity.

Jack Stewart, under whom MacKenzie had taught at Templehall School in Kirkcaldy, deplores the fact that MacKenzie did not get the full backing of Fife County Council in his efforts to explore new methods, and remarks on the deplorable conditions under which MacKenzie and his staff had to work at Braehead. He admires his courage in adversity, but feels that those in authority hoped that MacKenzie would eventually 'hang himself' in pursuit of goals he could never hope to reach through crucial lack of support from those in charge of education in the County Council.

The councillors that Bell interviews – Alec Eadie (who later became a Labour MP), Baillie Gough (Provost of Buckhaven) and Baillie Walker (Chairman of Braehead School Parent Teacher Association) all express sympathy in varying degrees for what MacKenzie was trying to do. Eadie regrets the fact that it proved impossible to find a place in the Fife education system for MacKenzie's ideas to be promoted. Gough takes the view that MacKenzie's 'failure' was due in part to the way he went about propagating his views, stirring things up, and alienating folk in the process...in effect, his demise, according to Gough, was largely 'brought upon himself'. Walker, whose son went to Braehead, appreciated what MacKenzie was trying to do in endeavouring to make his school turn out better persons rather than put emphasis on exam success and he defends MacKenzie's attempts to secure extra resources for his alternative curriculum. He also, as a politician, is more than aware of a powerful faction within the County Council who had little sympathy for what MacKenzie stood for and probably paved the way for MacKenzie's being sidelined at the time when Secondary education came to be reorganised in Fife.

Hamish Paterson, a former teacher at Braehead, when interviewed, commented on the deep divisions among staff at Braehead that MacKenzie's style of management seemed to provoke. In Paterson's view, MacKenzie was not a good communicator in the sense that he did enough to persuade staff of the need to support him. Paterson regarded him as being too 'remote', too authoritarian and too ready to side with pupils against the staff and not prepared to spend time consulting with staff about the efficacy of the changes he wanted to put into effect, for instance, with regard to the removal of corporal punishment. Paterson claims to have been on the staff for two years before he was made aware of the fact that there had been an experiment to do away with corporal punishment.

Three unnamed former pupils are interviewed very briefly in the broadcast. One of them comments on the way in which MacKenzie treated her and her fellow pupils as adults rather than children and on his willingness to have an argument with them. Another pupil takes the view that he did not get a proper education at Braehead, regretting not being able to study a language and expressing what he claimed was a widely-held view that Braehead pupils were looked down upon and made to feel inferior to pupils from the High School. And yet another pupil repeats the view that he did not get the 'right' education at Braehead compared with the High School, and, as if to prove his point, alludes to the old church hall that had to be used as a makeshift gym by Braehead pupils to show how poorly such facilities compared with those enjoyed by the pupils of the High School.

Douglas MacIntosh, who was a very high-profile Director of Education for Fife, before he became Principal of Moray House College of Education in Edinburgh, criticises MacKenzie's lack of rigour in setting out clearly his objectives in pursuit of the kind of educational experiences he wanted to put in place at Braehead and also his failure, in his opinion, to make any evaluation of these experiences. Moreover, MacIntosh reinforces the criticism that MacKenzie had too little regard for the concerns of parents who wanted their children to have the same chance of exam success as pupils in other schools and openly endorses the Authority's decision made in the light of MacKenzie's attitude to exams, to allow parents to transfer their children from Braehead to the High School if they thought they were being put at a disadvantage academically by remaining at Braehead.

In his reply to these criticisms, MacKenzie accepts, up to a point, many of the things said against him. He agrees that exam success was not his highest priority, and that parents would not have fully appreciated the implications of this policy on their children's job prospects. He grudgingly accepts that one consequence of this was the Authority's decision to allow parents to transfer pupils out of Braehead to other schools if they felt their own children were put at a disadvantage in academic terms by the sort of education they were getting at Braehead. Ironically, he illustrates this dilemma graphically in his admission that in real life his own wife had told him in no uncertain terms that when it came to the education of their own children, it was not their happiness that they as parents should be concerned about 'but their careers!'

He admits to failing to communicate effectively with his staff over the issue of corporal punishment and initiating new staff into the sort of 'ethos' he was trying to establish in the school, and sees in retrospect that such an approach had led to misunderstandings and a lack of consensus among staff as to what the school was actually setting out to do.

Remarkably, he confesses to Bell that the reason he had no set of clear objectives for the new curriculum at Braehead was because much of what he went on to do by way of experiment came about largely by accident: 'We didn't realise what it would lead to...we had no idea how far we were going to be driven by the course of events.' He would, therefore, if he got the chance to start again, have a plan and he would consult those around him. He would also do things more discreetly, avoiding confrontation...he had been badly bruised emotionally by attacks on all sides that had been made upon him, especially by sections of the press and by some of the County Councillors.

However, he goes on in the interview with Bell to deny the need to evaluate the learning experiences that pupils derived from his curricular changes. He argues that statistical analysis would be pointless and meaningless in that one cannot really gauge the effects such experiences would have on children in a measurable fashion – experiences undergone by pupils in hill-walking, in nature conservancy, in art and music, had as much to do with the human spirit and the 'good of the soul' as with 'learning' in a more conventional sense.

Continually, he had felt driven to do things by the sheer pressure of events and also by the nagging thought that his school might ultimately face closure. He had always considered himself to be a 'liberal' in education, but now he saw himself becoming an extremist. More and more he had come to believe that the overwhelming weight of the Establishment promoting the status quo fundamentally dictated the pace of change and that administrators, teachers and councillors were all of them totally constrained by these forces from questioning the nature of things, especially in education. For the underlying motive behind the authoritarianism of Scottish education with its insistence on maintaining corporal punishment and its antiquated exam system was to discourage children from thinking for themselves and instead to make them more amenable to accepting inherited values without question, and so relegating education to no more than a tool of the establishment.

This Open University interview took place not long after MacKenzie's appointment to the Headship at Summerhill Academy in Aberdeen. It shows that MacKenzie had, to some extent, been chastened by the bruising nature of some of his experiences at Braehead and that he had learned, superficially, at least, from the mistakes that he had made. Yet, as events at Summerhill were to prove, the strong, underlying restlessness to bring about change and a growing sense of evangelism were to drive Mackenzie ultimately to an even greater confrontation with the authorities that made events at Braehead pale almost into insignificance.

CHAPTER EIGHT

Mackenzie at Summerhill: The Calm Before the Storm 1968–1971

There was a real sense of shock amongst folk in the education world in the spring of 1968 when R.F. MacKenzie was made the new Headteacher of Summerhill Junior Secondary School in Aberdeen. Ian Flett, the former Director of Education for Fife, says as much when (in his memoir of MacKenzie) he not only expresses surprise at Mackenzie's appointment, but also at the fact that MacKenzie had not bothered even to ask him for a reference. The controversy surrounding his Headship at Braehead was well known throughout Scotland so that Aberdeen Education Committee knew very well in advance that there was a real element of risk in appointing a man like MacKenzie. Why then did Aberdeen take that risk?

From what one can gather from members of the ruling Labour group that were in power at the time, the reasons for his appointment were very much bound up with the process of Comprehensive reorganisation that the City was involved in then. Prominent members of the Labour administration who were on the Education Committee and influential co-opted members such as Dr Norman Walker of the University of Aberdeen, were keen to put Aberdeen in the forefront of education authorities in Scotland, all of whom were pursuing a similar policy in converting Senior Secondary and Junior Secondary schools into a Comprehensive system in line with the wishes of the Labour government, which, when it came to power in 1964, had made a manifesto commitment to implement Comprehensive education throughout the UK.

What the councillors saw when they interviewed MacKenzie for the Headship of Summerhill in 1968 was a man of undoubted vision who had close links with the North-East of Scotland. He had, more importantly, made a name for himself among those who favoured a change of direction in education away from rigid selection to a fairer, more egalitarian system in keeping with the movement in the 1960s to a more open and relaxed society epitomised by the rise of The Beatles and the popular image of the 'Swinging Sixties'. MacKenzie, as a reformer and innovator, would enable the Authority to be seen as 'progressive' and taking the government's policy very much to heart. Despite his reputation as a 'rebel', the Committee took the view that his experiences had probably 'mellowed' him and that his missionary zeal had been tempered somewhat by the harsh realities he had been forced to accept in recent years such as coming to terms with the failure of the Inverlair project and the closure of Braehead.

Anyway, had not MacKenzie given a clear assurance at his interview that he would give due regard to the need to present pupils for exams in line with the requirements of the Scottish Examination Board? MacKenzie, in his book *The Unbowed Head* which recounts his side of events at Summerhill, confirms the assumption that he had the full backing of Aberdeen Education Committee when he says:

> The Aberdeen chairman asked me what I understood by comprehensive education, thus giving me an opportunity to spell out clearly what I'd like to do at Summerhill. When they appointed me I was in no doubt that they would give me their full support and I entered the portals of Summerhill with a sober optimism.

The elements that were eventually to conspire to bring about the tragedy that engulfed MacKenzie at Summerhill can only be fully understood if we take into account the sort of school that Summerhill was before MacKenzie took it over and the nature of the staff who worked there at the time.

Summerhill Academy started out as a four-year secondary school in the early 1960s designed and built to serve those children in the Mastrick area of Aberdeen whose parents lived in a large council housing estate built in the 1950s. The school was a Junior Secondary that catered for the needs of those children in the area who, as a result of the 11-Plus exam that they had sat in Primary Seven, were allocated to a three-or four-year course of Secondary education as distinct from the other 25 per cent of the age group who would have gone on to follow a largely academic course in one of the city's Senior Secondary schools.

The new school was, when it was opened in 1962, largely staffed from teachers who had already proved their worth in Junior Secondary schools in the town. The Headteacher, Willie Christie, had previously been Head at Ruthrieston Junior Secondary School in Aberdeen and was well known as a strong and forceful character imbued with a great desire to push staff and pupils to their limits in pursuit of what he saw as excellence in all aspects of education. His appointments at Principal Teacher level mirrored the kind of man he was – they tended to be strong-minded individuals with a willingness, given Christie's drive and energy, to embrace change.

Willie Christie led by example. He set stringent standards of behaviour for all of the pupils. He insisted of parents that they support school uniform and set up in so doing 'contact' evenings for parents to come to the school and find out how their children were progressing – a practice that he initiated long before such meetings became customary in other schools, including Senior Secondaries. He also pioneered mixed-ability classes in the first year and persuaded his staff who took first-year classes to teach them a wide range of subjects such as English, History, Geography and Religious Education in order to reduce the number of teachers that pupils, fresh from Primary school, would have to get to know and to relate to in their new surroundings.

Principal Teachers, in particular, and staff generally were allocated additional duties which involved patrolling corridors and playgrounds in order to keep the school under strict control at all times during the school day. This was reinforced by Christie himself who characteristically used to make a complete tour of the school every day, entering each classroom and work area with a flourish, asking the teacher what was going on and making his presence felt among the pupils in a way that made them very conscious of his expectations of them.

Christie was a man who was forever on the move. He was of a restless disposition and was not happy unless he was doing something or getting someone to do something for him. He was held in awe, and, in some cases, almost in fear, by his staff, but generally he was respected for his selfless devotion to the school and his fundamental concern for the children in his care. He saw the Junior Secondary school as a place where children could get a chance to make up for what they had lost out on by not going to a Senior Secondary school. He also saw it as a place where innovative work could be done that was unlikely to be attempted in Senior Secondary schools because of the pressures in such schools to pursue academic attainments only. Christie himself in an article for the 25th anniversary magazine celebrating Summerhill's life as a school (1962 to 1987), expresses his basic aim for the school in a manner close to his personal beliefs as a Fabian socialist: 'Summerhill secondary school was built to serve a new housing estate. Families had been transferred from rundown city areas. Could we, as a school, help to make Summerhill a community and not just a collection of families living independently of each other?'

Perhaps the most interesting innovation that Christie came up with which bears a striking resemblance to aspects of MacKenzie's Inverlair project was the school's renting of a derelict cottage near Potarch (not far from Banchory in Aberdeenshire). The cottage was made habitable through the efforts of staff and pupil work parties, involving putting in a water supply, housing a generator for electricity and building a bridge over a ditch to provide access to vehicles from the main road. Visits were made to the cottage by two different school parties each week during term-time, involving ten pupils and two teachers, who shared the routine tasks of living together as a group (observing cooking and cleaning rotas, cutting wood for the fire) with trips to the hills and places of interest in a mini-bus that had been bought by the school from funds that had been raised in the community.

The school had been conceived by Christie not just as a focus for its community in the way it exercised demands on parents with regard to moral and financial support, but essentially as a work-place where everyone had a job to do. The pupils were expected by Christie to apply themselves assiduously to the work provided for them to do in the classroom; and as a result of the application exerted by both staff and pupils, high standards of achievement were reached, particularly in the practical areas of the curriculum, in Technical Subjects, Home Economics and in Art, Music and Business Studies. The school day tended to merge into the evening when various clubs continued after four o' clock; and even on Saturday mornings, staff volunteered to come along and supervise those pupils who turned up to make use of the Sports facilities that were made available to them, the perception being that facilities such as the swimming pool and the Games Hall should not go to waste simply because it was the weekend.

It was to this rather special example of a Junior Secondary school that I came to teach as Principal Teacher of English in December 1966. By that time it was clear that Summerhill was destined to become a fully comprehensive school under the plans of Aberdeen Education Committee for implementing Comprehensive education in the city. As a result, Christie was looking for people to add to his staff who had (as I happened to have) experience of presenting pupils for Higher Grade exams. I was duly interviewed for the post of PT English, being at that time a Special Assistant of English at Aberdeen Grammar School. I did not have a good interview, and it was only (as I learned later) that Christie insisted on having an Honours Graduate as his new PT English for the school (the other candidates being Ordinary Graduates with no Higher Grade presentation experience) that I got the job at all.

I found Summerhill School, when I moved to it, utterly different from

1. R.F. MacKenzie's parents on their wedding day, 1908.

2. His father, at Station House, Insch, Aberdeenshire.

3. Station House, Wartle.

4. The earliest photograph of MacKenzie.

5. Dux at Robert Gordon's College, 1927.

6. Graduation, Aberdeen University, 1931.

7. With his friend, Hunter Diack, at Insch.

8. With Diana (in Wrens uniform) and sister, Alice, *circa* 1944.

9. Robert and Diana MacKenzie's wedding, on 5 February 1945 at All Saints Church, Kingston upon Thames.

10. Flight-Lieutenant MacKenzie, late 1945.

11. Robert and Diana on holiday in Skunmaslov Strand, South Sweden, 1947.

12. On holiday at Bordighera (Italy) in 1948.

13. The MacKenzie family (from left to right), R.F., Neil, Diana (jun), Alasdair and Diana (sen), *circa* 1965.

14. R.F. MacKenzie's mother at Glentrool, Galloway, 1959.

15. The MacKenzie house at Upper Largo.

16. Family group at Upper Largo, circa 1962.

17. Robert MacKenzie's catchment area at Braehead, where he put his ideas into practice.

18. Teachers and pupils entered into a partnership.

19. Practically minded pupils built boats and canoes, fishing equipment and lobster pots.

20. An inspector who was invited to look at some outstanding art work by the pupils at Braehead complained because there was paint on the ceiling!

21. The English students produce a weekly newspaper.

22. The launching of the pupil-built boats.

23. Members of the Braehead School Council discuss the sins of omission and commission which have been perpetrated by fellow students during the week.

24. Scottish Secretary of State, Willie Ross, opens Summerhill Academy extension in November 1970. Also present (from left to right), Roy Pirie, James Clark and Provost James Lamond (*Reproduced by courtesy of Aberdeen Journals Ltd*).

25. The headmaster of Summerhill Academy.

26. MacKenzie at an educational conference at Stirling University in November 1974. On his left John Graham, Rector, Anderson High School, Shetland, and on his right, David Robertson, Director of Education, Dundee, and Jo Grimond, former leader of the Liberal Party.

27. On the Rhine, Germany, during his last trip abroad. December 1986.

28. At his home at Westcults Farm, *circa* 1986.

the rather staid and formal atmosphere of the all-boys Aberdeen Grammar School where I had spent the past seven years of my teaching career. Instead of the highly pressurised emphasis on exam preparation and performance that in those days characterised the ethos of that kind of school, here at Summerhill was a four-year Secondary that had a much more flexible approach to education. The pupils were more friendly and accessible as human beings and the staffroom was a place where open debate and discussion on a whole range of topics went on in a highly charged, almost hilarious, atmosphere. There were strong, and sometimes (even in those days) conflicting, personalities in the staffroom who used the one and only place in the school for staff to meet communally and relax at intervals and at lunch-time, and, frequently after four o' clock, as a forum for lively debate. Foremost among such personalities were Stanley Allan, the Principal Teacher of Physical Education and Ian MacDonald, the Principal Teacher of Science, who had just been appointed Deputy Headteacher at the time I arrived.

I enjoyed being at Summerhill. It had a great spirit about it. Willie Christie did not make life easy. He was always hectoring people, making them feel they were 'on trial', such was the way he pressurised them to get on with the job and do all the additional duties, such as playground supervision, that Principal Teachers such as myself were expected to do, as well as run their own departments. Attending contact evenings and meeting parents was an entirely new experience for me as well as was the expectation that you should take your turn at visiting the school cottage at Potarch with another teacher and ten pupils and learn as a consequence to drive the school mini-bus and come to terms with all the rules and regulations to do with managing pupils in such an environment, and with domestic chores such as duty rotas for cooking and washing up. And back at the school, I had to get used to long, arduous, weekly meetings of Principal Teachers with Christie where all sorts of original ideas were put forward for discussion, such as on one occasion, the pros and cons of setting aside somewhere in the school a 'quiet' room for senior pupils where they could learn the art of contemplation.

All this was set against the strong likelihood that the city authorities were about to implement a comprehensive system of education, which, as far as Summerhill was concerned, would mean the immediate development of a fifth year and a 'comprehensive' intake. This, in turn, would spark off a major additional building programme to accommodate a much increased school roll with specialist accommodation for the likes of art, the sciences and technology. However, just as this exciting prospect was about to materialise, at the start of the autumn term in 1967, Willie Christie suddenly announced that he was to take early retirement. Behind his decision to retire was the fact that his wife had become house-bound and he felt constrained to devote himself to look after her, giving her support and companionship. He remarks in the article he wrote for the magazine to mark the school's 25th anniversary. 'My retiral was marked by the dinner presentation in honour of my wife and myself by the parents as an expression of their gratitude for what the school had done in Summerhill...Much of our aim had been achieved. I was proud to have been Headmaster of such an excellent group of teachers, Parents and pupils.'

The news of Christie's impending retirement came as a total surprise to everybody at Summerhill – such was his identification with the school and the special ethos that he had helped to create there. His was the driving force that gave the school its sense of purpose and direction. The staff had mixed feelings about the prospect of his departure – some felt a sense of relief at his going in that they regarded him as a slave-driver who had little regard for the feelings of staff and rode rough-shod over them as and when it suited him to do so; others were worried that standards would slip and that the school would miss his strong hand at the tiller. Perhaps it was the pupils who were to miss him most of all, for he had the knack of getting to know them well and made them keenly aware of his expectations that they should always do their best – which was why, of course, he felt it so necessary to keep his staff on their toes all the time.

The news of R.F. MacKenzie's appointment as the new Headteacher of Summerhill was greeted with near disbelief and not a little apprehension by the staff of the school. Most of us had heard of Mackenzie, that he was a radical and a bit of a rebel. On reflection, we took it that the Labour-controlled Council had looked ahead at the prospect of implementing Comprehensive education in the City and that the appointment of a figure like MacKenzie was a gesture on their part that their hearts were in the right place with regard to that change politically. After all, he hailed from the North-East and would perhaps bring with him a fresh approach to education in the area in keeping with the spirit of the times.

I remember my first meeting with MacKenzie. It was a grey, coldish spring day in April 1968. It was the afternoon. Ian MacDonald, the Deputy, who had been Acting Headteacher in the interval of time between Christie's departure and MacKenzie's arrival, was showing MacKenzie round the school and introducing him to the staff.. I had not met him before, but had seen his photcograph in the papers. He struck me, when I met him, as a bit older than I had expected (he was 57 years old at the time) and he looked somewhat world-weary; but there was a warm benevolence about him and a strong North-East burr in his speech that was reassuring. His face and his features were craggy – that of a man of forthrightness and character; his build was solid and sturdy. I remember being surprised at the size of his hands. They reminded me of the muckle hands of an uncle of mine who, like MacKenzie, hailed from the countryside and conjured up in my mind a picture of someone more familiar with the hard, physical tasks of farming than the more refined work of a teacher and writer.

To begin with, things did not change all that much. The school (like most schools) had its own routines and like most Headteachers taking over a new school MacKenzie took his time to judge what was going on and to consult with staff about how they saw the job that they were doing and the task ahead, now that Comprehensive education was in the offing. One of the first things he did that gained the instantaneous approval of the staff was to rationalise the length of the school day. On certain days of the week, under Willie Christie, we worked a longer school day with a shortened lunch-hour. Instead of this, MacKenzie promptly opted for a uniform school day with a four o' clock finish (in common with other schools). It was a sensible move to make and was a gesture that earned him the gratitude of staff who inwardly resented having to work a longer school day than other schools on certain days of the week.

The degree of commitment that teachers had towards the job they had to do in schools such as Summerhill was to a large extent undermined by the lack of esteem associated with Junior Secondary schools in those days. Teachers in such schools tended to suffer from low morale which was largely brought about by a feeling that they were grossly underpaid and undervalued as a profession; there was a strong tendency for staff in such schools to look down on the pupils in their care as 'rejects' of the Secondary system and to have a very limited expectation of what their pupils were capable of academically. Discipline, to a large extent, was dependent on the exercise of corporal punishment by means of the tawse which was often used indiscriminately. Although Summerhill was an exception to the rule in many respects because of the unique ethos that Christie had created in the school mainly through sheer force of personality, yet, beneath the surface, the malaise that affected most Junior Secondary schools, still exerted an underlying influence in determining the outlook of teachers towards their job. The departure of Christie and the arrival of MacKenzie did in a very significant sense signal a change in the 'mood' at Summerhill. here was a relaxation in the atmosphere because Mackenzie did not exercise the same degree of control over the school that was the hallmark of the Christie regime. MacKenzie was content for a time to let the school proceed along the lines that had been set in motion by his predecessor. What helped him in particular to maintain a degree of stability in this initial phase of his Headship was the support of his Deputy Head, Ian MacDonald, who had been promoted to the post two years previously. He enabled MacKenzie to find his feet through his unstinting support and by using his knowledge of staff and pupils as a key factor in establishing a sense of continuity between one regime and the other.

Nevertheless, as time went on, there were mutterings among the staff at what was seen as MacKenzie's apparently laisser-faire attitude to disciplinary matters, especially among the more traditionally-minded who had strongly approved of Christie's high-profile approach to discipline and liked his strength of leadership. Prominent in this 'reactionary' element among the staff were the large number of male members who belonged, as I did, (though I did not consider myself as a 'reactionary') to the Scottish Schoolmasters Association. The SSA had more similarity to a trades union in its approach to teachers' pay and conditions than the monolithic Educational Institute of Scotland. The SSA was particularly well represented in Junior Secondary schools and, as a result, reflected the uncompromising views of those staff who had little time for child-centred education and were of the opinion that the status of the teacher depended on maintaining traditional codes of discipline in the school, embodied most aptly in the phrase 'in loco parentis'. This meant in practice that teachers should exercise the same control over a child at school as would be exercised by a parent over his child at home.

The Summerhill teacher who was at the hub of this powerful element of largely reactionary views about schools and the way they should be run was the Principal Teacher of Physical Education, Stanley Allan. Stanley had a high profile nationally in the SSA and eventually became its President. He was a big man physically and he had a strong presence. He liked to argue a case and to debate issues, often amusingly and articulately, in the staffroom; but there was no disguising his strong opinions about the lot of teachers and the need, in his view, to have their status and conditions improved by more effective political advocacy of their case. He had not got on well with Willie Christie. He had, in fact, conducted a long, drawn-out feud with Christie on various issues, but at the centre of it was the fact that they were both of them strong personalities and neither of them liked to be faced down by the other.

Over the course of the next three years the strength of the union-minded male staff in the school was to become a key factor in events as they unfolded in the deepening rift that was to open up in the staff between those who identified with what MacKenzie stood for and the resistance against him that owed a lot of its effectiveness to the organisational and rhetorical skills of Stanley Allan who presided at frequent meetings of SSA members called to discuss the growing crisis at the school.

However, any personal awareness on my part that such a confrontation would ultimately develop, did not enter my mind in the early days of MacKenzie's headship. I was much too busy running the English Department and trying to establish an interest in drama among the pupils by setting up a Drama Club in the school. This, in turn, led to an involvement on my part in producing an annual school play which usually ran in parallel with the other additional chore that was expected of the Head of an English Department in these days – the production of an annual school magazine. With the added burden of looking after the interests of 11 other members of staff who all taught English throughout the school, the pressures of the Principal's job were considerable. It was made even more onerous by the need to prepare the ground for presenting pupils from our first-ever fifth year for Higher English, now that the school was deemed to be 'Comprehensive'. I was totally convinced personally that Comprehensive education was the way forward for schools in Scotland. I welcomed, in particular, the opportunity, in a setting such as Summerhill,to develop the potential of pupils who had originally been designated as being fit only to do 'Junior Secondary' courses, but clearly had the talent to tackle courses at Higher Grade.

This opportunity came to me personally in school session 1970-71, when the school had its first fifth year of some 50 pupils. That coincided with the opening of the extension to the school which officially became Summerhill Academy in November 1970. The 'new' school was formally opened by Willie Ross, until recently Secretary of State for Scotland. Although MacKenzie himself had serious reservations about the efficacy of such a figure opening the school, given Ross's role in giving Fife County Council the go-ahead to close Braehead, the two men were in a conciliatory mood on this occasion and Ross made a genuine effort to support MacKenzie in what he was trying to do for Scottish education and wished him and the new school well.

I think we all shared a degree of optimism at this point in the school's history. We were buoyed up by the change in the status of the school and by the generosity of the authority in providing such a vast extension, comprising new facilities for Social Studies, a Youth Centre, a new Games Hall, and up-dated accommodation for Art, Home Economics, Science and Technical Education. If anything, the opening of this extension and the accompanying positive newspaper publicity marked the high point in the school's development under MacKenzie; but in other respects there was already cause for concern for the school's future well-being.

For one thing, the Education Committee had taken a decision to change the school's catchment area as from 1970-71 in such a way as to stop its intake from a 'residential' area not far from the school and put it instead into the catchment area of Hazlehead Academy that had been recently built at the West-end of the town to replace the former Aberdeen Academy. The result of this change was that Summerhill would in future have an intake that was almost purely drawn from the surrounding Council housing estates which meant the school did not benefit from having a social mix nor from a balanced intake, representing all abilities. Worse still was the fact that the new intake would very soon raise the school's population to well over a 1,000 which was bound to have a damaging effect on the school's ethos and the work involved in its daily management.

It was during the course of the 1969–70 session that MacKenzie and I had a row that at the time set me against him because of the way he reacted to the situation. The school magazine that I was responsible for producing that year had been given a new format – it was Donald Smith, the Principal Teacher of Art, who suggested to me that we go for a bolder, more imaginative cover design and a much larger page size than in past editions. The result was a much more ambitious production in keeping with the school's imminent development into a comprehensive school and it won an accolade from *The Scotsman*'s Annual School Magazine Awards as being 'light years' ahead of similar magazines being produced by the likes of Dundee High School in the private education sector.

However, my euphoria at the magazine's success was short-lived. One morning I was summoned to MacKenzie's room. He was in a seething temper. The magazine's editorial, which I had written, had deeply upset him. It mentioned the fact that the school council which MacKenzie had set up (much in the same way as he had done at Braehead) had been struggling in its efforts to gain the support of the staff and the pupils for what it was trying to do. A compromise had been reached whereby the prefect system that had been abolished by MackKenzie, when he came, was re-introduced in order to balance the kind of job the council was doing as opposed to that being done by the prefects. The editorial said, in effect, that there was room for both.

But to MacKenzie the admission I had made in print about the shortcomings of the school council was anathema. To him what I had done was to afford ammunition to the likes of the local press who, in his view, would use such evidence to disparage the democratic principles that school councils stood for; principles that he himself had fought for so hard at Braehead.

I was thunderstruck, I could not believe that he could become so incensed by what I thought was an objective assessment of how the school council experiment was working out at Summerhill. I was hurt too because the whole intention of the magazine had been to enhance the profile of the school and, to my mind, that had been more than justified by the national recognition the magazine had been given by *The Scotsman* in its Magazine Awards section that year.

In retrospect, what this incident shows was how scarred MacKenzie was by his experiences at Braehead. The bitter experience of being exposed to antagonistic press coverage at Braehead still haunted him. It was as if he felt that it was only a matter of time before the same process would start up again, and it showed a sensitivity to criticism that was out of proportion to the scale of the incident that had sparked off his fit of temper in the first place.

How far then, during the time I was there as Principal Teacher of English, until, indeed, I left in November 1971, was their evidence of a decline setting in at the school, culminating in MacKenzie's suspension in 1974, just two-and-a-half years later? Clearly, the day-to-day running of the school became much more difficult during the course of 1970–71, firstly because of the loss to the school through promotion of the strong and influential leadership of the Deputy Head, Ian MacDonald, and, secondly, because of the sudden and dramatic increase in pupil numbers. The least motivated pupils were already causing more and more problems for younger and less experienced staff, and the school became subject to frequent interruptions from fire alarms being maliciously set off. Each time this happened it meant evacuating the whole school and this had a very unsettling effect on teacher morale and on the pupils generally. Staff who had been brought up under the controlled authority of the Christie regime reacted badly to the increased numbers in the school and the apparent signs of disorder that seemed to reign in the school, especially at change-over times and at intervals.

Most of us were well aware of the impact that increased numbers would have on the running of the school and accepted that this would present a challenge, but we did not have any real fears for the school's future. Indeed, I had come to identify myself so closely with the school's life as a new Comprehensive that I found it extremely hard to put it all behind me when I left to go to Logie School in Dundee in November 1971. I enjoyed the company of the pupils, especially the ones I had worked closely with in the Drama Club in the years I was there, many of whom were in the school's first fifth year and had been in my class for Higher English. I also liked the way in which the new appointments in Guidance had been made. Known as Year Masters and Year Mistresses, these new appointments in some cases drew in fresh blood to the school and directly addressed the growing problem of increasing pupil numbers by seeking to establish good relationships with the pupils on an individual basis and to form links between the school and the home. Above all, I missed the camaraderie of the staffroom and the close friendships that somehow developed as a consequence of the adventure we were all mutually involved in, trying to shape and bring into being a new kind of school in difficult circumstances.

An invaluable insight into the way in which the change-over from the Christie to the MacKenzie regime was perceived from the pupils' point of view is provided by these recollections written by a former pupil, Raymond Hetherington, who attended Summerhill from 1966 to 1972. Raymond was also a member of the Drama Club and was in the class for Higher English that I taught in 1970 -71.

> When we children started at Summerhill School in August 1966, we were enthusiastic and generally obeyed the rules without question. Mr Christie was the headmaster. His 'reputation' was well known to all the kids. We regarded him as very much a disciplinarian. We kids were horrified by tales of older pupils being summoned to Mr Christie's office, more often on a Monday morning, to receive disciplining by physical punishment. The aura which emanated from Mr Christie was reinforced by his frequent visits to the classrooms of the school, in order that he might see for himself how the children were being taught, or were behaving. The school enjoyed a good reputation for the conduct of its pupils. We children were keen and proud to wear school uniform. After all, it was expected of us.
>
> For most of us there was no questioning of the system. What was being preached reflected that which had gone before in the Primary schools. Our parents were content with the system.
>
> Mr MacKenzie replaced Mr Christie upon his retiral in 1967. We were in our second year at Summerhill. I was disappointed that Mr Ian MacDonald, the existing Deputy Headmaster, wasn't replacing Mr Christie. Mr MacDonald was extremely popular with the pupils and staff. He had the confidence of the parents too. Ian MacDonald had helped establish the school

when it opened in 1962 and was familiar with the needs and abilities of the area's children. He had a good rapport with his pupils. I learned that many of the staff shared this disappointment too.

We were informed by our teachers that Mr MacKenzie had a distinguished career in teaching and that he had written several books on education. Mr MacKenzie was very open and relaxed in comparison with his predecessor. Mr MacKenzie would sit in on a class for a considerable time and earnestly communicate with the pupils. By comparison, Mr Christie, while I'm sure showing no less devotion to his pupils, was a dynamic person with little time to spend on individual pupils. Mr Christie was usually present in a number of classes over an afternoon, while Mr MacKenzie seemed little concerned if he spent the entire afternoon in only one.

During our time at Summerhill, the school leaving age was raised to 16 years of age, which was imposed upon all pupils whether or not they were destined for Ordinary Grade exam. This change occurred quite quickly, with little apparent preparation for accommodating pupils already at the point of leaving the school system. The lower achieving pupils felt very frustrated by this change and vented their frustration in any way they could. This usually took the form of disruption to classes.

With the benefit of hindsight, I feel that this rebellion might have been the catalyst for the later rowdiness and disruption which dogged MacKenzie's command of the school. This insurgence was also fuelled by the division in staff ranks.

Our year, and the following year's pupils (1966 and 67 intake) who had experienced Mr Christie's rule, liked Mr MacKenzie, and we appreciated what he was attempting to achieve for us with his more liberal regime. 'Younger pupils, however, came straight from the feeder Primary schools into this relaxed environment and tested the system to its limits. They were seeing division in the staff on the subject of corporal punishment, something which became apparent since Mr MacKenzie took over as Head.

The relaxed image of Mr MacKenzie was later accompanied by sightings of him in later years, usually in the corridors, on his way to, or from, placating a class, where he looked rather agitated and certainly disappointed. I can recall seeing him on a number of occasions with a rather glassy, hurt look in his eyes.

Thus the events leading up to MacKenzie's suspension in 1974 were part of a tragedy that enveloped not just MacKenzie, but his staff and his pupils as well. It is time that these events were examined closely, and at a distance from when they occurred, to see what significance we can attach to them 25 years later, that may help to illuminate aspects of the continuing debate about how best to educate our children; and what relationship between the State and the school can best provide the ideal balance between a school's autonomy to forge its own distinctive ethos and the state's continuing demand for uniformity.

CHAPTER NINE

Confrontation 1972–74

As I was to discover for myself, when I took over a school from another Headteacher in Dundee in 1971, there is a world of difference between starting off a new school where you can decide the way you want to go and shape events accordingly and having to pick up where someone else left off. At Braehead, MacKenzie's as its first Headteacher, had the crucial benefit of setting the tone of the school and, largely speaking, the school developed very much in his own image – a place which reflected his desire to try out new ideas free from the constraints of a curriculum oriented towards achieving passes in external examinations. At Summerhill it was totally different. MacKenzie had initially to follow in the wake of the strong and pervasive influence of Christie's personality. It was always going to be hard for anyone following such a person as Willie Christie, not to be compared unfavourably with him, in so far as his domination of the way he operated the school was concerned. MacKenzie, in making changes to the system, especially in disciplinary matters, soon got into bother with the staff. His unilateral decision to forbid the belting of girls, for instance, set the staff against him, not just because it was a decision that he imposed upon them, but because it caused difficulties in the classroom where girls had to be treated differently from boys when it came to the matter of applying sanctions.

The other decisive trend that he initiated was in his approach to the sort of job he expected his guidance staff to do with the pupils. For a school that was suddenly growing much larger numerically, it was essential that pupils had the benefit of the support of staff who could relate to them more effectively in the context of the ups and downs of school life in a large institution. The Year Masters and Mistresses who were appointed during the course of 1970–71 formed a core of staff who had the welfare of the pupils as their major concern. They were encouraged by MacKenzie to see their role as that of caring people who would act in a supportive role for the benefit of the pupils. Under no circumstances would this mean that they could employ corporal punishment as a sanction as this, in MacKenzie's view, would destroy the trust between teacher and pupil that such a system built its effectiveness upon. The Guidance staff concerned largely accepted this role. But it had a damaging effect upon the way the role of the Guidance staff was perceived by the rest of the staff. They took the view that the Guidance staff were, in a sense, undermining the role and status of the rest of the staff by cultivating the friendship of the pupils and, in some instances, allowing pupils to be on first name terms with them. Moreover, such Guidance staff who employed this overtly friendly approach to pupils tended to be staff that MacKenzie had 'imported' to fulfil this role and were seen by the more reactionary and traditionally-orientated members of staff as being identified with MacKenzie's 'soft' approach to discipline.

What also tilted the course of events at Summerhill in 1972 against MacKenzie and his efforts to steer the school in his direction were his absence through illness over a number of months that year (he had a slight heart attack) and the appointment of Alex Ritchie as the successor to Ian MacDonald as Deputy Head. Although events had not yet led to an open split in the school staff over MacKenzie's handling of discipline and related issues, his absence between February and June 1972 came at a bad time. It took him away from the school at a critical time in its development and, given that Ritchie had largely to take over the running of the school in his absence, it underlined intellectually, culturally and spiritually the appalling gulf between the two men.

Ritchie was basically a Technical teacher who had close links with Aberdeen Labour Party, having been at one time, a Labour councillor. He was chosen by a Staffing Sub-Committee to be the new Deputy Head a decision endorsed by the full Education Committee. The thinking behind his appointment was obviously dictated by a perception on the part of the politicians that MacKenzie was too much of a risk to be given as his Depute someone with views similar to himself. Ritchie, in effect, was chosen as a 'place-man' in order to counteract MacKenzie's libertarian tendencies as it was commonly known that Ritchie was an old-style,'hard man'whose outlook was that of many Junior Secondary teachers that a school needed to be run on strict disciplinary lines – he stood for just the opposite of what MacKenzie stood for. It was a scenario that was bound to lead to trouble for the school where the Headteacher and his Depute were so ill-suited and ill-matched. Ritchie had no finesse; he had little rapport with pupils; it is hard to imagine his having read any books on education, especially those of his boss, MacKenzie. Jenny Kinnon, one of the Guidance staff of the time, remembers Alex Ritchie only too well:

> It was the first day of the new term and I had my first year English class – apprehensive but keen, feeling grown up and looking forward to a new start. The Depute Head (Ritchie) appeared at my classroom...'Oh, yes, 1E, which of you is Smith? I know your, brother, lad. He's trouble – so you just watch it.' I saw the lad shrivel in front of my eyes. I suppose that was, for me, the first indication that things would not work out.

MacKenzie took the appointment of Ritchie as his Depute Head very personally. He was hurt to the core as well as inconsolably angry. He took it as a personal slight – had not the Education Committee promised by his very appointment to the post of Headteacher to back him and give him the sort of staff he would need to make the school successful? MacKenzie felt betrayed.

Much of this sense of betrayal comes out in a speech he made in September 1972 to the Comparative Education Society in Europe. In the speech he describes in detail the procedures that led to the appointment of Ritchie:

> There is a Labour Party Education Committee in Aberdeen and they say they reserve the right to add to our short-list anybody they want, and they did. Then the interviews came for four people, three of whom would have been to the Deputy Director and to me perfectly acceptable, and a fourth who was not...Well, the candidates had two questions fired at them and one or two other questions; no interview lasted more than 15 minutes. The four candidates retired. The discussion began, and then, as if to say well, we've had our discussion, the Convener of the Staffing Sub-Committee switched the thing off and said, 'I propose we appoint — [the fourth candidate]. The fourth candidate was a technical teacher; that does not necessarily exclude him; he had less experience, and the rest of us, that is the school and the Education Office were very much against his appointment. One Labour member, (the Convener) proposed that he be appointed, the other Labour member seconded. The Tory chap, the third one, objected, and finally, because he was a nice chap, and because they had more candidates to see, said, 'Alright I agree'. This chap (Ritchie), it was agreed, would be recommended to the full Education Committee which met the following week. I went and saw the Director about this and he said, 'Put it in a letter', I'll support you. But of course, what happened was that in the meantime the Labour Party met as a group to discuss this and, I believe, the fur and feathers flew, because the younger members were very much against his appointment. This chosen candidate had previously been a Labour member of Aberdeen Town Council and some of us thought that this was not in itself sufficient reason for appointing him to the job of Depute in a new Comprehensive. We tried to point out that the comprehensives were on trial in Aberdeen...it was by no means sure that they would be a success, and an appointment like this would not help. Well, the Education Committee met, but the Labour Party were bound by the group decision and they voted him in. This is the sort of situation that we are up against in the micro-politics of Aberdeen.

He then goes on to explain how the fact that his newly appointed Deputy Head believed in corporal punishment went right against what he as Headteacher was trying to do at Summerhill – abolish corporal punishment.

> When I went there I said there would be no corporal punishment of girls. When I said this in Fife there was a bit of a row. But it was nothing to the major battle which this raised in Aberdeen; and when in consultation with the Director, we decided that we would gradually reduce corporal punishment of boys, he suggested a novel idea...to start at the top end. The school was then a four-year school...and we said that besides not belting girls we would also not belt fourth year boys. When the school became Comprehensive, of course, it went without saying that having stopped belting them in fourth year we wouldn't start them in the fifth. So that was four, five and six. When we said this, there was a terrible battle. You can discuss politics, you can discuss religion and it will be a fairly vehement discussion, but it was nothing to the battle over corporal punishment...

What is important about this speech that he made in the autumn of 1972 is that MacKenzie had got to the point on his return to the school after illness when he no longer felt he could hold back on what he wanted ultimately to do at Summerhill. He was prepared to criticise the local authority publicly* for what he considered was their failure to back him up and he was prepared to take on the growing opposition to what he stood for in Summerhill rather than look for a compromise. The firmness of his resolve in this respect is reflected in the passage in his speech describing the work of the Guidance staff at Summerhill.

> The most effective work is being done by the Year staff...I told them that they are people who stand up for the pupils. Some of the pupils have nobody else at home interested in them. They are like a defence counsel...They will take an opportunity privately and quietly to tell a pupil off, but publicly they will always come out in defence of the pupil. I tell them any information they get they don't have to tell me, however important they may feel it is...It is in discussion between the Year Masters and pupils that the most important work as far as socialisation is concerned is being done in the school.

There is no doubt about the fact that at the core of the process that led to the split in the Summerhill staff was MacKenzie's passionately-held concept of the critical role his Guidance staff would play in the counselling of children at the school. The appointments made at Year Master level were largely MacKenzie's own choices and those appointments reflected willingness on the part of such staff to back MacKenzie's ideas, even if it meant being at variance with the rest of

*The speech was not, in fact, reported in the press until August 1973.

the staff. The suspicions of the rest of the staff as to MacKenzie's ultimate intentions for the school were further strengthened by the fact that some of the key appointments at guidance level and in the English Department, in particular, were teachers from England or from overseas. The teacher who succeeded me as Principal Teacher of English, John Roberts, was a case in point. With his prominent beard, Jesus sandals and his casual manner with the children, he gave the immediate impression of being trendy and 'left wing'. Worse still, John Roberts was also a forceful personality who was not afraid to speak up on behalf of MacKenzie's ideas at Staff Meetings and confirmed in the minds of those staff who resented MacKenzie's 'slack' attitude to disciplinary matters that the long-term MacKenzie agenda for the school was to replace the traditionalists with reformers and radicals who represented an alien 'English' culture, scornful of good old-fashioned Scottish common sense and conformity.

The flash-point for these growing tensions among the staff that grew inexorably during the course of 1972 were the Staff Meetings that MacKenzie regularly called once a month to discuss school issues. The Staff Meetings were where strong personalities such as Stanley Allan and John Roberts held sway – Allan representing the views of dissident staff and Roberts the faction, mainly from the Guidance staff and the English department, who supported the MacKenzie line. Although, in theory, such meetings were meant to reflect a democratic approach to decision-making and to allow people to air their views on school policy, in reality they became more and more a formal setting for a trial of strength between the protagonists on a 'for' or 'against' MacKenzie platform. The great majority of the 90-strong staff did not participate in these discussions; they were mere onlookers at the unfolding drama, but there was no doubt that the open conflict at such meetings ultimately helped to solidify opinion both for and against MacKenzie and what he stood for. In those days, there were no Board of Studies or Senior Management Teams where policy was hammered out, making Staff Meetings much less frequent and less crucial with regard to decision-making. MacKenzie's decisions, particularly on disciplinary matters, were, as he freely admits, not taken on a consensus basis, but were largely imposed because he knew he would otherwise be outvoted. This authoritarian approach on the part of a man so outwardly in favour of democratic procedures, left MacKenzie open to damaging criticism from the majority of his staff and exposed him ultimately to the threat of intervention in the running of his school from the local education authority itself.

Pressures also continued to build up during 1972 as a result of the larger intake and the resultant strain on the day-to-day school management and on the Guidance system generally. The perception of the pupils increasingly was that MacKenzie and the Guidance staff were largely sympathetic to their welfare; whereas other staff were not. An extreme but nevertheless important example of this dual application of standards took place in 1972 in connection with the year group who were the first to form a fifth year at the school.

The incident arose out of a complaint made by members of this year group to MacKenzie that they saw no point in attending a class on social dancing that was taken by Stanley Allan as part of his duties as PT of Physical Education. The social dancing comprised a mixed group of boys and girls, boys on one side of the gym and girls on the other who were being instructed on how to do Scottish country dances. It had not been an option on their timetable – it was simply a 'fill-in' that they were timetabled for as part of their PE programme. The boys were especially reluctant to take part and felt it to be a 'waste of time'. They felt their time would be more constructively spent studying in the library. Stanley Allan, on the other hand, regarded the social dancing as part of his responsibility as Principal Teacher, and, when some of the boys openly refused to take part, he stormed out of the gym and went to fetch MacKenzie to sort out the matter. Mackenzie came along to the scene of the dispute and asked to hear what the boys and girls had to say by way of their objections to the lesson. After listening to their explanation for not cooperating with Mr Allan, MacKenzie said that he agreed with them and the class, much to Stanley Allan's anger, was discontinued. Such an intervention said a lot for MacKenzie's willingness to listen to what his pupils were saying and to come to their assistance if he thought they were being treated unfairly, but in regard to stoking up resentment to his way of running the school, such an intervention, involving the chief source of resistance to him within the school, could only confirm the worst fears of the silent majority of the staff that he cared more for the pupils than he did for the staff when it came down to matters of principle.

Towards the end of that year, MacKenzie, still in a state of frustration about the imposition upon him of what he considered to be unsympathetic staff, had an interview with the Director of Education, James Clark. During the course of their discussions about staffing, Clark suggested that within Aberdeen authority there was a policy of inviting staff who were unhappy with their lot in a particular school to be asked to be transferred to another. Not long afterwards MacKenzie addressed a Staff Meeting at which he said, 'If there are members of staff who don't feel able to work in this more permissive climate, they should feel free to ask for a transfer.' There was some dispute concerning MacKenzie's use of the word 'permissive'. He claimed later that he had meant to use the word 'progressive' rather than 'permissive'. However that may be, for the majority of staff in the school who were by this time largely against him, the word 'permissive' meant ultimately getting rid of the belt. This speech was also interpreted by the hard-liners on the staff as an ultimatum to conform or get out. Early in 1973 it led to Stanley Allan, as the leading member of the hard-liners writing to Clark on behalf of 49 members of staff (more than half) protesting at MacKenzie's 'ultimatum'. Not long afterwards Allan and seven other members of the 'hard-liners' had a meeting with Clark at which they presented him with a document listing areas where, in their view, discipline had broken down. However, all sides were still prepared to be conciliatory at this stage. Clark, in particular, was anxious to avoid further confrontation and even MacKenzie and Allan were prepared to look at ways of resolving some of the differences through discussion groups. However, just when it looked as if a compromise might be reached as to how such discussion groups might be set up, MacKenzie and Allan reached an impasse over what role the hard-liners should be allowed to play in such discussions. As a result, their patience now exhausted, the hard-liners presented to Clark and MacKenzie on 5 June 1973 what has come to be called 'The Document on Discipline'.

This document claimed to encapsulate the views of more than half of the staff about their concerns for the school and where it was going. It also claimed 'to reflect the views of many parents and even many pupils, many institutions and other agencies local and otherwise, that the policies of the school were likely to add to the continual and rapidly deteriorating situation presently existing in many areas of the school's functioning.' They felt that the root of the problem lay in the question of authority and claimed that 'so-called anti-authoritarianism is fashionable and that the collapse of secular and learned authority in our society has inevitably affected our schools. It is the basic premise of this document that authority must exist because it is necessary for the maintenance of any form of pluralistic society and that is particularly relevant to the specialised society of a school.' There followed a report of the type of incidents which had caused consternation to half of the staff.

Their statement listed apathy to work, recalcitrance, dress, manners, obscenities, vandalism, violence, intimidation, extortion, theft, truancy, dangerous behaviour, the number of pupils who did not accept reprimand. Other less important but nevertheless significant factors that had caused staff concern were 'pupils' speech and a lack of manners and courtesy'. especially in their dealings with staff. The staff document listed the demoralising effect that pupils were having on some members of staff, claiming that teachers were losing heart, turning a blind eye to misdemeanours, feeling that their status was being lowered. One sentence said, 'They object to their professionality being questioned and unrecognised.' And they claimed also that MacKenzie supported the pupil against the teacher, appeared to be 'interested only in the recalcitrant', discouraged the use of sanctions and 'denied the professionality of teachers who refuse to accept offensive insults from pupils.'

Although MacKenzie deplored very strongly the viewpoint expressed in 'The Document on Discipline', he agreed that it well represented the views of his opponents. It signalled in the context of the school itself, a formal recognition that the staff was now hopelessly split into two camps on ideological lines, and any chance that there might yet have been a meeting of minds on what divided them as a staff, came to an end near the end of June 1973 when *The Press and Journal* published the full details of 'The Document on Discipline' and of the tensions in the School. The information was apparently leaked from someone on the school staff – possibly close to the Allan camp. The story hit the streets accompanied by a whole series of adverse comments on the school by a Conservative councillor. At a stroke the running of Summerhill Academy was now a political matter. The leaders of the controlling group had no option but to respond to the situation.

This the Labour group did during the summer vacation in 1973 when a Sub-Committee under the chairmanship of the Education Convener, Roy Pirie, met to discuss what to do about the 'Summerhill crisis'. The recommendation was that real staff discussion groups be set up so as to deal with the problems on a 'consensus basis'. As the meeting broke up on 3 July, journalists handed the committee copies of a petition that a local newspaper had that day received from 150 households in the Mastrick area. A fortnight later the Conservative group sought to embarrass the ruling Labour group further by launching a petition to the then Conservative Secretary of State for Scotland. This called for an enquiry into the allegations of smoking, drinking, gambling – even gang warfare – at Summerhill, and to make matters worse, church leaders in the Mastrick area also began to voice the concerns of some of their parishioners, both in what they saw as the breakdown of discipline and the inclusion in the curriculum of activities they saw as morally dangerous. The English Department, for example, was accused of encouraging the pupils to write pornography, although the truth of this allegation has never been properly investigated.

When the new term began in August 1973, there was still an outside chance that MacKenzie and Allan might have somehow found some common ground for conciliation along the lines suggested by Convener Roy Pirie that the staff engage in a consultation exercise on those issues that divided them. However, the whole situation was worsened further by a press relevation in *The Scotsman* of MacKenzie's speech made in September 1972 at the European Comparative Education Conference in Edinburgh which had openly criticised the Labour Party in Aberdeen concerning Alex Ritchie's appointment as Depute Head earlier that year. Hence at one blow, MacKenzie had ranged against him virtually the whole of the Aberdeen Establishment. The Labour Party, for a start, could not be expected to take kindly to his accusation of political manipulation in staff appointments. The churches were already up in arms over what they say as the immoral dangers of some of the happenings at Summerhill, while the full-time education officials resented his implications that they had failed to support him. To make matters worse, the day after the publication of *The Scotsman* article the parish ministers in the school's catchment area in Mastrick launched their own petition to the Secretary of State claiming to represent parents' views on matters of curriculum and discipline.

Internally, staff relations continued to be strained, not just because of the fact that a lot of what was going on in the school had become public knowledge, but because of the continuing clash of personalities within the staff who held very different ideological views. In August 1973, Edna Smith, the woman Depute Head, who had been in the post since 1971 (when an additional women's post had been put into effect) left to take up a post elsewhere. She was replaced by Elizabeth Garrett, a 'MacKenzie' appointment who was specifically put in charge of Guidance. Garrett had held posts in Senior Secondary schools prior to coming to Summerhill and had also at one time been Education Officer with Grampian Television. She was a self-confessed admirer of MacKenzie and set about her task at Summerhill with zeal and absolute commitment. She quickly identified herself with the principles upon which the Guidance system operated in the school and with the MacKenzie faction on the staff. She powerfully supported the work that the Guidance staff were doing in the school and went out of her way to provide support to the many girls who had behavioural problems. Garrett was resented by the traditionalists for her open and enthusiastic identification with what MacKenzie stood for, and her intellectual calibre and academic background which related more closely to that of the other MacKenzie supporters such as John Roberts and added to the undercurrent of resentment among the traditionalists that the school was being taken over in key positions by MacKenzie appointees from outwith the local establishment.

In his book, *The Unbowed Head*, about the Summerhill conflict, MacKenzie seeks to show how, in retrospect, the various forces lined up against him by the autumn of 1973 were for a time held at bay by the intervention of the Education Convener, Roy Pirie. MacKenzie describes Pirie as well-meaning: 'He believed the teachers (the staff of the school) in conference could settle their differences and reach what he called a 'consensus' and to this end he divided them up into small groups and set times for regular discussions that lasted several weeks. They were to work out a 'draft code of principles of conduct for pupils'. However, MacKenzie makes it plain that in his view and in the view of the staff minority supporting him, 'the difficulties could not be settled by the imposition of new code of rules.' MacKenzie, while recognising the amount of time and effort that went into the 'consensus' document, took issue with its concern for reimposing a traditionalist approach to education in the school. He takes issue, for instance, with the first statement of the document where the aim of what follows from the staff's deliberations is to 'establish a healthy climate in which learning and teaching can most effectively take place within the school community.' MacKenzie sees such emphasis on 'learning and teaching' as a backward step, where quietness in the classroom would be re-established so that the age-old Scottish tradition of putting information into children's heads, a transfer of information, 'could proceed without unseemly interruption.' And he also takes issue with the document's attempt to define the sorts of actions that pupils would be punished for: 'lying, stealing, swear ing, persistent bad conduct, disruptive or improper behaviour – e.g. acts of violence, bullying, intimidation, extortion, truancy, vandalism, smoking, consumption of alcohol and misuse of drugs.'

MacKenzie quotes an Aberdeen educational document of 1675 in response to the litany of offences for which children could be punished in the Summerhill report of working parties.

> In 1675 the Synod of Aberdeen asked its Presbyteries only to demand three questions of the School master: whether he makes the bairns learn the catechism, whether he teaches them prayers for morning and evening and a

> grace for meals and whether he chastises them for cursing, swearing, lying, speaking profanitie, for disobedience to parents and what vices that appears in them.

MacKenzie uses this 300-year-old advice from the Aberdeen Synod to illustrate how deep the tradition of sin and punishment in Scottish education still is and claims that 'the rebuke of a 17th century minister of the kirk could be heard in the sentences from the 20th century document.' MacKenzie was also unable to accept the document's insistence on leaving no room for dissidents in the school community. He asks, 'Do we impose order and crush the exasperating dissidents? Or do we undertake the much harder job of creating a society capable of containing in harmony people of widely varying outlook?' In the same way he found it unacceptable the statement in the document that disruptive and disturbed children were to be readily identified in the sense that in his experience once such children were identified, some teachers took it out on them by victimisation. He also finds unacceptable the right of any teacher without consultation to contact the police, which previously had only been done as a last resort and the demand that there be regular staff meetings 'to check on implementation of rules.' He wryly remarks, 'It was not only the pupils who were to be checked up on, it was also the teachers. Once you make rules for teachers (as well as pupils) you have to set up machinery for ensuring they are followed...that is how the Covenanters imposed their rules of righteousness on backsliding sinners.'

He also takes strong exception to the arbitrary way the rules would be imposed upon the pupils. Although the document stressed the need 'to win the support of the pupils for the rules' which could be discussed at the school council and at form or year meetings, yet it was also saying, 'Every opportunity should be taken to emphasise that Headteacher and staff agree with these rules and expect them to be observed.' The document was saying to the pupils, 'Here are the rules. Discuss them. But remember that we expect you to obey them.' For MacKenzie this approach to discipline was anathema. In such a scenario he saw the powers-that-be using the school council as part of the machinery of 'government', much in the same way as a colonial power tells a native council the way it is expected to operate.

The 'Consensus Document' did not, of course, reflect the views of the minority group of teachers who supported MacKenzie. As a consequence, the minority group drew up its own report. They took issue with the principle of establishing a set of school rules, agreeing that, 'The children's values do not coincide with the values of the school because the goals of the exam obstacle race are unobtainable by them and its problems considered irrelevant or difficult.' The minority report proposed to regard each child as 'unique' and put the emphasis for successful discipline upon the individual child's willingness to make decisions about what is appropriate behaviour by himself:

> Discipline, Justice, right and wrong cannot be simply codified – relevance, modification, and flexibility are more important than some arbitrary and authoritatively imposed correctness. Although pupils and teachers need some form of security, a code of security, a code of discipline with specific rules removes personal responsibility from the teacher. How then can we pretend that we are trying to promote personal responsibility in the pupil? Rules protect people from decisions they should be encouraged to make for themselves.

The envelope of documents that the Director of Education, James Clark, sent out to the members of the Education Committee about the state of affairs at Summerhill contained this minority statement but it was largely ignored thereafter as far as any public reference was concerned. MacKenzie was of the opinion that the Education Committee gave it little attention. The other documents that were sent to the Education Committee by the Director contained the majority statement, histories of disturbed pupils and a letter from MacKenzie justifying the work they were doing at Summerhill.

Clark's advice to the Education Committee out of the 'evidence' that had been given to him came very much down in favour of the staff majority. He said, 'In my opinion at this time Summerhill lacks a basic framework of procedures regulating the daily routine of staff and pupils – attempts at innovation can be almost counter-productive if they produce unease among the staff. In stating my own views here I am not denying the changing nature of authority, but there must be authority which is recognized. He went on to say that, 'Only after decisions made and implemented on what is permissible and what is not, can the Headmaster and his staff go forward together to deal with the educational issues.' MacKenzie saw the Director's advice to the Committee as being superficial 'written by a man in an office who spent his life with circulars and committees and reports. He had little intimate understanding of the turmoil in the lives of some of our children. He and we meant different things by education.'

Clark, in MacKenzie's view, had totally misconstrued what MacKenzie was trying to do at Summerhill by failing to acknowledge the need in a community situation such as a school to work out with the pupils how everybody could live in friendship and harmony together.

The Education Committee, when it met, accepted the advice of the Convener's motion, 'that the Sub-committee, being of the opinion that the recommendations contained in the report by the working parties are likely to create an atmosphere and framework conducive to the successful attainment of the aims of the Headmaster, resolves to recommend that the Education Committee indicate their approval of the recommendations contained in that report.' An amendment that was proposed suggesting that the Committee should not approve the extension of corporal punishment beyond the regulations in force at Summerhill and recognise that there were other means of dealing with anti-social behaviour was narrowly lost. MacKenzie who had been invited to be in attendance during the meeting was not called (he had been kept waiting in an ante-room). If he had been called, he would have challenged the misrepresentation contained in the wording of the motion. It was saying, in MacKenzie's view, that that the introduction of authoritarian methods were 'conducive' to the aims of the Headmaster – 'In particular, the Education Committee were saying that they supported me in seeking to reduce corporal punishment, but the best way to reduce it was, for the present, to increase it.'

Mackenzie was firmly of the opinion that the Labour administration had not really thought through the implications of comprehensive education if, in effect, they should have seen it as a step towards the emancipation of the many as opposed to the few – the setting up as in Summerhill of a freer, more just society where a more enlightened form of education could take place based on a really close relationship between teacher and pupil. Instead, MacKenzie saw only among the politicians and administrators a preoccupation with keeping intact the values in education associated 'with a previous dispensation'. There was a strong identification in their minds of equating leadership with the business of maintaining the status quo and so in those terms they found MecKenzie very much lacking in these qualities. The Convener said that 'firm and effective leadership would have prevented this situation from reaching crisis proportion'. MacKenzie had shown an 'inability to be the leader of the team'. He had been guilty of 'woolly theorising' and had not been 'sensitive to staff views'. Their idiom, their ways of thinking, their philosophy of life identified them with the old system. It was the view that came across at a staff meeting in Summerhill towards the end of 1973 when the staff was addressed by Roy Pirie, the Education Convener. In his address Pirie offered little in the way of consolation to MacKenzie, confirming in the tenor of his remarks the Committee's view that MacKenzie had largely only himself to blame for not commanding the support of the majority of his staff in his efforts to carry out his policy. On the other hand, Pirie did admit in public that the majority document had failed to achieve consensus.

Even against the background of the turmoil in the country as a whole early in 1974 when the Miners' Strike led to a General Election and the return of a Labour government under Harold Wilson, the events at Summerhill still commanded a lot of press attention and speculation. The tenuous position of MacKenzie himself was further eroded at a meeting for Summerhill parents that took place at the school on 19 March 1974. No more than 200 of the 2,000 parents attended this meeting which was called by the Education Committee and was chaired by Councillor Pirie and at which two other councillors, the Director and his Senior Depute, MacKenzie and his Depute Head were present.

The purpose of the meeting was to give parents the opportunity 'of indicating views on various aspects of the school which they would wish to bring to the attention of the Committee representatives.' The parents' contribution to the meeting dwelt mainly on concerns about discipline at the school. For instance, widespread exception was taken to the practice of allowing pupils to address staff by Christian names. This was held to undermine discipline and respect. There was also a general concern about teachers turning a blind eye to the behaviour of pupils and the Headteacher of condoning such inaction or not being aware of many of the incidents taking place at the school that had been causing alarm among parents. There was also considerable disquiet expressed about apparent lack of academic progress on the part of pupils, lack of homework and few books being taken home by pupils for study. As well as that were complaints of excessive turnover of staff and of reports of staff wanting transfers away from Summerhill because of its bad working conditions. There was also criticisms of the Education authority for not acting quickly enough to resolve the problems at the school. A few parents were unhappy about the singling out of Summerhill Academy by the Committee.

Mastrick, it was said, had problem families but that was no reason to blame and denigrate the school. Some things could be improved but this was true also of other schools. The Convener replied that only in Summerhill had parents requested a meeting, and only in Summerhill had some of the staff lodged a memo with the Director. The majority of the parents present, however, appeared to support a demand for immediate action by the Committee.

In response to this, MacKenzie was given the chance to speak. He made an impassioned plea in defence of his opposition to corporal punishment, pointing out how much the need to belt children in Scotland was entirely the wrong approach if society was to attempt to bridge the gap that now existed between our disaffected young people and the adult world. He referred to the incident in the school where the school had for the first time fifth year non-academic pupils with the raising of the school leaving age. Before leaving at Christmas they tore down the curtains in their social area because they felt rejected and 'hated our guts'. He made an appeal to the parents to help tackle the problems the school was facing; the school was working on a shoestring on projects like Inverlair – the parents with the agreement of the Education Committee, could act as a board of governors...He ended by reiterating the need to tackle the fundamental problems facing society of which the crisis at Summerhill was only a part; and he ended on a typically defiant note: 'The Committee can sack me but the problems will remain!'

The Convener ended the meeting by stressing that the Committee was not interested in supporting one type of educational philosophy against another, but the school must be seen to be operating in a normal manner with pupils, Headmaster and staff working in accord for good order and discipline. He promised the parents that firm decisions would be taken by the end of the month.

As MacKenzie wryly confessed in *The Unbowed Head* the outcome of the meeting with parents on 19 March was enough to persuade the Convener and the Director that they had heard 'the authentic voice of the people', since clearly a majority of those who spoke were in favour of corporal punishment and more discipline. There was no doubt either in the minds of the Convener and MacKenzie himself that the only possible way forward was for MacKenzie to be sacked from his job. It was now only a matter of time. However, there first followed an exchange of letters between MacKenzie and the Director which could have led to a rapprochement had MacKenzie been willing, at the last, to recant by accepting the will of the majority and gone along with the terms of the 'Consensus document'.The pressures on MacKenzie to compromise were immense. He did not want in a sense to go through with the ignominy of being sacked if it meant abandoning the school and the children he wanted to protect, leaving them to the mercies of the reactionary forces of the establishment. On the other hand, to compromise would go against all he had fought for over the years, and to relent now would surely undermine the position he had fought so hard to establish and would be seen as capitulation, an admission of defeat, a decisive blow against his radicalism. Even so, the temptation to compromise remained, 'I was fortunate in having the full support of my wife and family, and deeply grateful. Otherwise I would have had to capitulate.'

The Education Committee for its part found itself moving remorselessly towards suspending MacKenzie from his post. There was already considerable expectation among parents that this would happen and in church circles locally where Mr Tyrell, the Mastrick minister, had openly opposed MacKenzie and what he stood for and had encouraged parents to lobby for MacKenzie's removal. The teachers' unions similarly vigorously supported the teachers' right to belt pupils and opposed any suggestion that a record should be kept of the occasions on which it was used. On 29 March 1974, MacKenzie appeared before the Staffing Sub-committee to explain his position of his non-acceptance of the 'Document'. Despite the protests of some Labour members, the Committee recommended MacKenzie's suspension. The recommendation went, three days later on 1 April 1974, to the Education Committee. The Convener spoke of 'Growing concerns about the practical aspects of policy implementation at the Academy', and said there had been a consequential disorientation of approach by the teachers individually and the eventual polarisation by significant numbers of the staff into 'pro' and 'anti' MacKenzie groups. He said that when the Committee had imposed the staff Majority Document on the school, MacKenzie was morally obliged to carry out the terms of that document as a matter of urgency. Because he, as Headteacher, had refused to do so, the exercises of last autumn (involving staff working parties) had been rendered worthless. The Convener concluded his attack with five points:

> There is no evidence of an acceptable framework of order in the school. There is marked lack of respect between pupils and teachers, pupils and pupils, many teachers and pupils and the Headmaster. There is confusion about the real meaning of discipline and a false equating of discipline with corporal punishment. There is a demonstrable lack of confidence in many parents in the educational provision for their children at Summerhill Academy. There is a grave loss of morale among staff.

After two hours of debate during which an amendment put forward by Councillor Robert Middleton that the whole matter be referred back to a Sub-Committee for future consideration was defeated, by a vote of 16 votes to six, MacKenzie was suspended from duty on full pay.

CHAPTER TEN

Aftermath 1974–76

On the morning after MacKenzie's suspension from duty, the tune 'The Party is Over' was played at Assembly in Summerhill Academy. It was a long-held tradition at the school that a piece of music specially requested by a pupil was played over the public-address system at the end of Assembly in order to set the 'mood' for the day. Whether or not the choice of music on this occasion was that of a pupil or not is hard to establish. However, it did not take the pupils long to react to the news of MacKenzie's suspension, once they were made aware of what had happened.

Rosalie Martin, a third-year pupil at the time, who very much identified herself with what MacKenzie was trying to achieve at the school, recalls very clearly the situation that developed during the course of that day.

> The girls all got together in the toilets and hatched a plan, a school strike. Lots of us felt the same. We wanted our 'Headie' back in charge. It was the pupils' school; it should have been for us to sack him. We went out on strike after the morning break on the same day as the announcement at Assembly that he had been sacked. My job was to run through the third floor of the school, open up all the classroom doors and tell the pupils who did not know that we had decided to strike. Those who were not sitting exams followed and the teachers did not try to stop them; other girls took charge on the other floors of the school and others went out to the grounds...so that we could make a stand in public.
>
> We stayed out for days. The teachers tried to talk us into going back in; we were not having any of it. We decided to contact the press; this was a good move in one way and a bad move in another. We got the publicity to our cause but certain journalists thought they might spice things up a bit by offering some of the lads tins of beer and that they would take a photograph of them holding them; this was quickly recognized and the reporters were told to 'get lost'. We stayed out until the school broke up for the holiday break and when we came back most pupils had forgotten about the upset and decided to resume as normal. I, however, thought about Bob's sacking for much longer...

Ironically, Elizabeth Garrett, Depute Head, and one of MacKenzie's strongest supporters had been put in charge of the school as soon as

MacKenzie's suspension had taken effect. Bill Henry, the Senior Depute Director of Education for Aberdeen, had been the Education Committee's immediate choice as Acting Headteacher, but because he was due to go off in charge of an educational cruise to the Baltic, Elizabeth Garrett was asked to deputise for him. She recalls the day of the strike vividly, describing it 'as a terrifying experience'. She telephoned Clark, the Director, about the situation, but was told, 'I'm sure you'll manage beautifully.' Suggestions from the staff about how to deal with the strike included advice to 'turn the fire-hoses on them'. But her advice to the staff was to adopt a 'softly, softly' approach and to have staff meet dissident pupils in the playground and, as a result some effective informal education was achieved in these odd circumstances.

The symbolism associated with the appointment of Bill Henry as caretaker Headteacher was not lost on Mackenzie nor those on the staff who still supported him. The whole point of Henry's appointment, as MacKenzie states quite categorically in *The Unbowed Head* was to re-introduce law and order to a school described as 'chaotic' and 'anarchic'. Henry was an out-and-out traditionalist. Thin and spare in appearance with a small military moustache he looked exactly what he was, a charmless bureaucrat who had no time for MacKenzie's liberalism. It came as no surprise to MacKenzie, therefore, that Henry in pursuing his policy of restoring what he regarded as 'order' to the school, was guilty of blatantly flouting some of the key provisions of the 'Consensus Document' which MacKenzie's refusal to accept had led to his own downfall. Near the end of June 1974, Henry called a Staff Meeting. After it was over he ordered the final staff discussion should be struck from the record. The Staff Meeting had voted by a majority that the new Headmaster would not be bound by the document, and would not have to implement it. Recommendations had been included in it to placate MacKenzie's supporters. One paragraph stated, 'When corporal punishment is used, a detailed record be kept of its use and the reasons for its use.' There was no attempt or intention to abide by this decision. When a query was raised, the reply came, 'The document says "should" not "must".' Other recommendations such as the setting up of a unit for children with problems, an increase in the number of remedial teachers, staff discussions on Primary-Secondary liaison never came to be implemented.

Under Henry's regime Staff Meetings became infrequent (not once a month as they had been under MacKenzie) and were no longer held in the comparative intimacy of the staffroom, but in the large Assembly Hall where staff were drawn up in three rows across the entire width of the hall. Discussion was discouraged and decisions already made at senior level were imposed. Teachers, particularly those who had supported MacKenzie, who expressed opinions contrary to the principles of the new regime, were accused of being 'divisive of staff unity'. Such an approach to the situation within the school in the aftermath of MacKenzie's removal as Headteacher exacerbated the deep feelings of pain and bitterness that MacKenzie supporters experienced as a consequence of the course of events leading up to and immediately after MacKenzie's departure. Even after the passage of many years, teachers in the MacKenzie camp, a very tight-knit group that used to meet socially outwith school and have kept in touch with each other ever since, have told me how deeply affected they still are about the issues surrounding MacKenzie's downfall and how these same feelings of pain and bitterness are likely to return if they happen to meet by chance in an Aberdeen street any of the teachers closely associated in their minds with the campaign in the school against MacKenzie.

This abiding feeling of conflict relating to MacKenzie and what he stood for comes out very clearly in the course of the Open University broadcast that Bob Bell did with some of the main protagonists of the Summerhill affair two years after MacKenzie's dismissal. Bell interviewed Roy Pirie, the Education Convener, Mr Tyrell, the local minister, Stanley Allan, the leader of the opposition to MacKenzie at the school, Andrew Walls, a co-opted member of the Education Committee and a MacKenzie supporter, and Bill Henry, the Senior Depute Director of Education, who took over as caretaker Headteacher after MacKenzie's departure.

What Bell is able to establish in the course of this radio broadcast called 'Bon Accord' on the topic of the curriculum is an apparent confusion in the minds of some of the main players in the drama that took place at Summerhill in 1974 between MacKenzie's alleged weakness as an administrator and manager and fear of the long-term consequences of MacKenzie's approach on the educational service, especially at Summerhill. Pirie, Tyrell and Allan all highlight MacKenzie's inability as an administrator as the main contributory factor in his downfall, although each expresses sympathy for his ideas on education and his overall philosophy. It is this so-called distinction between what his detractors saw as curricular or educational issues, on the one hand, and what they saw as purely administrative on the other, that Bell brings out in his programme. He argues that few modern writers on the curriculum would believe in this distinction. And he pursues the point in taking evidence from Andrew Walls who held the post of Head of Religious Studies at Aberdeen University.

Walls sees the confusion coming about as a result of a basic lack of communication between MacKenzie and the Education Committee in the sense that MacKenzie insisted on talking about education at a time when the Education Committee was talking about administration. They were on the wrong 'wavelength' for a long time. Also he is of the opinion that the Committee underestimated the problems that began to manifest themselves at Summerhill as a 'little local difficulty' and by the time they did act, it took the form of an intervention (the 'Consensus Document) in the actual government of the school – effectively taking away the Headmaster's authority by imposing the document and blaming the Headmaster thereafter for not exercising authority.

Bell elaborates further on this theme of MacKenzie's being indicted on administrative grounds by describing how, in effect, those who had appointed him on the basis of his progressive ideas were reticent to accept that these progressive ideas themselves were now alienating many teachers and parents and were causing political embarrassment. It boiled down to an acceptance on the part of the Committee that people like Stanley Allan were right in claiming that MacKenzie had over-stepped the limits of what was acceptable in regard to the implement ation of his ideas in a school context, particularly in respect to pupil behaviour and the relationships between teacher and pupil. As Bell puts it, 'It suited MacKenzie's opponents in the Council and the Education Office to portray these 'limits' as a boundary imposed by administrative necessity.' Walls admits to the fact when it came down to it, the Labour-controlled Education Committee, although outwardly 'progressive' in its ideas about education, yet was essentially 'conservative' about what they saw as education in practice 'What they wanted really', says Walls, 'was a general access of the same opportunities as had been presented by the Senior Secondary schools of the old system.'

A very powerful contributory factor leading up to the eventual suspension of MacKenzie from his post, Bell claims in the broadcast, was that of parental pressure. Unlike his predecessor, Christie, MacKenzie had tended not to exploit the undoubted support he could have been expected to have obtained from the parents of those children who were doing well at school. Instead, he had championed the cause of the under-privileged youngsters at the school and the 'misfits' whose predicament was largely due to inadequate parental support at home and consequently when it came to a crisis of confidence, MacKenzie could not call on the support of those parents who could have swayed the balance in his favour. To make matters worse, the pressure among parents to have MacKenzie removed was further intensified by the charge that the English Department at Summerhill had encouraged the children to write what was described as 'pornography'.

Bell quizzed Clark and his Deputy, Henry, about the way the charge was investigated. Henry, in particular, was evasive in his answers. The investigation was put in the hands of the chief adviser who interviewed MacKenzie and possibly John Roberts, the Principal Teacher about it. But the evidence of such writing, when it emerged, seemed to have come about as a result of the actions of an un-named member of staff who 'came across' samples of what appeared to be confidential diaries being kept by pupils and submitted them to the Education Office for investigation. According to Henry, the material was 'offensive' but no real effort was made to discuss it with the teacher concerned or to establish the context in which such writing was attempted. Instead, the episode gave rise to damaging rumours and speculation about what was going on in the school and fuelled the energies of those parents who wished to see the back of MacKenzie.

Henry is then tackled by Bell on the issue of the 'Consensus Document' with regard to the fairness of imposing it on MacKenzie against his will. In reply, Henry testily declares his complete support for the document and reveals his antipathy towards MacKenzie by stating quite candidly that had he been in MacKenzie's position, he would not have allowed the situation to deteriorate in the way that it did – with MacKenzie's having to put up with the embarrassment of the 'Consensus Document' being imposed upon him. In addition, Henry had also been largely responsible in preventing the appointment of a former Jesuit priest to the post of Teacher of Religious Education at Summerhill on grounds that he, Henry, thought him unsuitable because the priest had been laicised by his Bishop for his political activities and that it was inappropriate in his view for a Roman Catholic to be in charge of charge of RE in a non-Catholic school. Be that as it may, the Jesuit priest would have been MacKenzie's choice; but once again, as in the case of Ritchie earlier, the Authority exercised a restraint on MacKenzie's freedom of choice with regard to the sort of staff he wanted to further the sort of education he felt was appropriate for Summerhill. In other words, MacKenzie's suspension owed as much to a feeling of fear and alarm among the Education Committee and among some of its officers that he had gone too far in the sort of educational philosophy he wanted to promote at Summerhill as the commonly-held perception that he was not up to the job as a manager and administrator. As it was, there was a terrible irony in the fact that a so-called enlightened Labour-controlled authority should end up replacing MacKenzie, the most charismatic, forward-looking Headteacher of his generation with an out-and-out bureaucrat, well-known for the sanctimoniousness of his views. Andrew Walls, in his final speech to the Education Committee prior to his resignation from it over the MacKenzie affair, told them he saw little consolation in the City, 'stoning its prophets when one day it would have to gild their tombs.'

The extensive coverage of MacKenzie's downfall at Summerhill, not just in the local newspapers but in the national dailies and in the quality press reflected the country-wide interest in the drama that accompanied MacKenzie's sacking and the outbreak of pupil disorder in the playground. It also subjected the local authority to a lot of unwelcome publicity in that the sacking of MacKenzie to the opponents of Comprehensive education – and there were many – seemed a vindication that Comprehensive in a 'liberal' form just would not work. The fact that the school still had within it a minority of teachers from the MacKenzie camp who continued to teach there after MacKenzie's departure also kept the school under the microscope. For, although the appointment of Henry was seen as a fairly cynical attempt on the part of the authority to re-introduce the sort of regime that had flourished under Christie (MacKenzie's predecessor), the teachers in the minority group were unwilling to put up with what they saw as the imposition of unjust measures against the pupils in order to establish in the eyes of the outside world an atmosphere of harmony and a return to 'blessed normalcy'.

This simmering discontent with the way the new regime operated was never far from the surface and is clearly illustrated in a letter written to *The Press and Journal* in May 1974 by Mr Sutherland, a member of the Maths department and a MacKenzie supporter.

> Does anyone want to know what is happening at Summerhill? When R.F. MacKenzie was suspended, there was much comment about the implications of the future of comprehensive education and progressive schooling. Since then there has been an almost indecent silence.
>
> Presumably the Education Committee and others involved in the solution to the 'crisis' school are congratulating themselves on the success of their moves. The place is not in the headlines and all appears quiet. As the Acting Head has told us, 'We are becoming a good school and making progress towards civilised behaviour.'
>
> Unfortunately this 'barbaric behaviour' implied in this statement about Summerhill under MacKenzie is still continuing. The difference is that those who before worked to publicise it, now want to conceal it. There is still vandalism, stealing, swearing, extortion, gambling, etc. and some teachers ate still unable to cope with their classes.
>
> Yet strangely we have no complaints from those who were most vociferous

> in their condemnations of the school under MacKenzie. Perhaps they are scared to voice their criticisms since the Acting Headmaster is also the Senior Deputy Director of Education, and one of those involved in the promotion of teachers in Aberdeen?
>
> Already several dedicated teachers are leaving and more resignations seem imminent. These teachers are leaving...because what they want to do is contrary to the new spirit of the place which seems to discourage new attitudes.
>
> Relationships between teachers and children are deteriorating as teachers are forced to become more authoritarian...some teachers who feel themselves to have been vindicated by the dismissal of Mackenzie are active outwith their areas of responsibility and in some instances are harassing probationer teachers whose views they disagree with.
>
> MacKenzie was suspended partly because he refused to implement the staff's document which was accepted by the Education Committee. One item in this document was that a detailed record of corporal punishment had to be kept and the machinery for doing this was set up. Despite the fact that children have been belted in the past few weeks, there is no record of this. What is the Education Committee's attitude to those teachers who are not implementing this part of the document?
>
> Soon the appointments of a new Depute Head and Headteacher will be made. Will they be men of vision who support MacKenzie's principles, as the Education Committee have so often asserted they themselves do? Or will they be 'yes' men to whom it will be safe to entrust responsibility, who can be relied on not to rock the boat?
>
> The Convener of the Education Committee claims that Aberdeen has not rejected Mr MacKenzie's educational methods; he said, 'Mr MacKenzie was just not successful in implementing his own philosophy.' In these two new appointments we shall see how much he meant it, and whether Aberdeen really is in the forefront of educational innovation.

Mr Sutherland's fears as to the sort of direction the future of Summerhill would be heading for in the light of new appointments at Headteacher and Depute Headteacher level, following upon MacKenzie's dismissal and the death of the former Deputy, Alex Ritchie, (from a heart attack early in 1974) were soon to be realised. At the beginning of June 1974, in somewhat farcical circumstances, Mr David Kinmond was proposed as Headmaster Designate, even though he had not applied specifically for the job. This proposal came about, strangely enough, at a time when both Clark, the Director, and Henry, his Depute and interim Headmaster at Summerhill were on an educational cruise in the Baltic. Technically, according to the Education Committee, the Summerhill post could not be advertised until the suspended MacKenzie had officially retired in April 1975. Hence Mr Kinmond, who had spent the whole of his career in Junior Secondary schools and was formerly Depute Head at Powis Academy in Aberdeen, came as Headmaster

Designate to Summerhill in August 1974. Just prior to that, in the middle of June 1974, Douglas Thomson, Deputy Head at Old Aberdeen Junior Secondary, had been formally confirmed as the new Depute Head of Summerhill Academy.

The appointment of Kinmond and Thomson signalled the complete capitulation on the part of Aberdeen Education Committee to the reactionary forces at work in the wake of the MacKenzie Affair. Although Kinmond was generally well-liked and well-thought of as an individual among the teaching fraternity, he was very much a 'safe' choice. His appointment would be well received by the strong traditionalist element in the Summerhill staff, particularly with his 'sound' Junior Secondary background. Moreover, his Deputy, Douglas Thomson, was well-known as a 'hard' man, very much in the mould of Alex Ritchie, who could be relied upon to wield the big stick. In these circumstances it did not take long for the MacKenzie supporters on the staff to react publicly to what they saw as the imposition of a reactionary regime at the school based on what Henry had already tried to put into practice. Fourteen MacKenzie supporters on the staff at Summerhill wrote to The Press and Journal on 19 September 1974 disputing claims made at an Aberdeen Town Council meeting earlier that week that there was now a 'different atmosphere' at the school and that things 'were settling down very well'.

The fourteen signatories wrote:

> Yes, there is a different atmosphere in Summerhill now. It is a place which is easier for teachers to be in, because fear is used to control pupils. The belt is used frequently...the atmosphere is one where teachers are encouraged implicitly to seek the easiest solution to their problem...belting. The spirit of the Aberdeen regulations on corporal punishment is not being adhered to. Belting is not used as anything like a last resort.

The 14 also alleged, 'that contact with parents is being reduced for the guidance staff whose role more and more is simply to administer and to deal with human problems. Far from offering help, the school just increases the pressure' and the teachers conclude, 'Yes, the atmosphere is different, a different set of values is at work.' Paper efficiency is what is important. To treasure people as human beings is less so.'

As a result of the letter's publication openly criticising the authority's stance on the state of affairs at Summerhill, each of the 14 teachers received a letter from James Clark, the Director of Education, suggesting that they should conscientiously wonder whether they could continue to teach at Summerhill. Part of the letter read:

> I have been informed that you were one of the signatories of the letter sent to the Press and Journal and printed in the issue of 19 September 1974. In

> my view such conduct was unprofessional in that you have participated in a public attack on the school and on the attitude and integrity of many of your colleagues.

The actions taken by the 14 MacKenzie supporters in writing publicly about their concerns reflected the very real tensions that still existed among staff six months after MacKenzie's departure. Similar tensions likewise affected the Education Committee where supporters of MacKenzie such as Councillor Robert Middleton proposed a motion to the effect that the Education Committee find ways of employing MacKenzie 'in a meaningful way'. This motion, which was turned down, coincided with the resignations of two external members of the Education Committee, Mrs Joan MacDonald and Mr Andrew Walls, who had asked to have their dissent recorded when MacKenzie was suspended in April 1974 and had made several unsuccessful attempts to have his suspension reconsidered.

Further acrimony among staff at the school was provoked by the decision of a senior member of staff in the wake of the publication of the letter in *The Press and Journal* by the 14 dissident members of staff, to report the 14 to the General Teaching Council for Scotland for what he described as 'infamous conduct'. The General Teaching Council referred the matter to its investigating committee, but since no evidence was produced which appeared to support the case against the teachers, no further action was taken. This verdict came just before Christmas 1974 and was the sad culmination of a year which saw the demise of MacKenzie and his hopes for what he aimed to achieve at Summerhill, the break-up of his staff into two bitterly opposed camps and the humiliation of the Labour group on the Aberdeen Town Council in their having to suspend their own choice of Headteacher in circumstances extremely damaging to their credibility as a progressive authority.

Although the events at Summerhill in 1974 did not lead in any sense to the end of MacKenzie's activities in the education world, nor his work as a writer, nevertheless it did mark the end of his controversial life as a Headteacher in the State system. Suspension, of course, meant that it was not until May 1975, when he was 65, that his teaching career ended in actuarial terms; but, to all intents and purposes, the decision of Aberdeen Education Committee on 1 April 1974 to suspend him meant his dismissal from his post as Headteacher – any attempt by the Authority to have sacked him as such would have enabled him to appeal to the Secretary of State which the Education Committee wanted to avoid given the embarrassment they had already suffered in regard to the symbolism associated with his appointment in 1968 and their volte face six years later.

Looking back at these six years, it would be interesting to know how far MacKenzie himself could have imagined how events would conspire to make him the leading figure in the tragedy that finally engulfed him in 1974. The evidence of the Open University broadcast in 1968 strongly suggests that MacKenzie had had enough of the controversies that had dogged his days at Braehead in Fife. He says candidly that he would have wanted to do things differently – having a plan and trying to take people along with him. We all of us knew from the start in 1968 that MacKenzie wanted to change the school to fit in with his distaste for corporal punishment and to broaden our concept of what education was about; but there was no hint, certainly to begin with, that everything would end in the sort of tragedy that eventually came about. What he was unable to predict was the scale and strength of the opposition that gradually grew and was so effectively articulated against him within the school itself and how this in turn fed into a broader reactionary coalition against him involving not just the parents but the local churches and, crucially, the local Labour authority itself. His career as a Headteacher in 1967 had seemed to be at an end until his appointment to Summerhill had, as it were, came out of the blue. It offered him an enormous opportunity to re-instate himself and to be in on the adventure of helping to establish a comprehensive system in one of Scotland's major cities. His great achievement at Braehead had been to break through the barriers of conventional education by making a plea for a shift in educational values away from the academic to a more child-centred approach rooted in the concept of discovery in a countryside setting. Summerhill did not offer the same challenge – it already had a history of fairly radical educational innovation under Christie – and so the struggle that ensued within the school became associated with 'discipline' at a time when Summerhill was in the midst of traumatic change anyway from going Comprehensive and growing considerably in size.

At the heart of the problem was the fact that MacKenzie was to a large extent an isolated figure, not just among his fellow Headteachers who tended to regard him as a maverick, but in Summerhill itself where he never really enjoyed the support of the staff as a whole. The key staff he needed to support him were never there in sufficient numbers to ensure he could forward his aims; although he actively 'recruited' the sort of people he needed, there was never enough of them to enable him to carry the day against the reactionary elements in the staff as a whole whose actions were orchestrated by Stanley Allan, surely one of the most formidable adversaries on the side of the establishment that MacKenzie had ever come across in his teaching career.

Besides, most of the staff who supported him were concentrated in the Guidance system and caused divisiveness in that other staff interpreted their pupil-friendly approach as undermining the discipline of the school and cutting across their own more formal relationships with the pupils. The result was that pupils got contradictory messages about what behaviour was acceptable, depending on each individual teacher's stance in the ongoing feud between the pro-MacKenzie faction and the majority of the rest of the staff. MacKenzie also did his own cause no favours by being seen increasingly not just to identify himself with those staff in Guidance and in the English Department who openly supported him, but to be seen to confide in them in such a way as to make those staff who were on the sidelines and uncommitted to either cause feel undervalued and thus more likely to align themselves with the dissidents on the staff than give their support to their increasingly beleaguered Headteacher.

MacKenzie's state of mind during this last phase in his battle against the establishment was that of a man at bay. Following upon his illness in 1972, he seemed to staff who knew him well, inwardly more determined than ever to press on with what he saw as the need to reform the system – even though it meant untold strife and disruption in his own school. He became more and more sensitive to criticism and was under constant pressure from the Education Authority to compromise. In the end, he took the view that he had compromised too much. He must have been aware that time was running out for him; he was, after all, in his early 60s, less than two years away from retirement. He had taken up a position which he must have known was untenable (his refusal to go along with the 'Consensus Document') and that the likely outcome would be the loss of his job. He knew in his heart of hearts that this was going to happen and that he would be facing a sort of martyrdom for what he believed in. He also knew that the scandal would create a lot of publicity for his views and confirm his standing as a rebel against the powers of the Estalishment. That is why, as he faced the Committee at his suspension, he was seen to the Convener, Roy Pirie, to be 'speaking in parables' when his job was on the line. MacKenzie held on to his ultimate conviction that in principle what he was doing was right.

The events of 1974 still need to be examined in the light of what actually happened and in terms of their significance for us now in retrospect both as human beings and as educators. MacKenzie himself at the conclusion of *The Unbowed Head*, had no doubt that the events were indeed a milestone on the way towards what he calls a 'cultural revolution':

> In Scotland the forces resisting change are still powerful and as at Summerhill, determined to keep control wherever they are challenged. The battle at Summerhill is likely to be repeated in other schools...It's a simple choice for the teachers. Do we agree that the key to a deeper insight into human behaviour is not technical proficiency but simply love? If we agree, for the first time in our history the majority of Scottish children could be entering on a cultural revolution.

CHAPTER ELEVEN

Life After Summerhill 1976–84

MacKenzie, in the aftermath of his suspension from his job at Summerhill in April 1974, spoke understandably of how dark a time this was for him personally. The strength to survive the crisis that all but overwhelmed him physically and spiritually during those dark days in the spring of 1974, came not just from his native stubbornness and ruggedness as an individual, but essentially from the support he received at this time from the abiding love and devotion of his wife and family. Diana had long shared the ups and downs of MacKenzie's life, especially the trials and tribulations that came their way in Fife, and had sustained him in times of stress with her natural warmth and optimism. Now with the children nearing adulthood – Neil was at Edinburgh University studying Medicine, Alasdair was in his final year at school and Diane was in her fourth year – they gave their dad the kind of support that drew on the feelings of love and deep affection that he had lavished upon them as infants and had expressed so lovingly in the diaries he wrote about them at that time in their lives.

The MacKenzies had always been a close-knit family, stretching back to their days in Fife, where, after having lived in a Council house in Glenrothes from 1952 to 1957 when the children were just infants, they moved to a house that MacKenzie had bought in the village of Upper Largo on the Fife coast. This house was where the children spent their formative years (from 1957 to 1968) and enjoyed the run of the place. Upper Largo was a quiet and friendly village that gave the children at that stage in their lives the opportunity to roam about freely to their hearts' content in the surrounding woods and down by the beach. Although the house was on the main street, it had a large walled garden at the rear that provided privacy and gave MacKenzie the chance to indulge himself in one of his favourite activities, gardening. He loved to prepare the ground for planting, such as in the same way his forebears on the land had done back in the North-East of Scotland. He took immense pleasure in growing vegetables, monitoring their growth and weighing the produce at the end of the season.

Family holidays to begin with were spent under canvas (an ex-army bell tent) in various parts of Scotland. But, as the children grew older, the MacKenzies exchanged houses with families who lived on the continent and this resulted in family trips during the summer holidays to countries such as France, Spain and Portugal where MacKenzie delighted, as he always did, in visiting places of historical and cultural interest and passing on to his children his knowledge of such places and their historical significance.

Inevitably, the MacKenzies also got involved during the Braehead years in various school trips to the Highlands and family holiday trips to the Braehead school cottage in Rannoch and the lodge at Inverlair. All of these family excursions meant a great deal to MacKenzie and to the children individually who remember this period of their life with great fondness. It was an upset for the two younger children, Alasdair and Diana, therefore, when the family moved to Aberdeen. Neil, the oldest, now 17, was destined to go to university, but his younger brother, Alasdair, found it difficult to settle down at his new school and Diana, the youngest, who spent a short period of time at St Nicholas School (a small independent school run by Jean Allan, the wife of writer John R. Allan), initially found it hard to make friends, when, at the age of 12, she went into the first year at Cults Academy.

MacKenzie's choice of a new house – the old farmhouse at West Cults on the outskirts of Aberdeen – when he moved to take up his post at Summerhill Academy, was just what he wanted. It was not just roomy, a real family house, but it also provided privacy, as it was on its own at the bottom of a twisting road, leading down to the River Dee at Cults. It was comfortable and had the advantage of being a traditional farmhouse which appealed to MacKenzie's Aberdeenshire roots. It allowed him to relax and wind down after the tensions of the school day and to keep things in perspective. Often, he found relaxation in walking the three to four miles over country roads between Cults and Summerhill rather than go by car which enabled him to take in what had always fascinated him as a boy and as a man, the sights and sounds of the Scottish countryside, whatever the season of the year.

In the comparative seclusion of the farmhouse, away from the gaze of the media and the furore surrounding his departure from Summerhill, MacKenzie came to the conclusion that the principles he had fought to uphold throughout the dispute with the Education Authority were still worth fighting for. So he relentlessly bombarded the Authority, the politicians and the education officers with letters and comments through the medium of the press, criticising the way in which they were handling the 'fall-out' from the Summerhill affair, particularly the installation of

Henry as a 'trouble-shooter' and their cowardice in going back on their original pledge to continue with a liberal regime at Summerhill – bearing in mind their claims that it was not MacKenzie's ideas that had got him the sack, but his lack of administrative competence. He supported the efforts of the tightly-knit group of his supporters still at the school to resist the gradual decline of the school into a conventional institution where corporal punishment and the application of traditional disciplinary methods very rapidly undid a lot of the experimental work that he and the guidance staff had tried to put into practice over the past five years to enrich the lives of 'the dissident minority'.

The appointment of David Kinmond as Headteacher in August 1974 and Douglas Thomson as his Deputy Head more or less formally ended the MacKenzie experiment. Already some of the MacKenzie supporters on the staff had signalled their intention to leave. It was all too evident, after the incident of the 14 MacKenzie supporters being taken to task by the Director over their comments to the press about the Council's policy at Summerhill and their subsequently being reported to the General Teaching Council for unprofessional behaviour, that it was only a matter of time before all of them would eventually leave Summerhill and pursue their careers elsewhere.

To mark the occasion of his 65th birthday and what would have been the time that he would have actually retired from the teaching profession, MacKenzie and his wife and family were invited to a party at the home of Elizabeth Garret, his former Depute Head, in May 1976. Here more than 50 friends and colleagues gathered to pay him tribute. The occasion was described by John Roberts, Principal Teacher of English at Summerhill and one of MacKenzie's most ardent supporters:

> Was it a sad or a happy occasion? It was certainly a splendid occasion, a banquet. It was a gathering of people who believed in him and had been sustained by him, people who loved him and found joy in being with him.
>
> It was an evening of liberation, the words were of growth, warmth, love, independence, happiness. Jean Allan, (the wife of John R. Allan, the Scottish writer and herself the Headteacher of an experimental school) spoke of him as an enabler; John Aitkenhead (Headteacher of Kilquhanity School) spoke of his wondrous curiosity for life. Colin Sangster, a guidance teacher at Summerhill, described him as a listener, especially the listener to children, Betsy Cumming, another guidance teacher made the presentation and spoke of his inspiration to those who worked with him.
>
> R.F. tonight amongst his friends spoke of the spirit of children, of the goodwill in children that the school system gives no opportunities for, of the fine men and women whom education administrators indifferently pushed out of schools. He was happy in the rejection of schooling by increasing numbers of children.
>
> It was sad because we remembered what it was like working with him –

his openness, gentleness, refusal to compromise. Those qualities are absent in those who had the power to manipulate his dismissal. It was sad because we remembered he had been deprived of his school.

It was happy because he was not defeated. What he said lived in us and would support us. He has shown us the road.

We talked of children, of power and politics, of travel,of education – not teaching. We laughed at the verses written for the occasion, bawdy, libellous portraits of friends and enemies. We sang songs, including one of his favourites:

One man's hands can't tear a prison down,
Two men's hands can't tear a prison down;
But if two and two and fifty make a million,
We'll see that day come round.

That was the hope.

And as the party ended, there was sadness as R.F. looked at the people gathered there. 'What a waste', he said quietly, 'they stopped us from doing so much.'

But 'they' weren't there. It was not an official occasion.

Dawn was breaking as he and his family returned home. Monday morning would be very cold. He is a man to be with.

The corporate feeling of sadness experienced by the MacKenzie supporters at Summerhill at the course of events during 1975 when the regime of first Henry and then Kinmond took their toll of what MacKenzie had tried to put in place, was also reflected in the departure gradually of most of those staff to other posts or, in some cases, out of teaching altogether. Elizabeth Garrett, his former Deputy, was so disillusioned by the train of events that she left Summerhill in the autumn of 1975 to take up a new career as a student in the faculty of Law at Aberdeen University. In an emotional article for the *Times Educational Supplement* in August 1975, she expresses her very mixed feelings at leaving teaching and the debt she owes MacKenzie.

Those of us who knew him from the every-day living in a school community are never going to be quite the same again because of his clear insight, his gentle care for people and his certainty about the things he believes in. His pupils recognised his qualities, 'You know the Headie really listens to what you say', said one girl. 'He doesn't wait till you've finished like most folk, so that he can start saying what he thinks.'

There is fine talk...about our developing the potential of all children, each according to his ability There is not so much talk about developing the potential of adults who work with these children. The hierarchical pyramid of the secondary school, strengthened and finally petrified by the mass of promoted posts, reinforces each teacher's place in the structure...the waste in human initiative inspiration and imagination is wicked, but inadequate teachers feel safe: their stone in the pyramid is clearly marked and defined. Wasn't there something about the pyramid being a burial chamber?

> It is much safer and more comfortable to teach in schools where the value of what we are doing is never questioned; where there is 'normal discipline' based ultimately on punishment and physical force (we believe in guidance after punishment). You can feel secure in a school where teachers and pupils know their place...it is a comfort to know that whatever happens, your colleague will be 'professional', back you up, hush up your difficulties...
>
> I have muddled emotions about leaving teaching; but some things are certain and clear. MacKenzie's Summerhill was different, exciting and important – it should have been encouraged to develop. Can we really hope for any change or experiment within the State system until all concerned are prepared to look honestly at what is happening and accept criticism and questioning?...Maybe it is not surprising that teachers show more enthusiasm for a school fair than for major curriculum development. Is it any wonder that educational theory is remembered as a course from Teacher Training College but not anything to do with getting through the school day? Depressing thoughts; depressing times.

Garrett's feelings of depression for what was happening in education, particularly in relation to what was happening at Summerhill was ominously close to the truth when one observes the later history of events at the school. MacKenzie's immediate successor, David Kinmond, died after only two years in the post in 1976, and his successor, Bill Henry, the former Depute Director of Education, who was sent in as a 'trouble-shooter' to quell the school's discipline problems after MacKenzie's sacking, was appointed Head in 1976. That the future welfare of the school should be entrusted to a man widely regarded as a charmless bureaucrat, openly contemptuous of the liberalism that MacKenzie stood for, showed the depths to which the local authority had sunk in its estimate of the kind of educational leadership needed to restore the school's fortunes in the eyes of the public. Neither his stop-gap Headship from 1976 to 1980, nor the appointment of Ms Pat Cormack as his successor, thereafter, could halt the steady decline of the school as a place which enjoyed the confidence of the local population in its ability to provide as good an education as elsewhere in the city.

As a consequence of the new Conservative government's Parents ' Charter, Mastrick parents began increasingly to send their children to other schools such at Aberdeen Grammar instead of their catchment area school, Summerhill. So the roll began to fall rapidly during the 1980s, and it came as no great surprise in 1987, when, after a lot of rumour and speculation, a decision was taken for the school to be phased out as a school in its own right by the end of the decade. The terrible irony was that the announcement about the school's imminent closure was made on the very same day, on 4 December 1987, that MacKenzie died.

It was during the late 1970s and early 1980s that MacKenzie had a great surge of energy. Freed from the constraints of running a school, he liked nothing better than to travel the country, lecturing and taking part in debates on education. Besides that, he took every opportunity that he could by writing articles and letters for the newspapers and in broadcasts on the radio and television to record for posterity what had happened at Summerhill. Hence, during the course of 1976, not only did he have his own personal account of events at Summerhill published in a book entitled *The Unbowed Head*, but he took part in a television programme under the auspices of the Open University in which he was interviewed at length on the Summerhill story. At about the same time, Bob Bell, who was largely responsible for the TV programme, also made a radio broadcast for the Open University in which he interviewed some of the main figures (other than MacKenzie) in the events as they unravelled at Summerhill.

The publication of *The Unbowed Head*, in 1976, in a sense, not only rekindled, to some extent, the controversies of 1974, but it also allowed MacKenzie to set the record straight as far as his own version of events was concerned. Much the most interesting of the reviews that were done of the book was that written by Max Paterson who reviewed it in *The Times Educational Supplement* in December 1976. He does not see MacKenzie as a 'prophet'...'to do so is to diminish...and to denigrate his work.' He sees MacKenzie rather as a social revolutionary. This Paterson deduces from the fact that MacKenzie is not so much interested in events but in their significance.

> Gradually I realised the full significance of what was happening when the pupil(William Brown) shouted back to the teacher...it is part of a world movement. In Chile and the Dominican Republic peasants learning to read were beginning to think their own thoughts and were refusing to be cowed...there was an awakening of awareness in which a human being recognises himself as a person, an active subject rather than a passive object; aware that he can improve human situations, and, acting with others, change society and make life truly human.
>
> I began to realise not only that our pupil, William Brown, and others like him were standing shoulder to shoulder with peasants of the New World, but also that Scottish education was standing shoulder to shoulder with the oppressive regimes of Chile and Dominica. People need to abandon the stooping gait and walk tall: they have the ability to cope with the problem of living. If a civilisation doesn't give them that...it denies them the vital thing...and that society is tyranny. Because it denies this to its young people, Scottish education is tyranny.

As a result of this, Paterson argues:

> We must judge MacKenzie as a social revolutionary. Certainly this provides a perspective. Summerhill was not an experiment in education as the

> councillors and educationists of Aberdeen might have been expected to construe experiment. Perhaps this was as MacKenzie himself viewed it in the beginning, for he characterises his thinking as 'gradual' and 'later'. But in the event MacKenzie has identified with the rebel and his book is a book of rebellion.. It has the conviction, the indignant anger on behalf of others, the identification with the oppressed, and it has the over-simplifications historically present in revolutionary movements...MacKenzie, the rebel, takes us further into conflicts, not only between ourselves and others, but, as we read, within ourselves...This book I see as a personal release and a prelude. It has revealed much of the man. We await the vision and the means.

Max Paterson's analysis of *The Unbowed Head* raises issues which take the whole question of what MacKenzie stood for and his consciousness of the role that he saw for himself into areas of our civilisation that go well beyond the perceived boundaries that encapsulate the process we have come to know as 'education'. As with the Braehead experience, a lot of what happened there resulted from the energies and actions that MacKenzie, because of the sort of man he was, triggered off in other people – for instance, the richly rewarding developments in art and music and, above all, the break-out from the confines of the town into the Scottish hills of the scores of youngsters that Hamish Brown introduced to the wonders of climbing, bothying, hostelling and adventure. So also at Summerhill, much of what actually came to pass did not come about, as a result of a MacKenzie master-plan, rather did it come about, as it did at Braehead, out of the impact of MacKenzie's personality and sense of mission upon the staff and the pupils over a period of time. That it developed in Summerhill into a tragedy because of the conflicts that MacKenzie's influence brought about in the way things worked out at the school, owed as much to the reactions of people drawn into the conflict, as it did to MacKenzie's own control over events. Only, as Paterson argues, in retrospect did even MacKenzie himself come fully to realise what the significance of the struggle that had taken place at Summerhill meant in broader human and social terms.

The publication of *The Unbowed Head* more or less coincided with the opening of Whitfield High School in Dundee which was the school that I came to be in charge of after the phasing out of Logie Secondary earlier that year. MacKenzie wrote to me in December wishing me well in the 'new school', knowing full well that I would meet similar problems as he had done himself in establishing a comprehensive school in a catchment area that, like Mastrick, had no shortage of social problems. I was glad some five years later to hear from him once again. I had recently written to The Scotsman complaining about the bad press coverage that the Whitfield Housing Estate was getting which took no account of all the good work that the school was doing with the young people there. I took the writer of the offending article to task, mentioning the fact that the school did not share the apathy and despair that was rife among the adults on the estate, but had its own ethos, and, in cultural terms, not only ran its own theatre shows and orchestra, but had two newspapers. MacKenzie, ever alert to what was going on, wrote to me in encouraging terms, telling me 'to keep up the good work'.

Not long afterwards he paid a visit to Whitfield High, and spent the day with us. The highlight of his visit was not, predictably, seeing round the school, but joining a first-year class and sharing the children's delight at meeting George Reid, the Countryside Warden from Camperdown Park, Dundee, who had brought along with him animals and birds as part of a Biology lesson, enabling these town children to see and touch such creatures as owls, rabbits, rats and mice for the very first time in their lives.

Of continual concern to myself as a Headteacher, as it was to MacKenzie both as a Headteacher and a polemicist, was the vexed question of the use of corporal punishment in Scottish schools. His own attempts to ban it at Summerhill, it is fair to say, led directly as much as anything else to his ultimate dismissal from his post in 1974. For me, as a practising Headteacher, its use was inextricably bound up with the way we kept control of our schools in those days. Very few Headteachers, myself included, were at all comfortable with the thought of running a school without recourse to the use of corporal punishment. However, the judgement of The European Court of Human Rights in March 1982 that two Scottish parents had the right to insist that their children were not disciplined by the strap meant more to MacKenzie than most. When the historic decision was announced, MacKenzie had the satisfaction of getting centre-page billing in the Aberdeen *Evening Express* that just eight years previously had taken up much of its similar space to proclaim his dismissal from his post as Headteacher at Summerhill. A local journalist, Mary Riddell, interviewed him to get his reactions to the Strasbourg Court's decision. Typically MacKenzie illustrated his response by telling a story set in the context of his early days in the North-East of Scotland:

> The small boy returned home after his first day at school to the solicitous inquiries of his parents, 'Hiv ye hid yer licks yet?' they asked. On the second day, and the third the question was repeated, and the response was still negative. By the fourth morning the new boy could no longer tolerate the school's blatant neglect of his educational needs.
>
> 'Fan div I get my licks?' he asked the teacher, rather plaintively.

Mary Riddell's article continues:

> Robert Mackenzie tells this story as an indication of how the belt had been a way of life for generations of North East youngsters. He tells it on a day when the next lot of fledging school children can look forward to a less painful future...he welcomes the Strasbourg verdict not so much as a personal vindication, more as a step away from a system which may have been beaten at its own game. For it looks now as if the strap will be outlawed in schools throughout Britain and Mr MacKenzie is naturally delighted.
>
> 'This is a historic day in the annals of Scotland, a major change in direction. What I guess will happen is that after a lot of huffing and puffing people will just accept it...teachers are not cruel people They are just part of a system which condones beating, conformists in the manner of the slave-owners and the pharaohs...nice chaps at heart.'
>
> Years ago, Robert MacKenzie was prophesying doom., 'We need a change of heart', he warned. 'Otherwise there will be a time of great tribulation. Only time will tell.'
>
> Now he says the Court decision may be too little too late. This is only the beginning of a major change. People will ask what we put in place of the belt, which implies that education is a punitive thing...alternative punishments are not the answer. He quotes Sir James Robertson, former Head of Aberdeen Grammar School, as talking about the gaunt, arid intellectualism of education in Scotland. He talks of Calvinism and the kirks, of the rise of the dominies and of how the North East has been called the black spot of this unpromising terrain...Grampian is likely to be that last ditch (in moves to finally abolish the belt)...However, he will not admit to any sense of personal triumph, 'I just feel relieved that Scotland is going to be the sort of country I always knew it was possible for it to be.'

For all MacKenzie's optimism about the way in which the Strasbourg ruling would ultimately change the face of Scottish education once and for all, he soon revised his opinion in the light of events. In the mid-1980s tensions began to develop between the teaching profession in Scotland and the Thatcher government over the matter of the implementation of the proposed new system of assessment of pupils at the age of 16 to take the place of the Scottish Certificate of Education 'O'-Grades that no longer met the needs of the vast majority of pupils in Secondary schools. The additional work involved in putting into effect this new system met with concerted resistance from the Teaching Unions in Scotland, particularly the largest one, the Educational Institute of Scotland, as its imposition further antagonised teachers who felt undervalued and underpaid by what they perceived as an insensitive and arrogant style of government.

The unrest spilled over into a period of industrial action that saw them over a lengthy period of time in the mid-1980s conduct selective strikes and 'work to rule' that held up the introduction of the new exam system for two years. The dispute also eroded a lot of goodwill in the schools that had been taken for granted over the years and consequently destroyed, almost for good, a lot of voluntary activities that teachers did as 'extras' without pay, such as running clubs and sports teams. At the heart of the dispute was a reluctance on the part of the Government to pay teachers the going rate for the job and an insensitivity to the teachers' complaint that the changes involved in going over to the new system of assessment meant a lot more work for teachers who thought, justifiably, that they were already undervalued as a profession and stretched to the limit, now that corporal punishment had been abolished, keeping order in the classroom.

MacKenzie could have been forgiven for feeling somewhat bemused by all of this. Characteristically, he saw the proposed changes in the 'O'-Grade system as no more than papering over the cracks – the system, as he saw it, was flawed anyway. In an article for *The Scotsman* in April 1983 he argues powerfully that the lesson of history is that education has not been accorded its proper place as a liberalising influence on people, but, instead, has been used by the ruling élite as a means of exercising control principally through the imposition of a narrow curriculum coupled with an external exam system. He goes on:

> One reason for the failure of the French, American and Russian revolutions to achieve their political purposes was that they shunted school education into the sidelines. In France, the USA and Russia the dominant few wanted to maintain decision-making in their own hands without much reference to the majority. Thus, what aimed to be major political changes resulted only in the replacement of one controlling minority with another. A new minority took over the seats and privileges of power. Cynically the French said, 'The more it changes, the more it remains the same.' France slid into the hands of Napoleon the Third, George Washington gave Tom Paine the brush-off and resumed at Mount Vernon the style of the English gentleman, Lincharsky's Ministry of Enlightenment was darkened by the clouds of Stalinism.

Thus MacKenzie sees the role of education being diminished and distorted by the control exercised upon it by the State. Instead of education acting as an enlightening experience that encourages us to cooperate with each other, it does the opposite – creates a competitiveness that is part of the exam system, inhibiting debate and enquiry, but sanctioning instead an unquestioning acceptance of the status quo. Hence, to replace the 'O'-Grades with yet another system that ultimately depends on some sort of external testing is merely to replace one discredited system with another:

> The possibility that there is something wrong in basing almost the whole of Secondary education on external examinations is not one that recommends

itself to the educational administrators. When the exams are seen not to work, they react by developing a still more convoluted system of exams, new certificates, one of them at Foundation, General and Credit levels, and the other made up of modules. And similarly when corporal punishment is abolished, they concentrate on other punishments. The possibility does not occur to them that it's the requirement to drill dull information into unwilling heads that forces teachers to use punishment and distorts education. The abolition of the examinations would reduce the need to make schools punitive institutions.

And he concludes: 'I know of no single measure that would do more to release the flow of initiative in our society than the unblocking of ideas in the school – the abolition of the external examination.'

Mackenzie, in his constant campaigning against what he saw as the debilitating effects of the establishment on people's ability to question and challenge the assumptions underlying the way we are governed and what passes as 'established truth' on television in the press, got considerable sustenance from keeping in touch over the years with other educational radicals such as John Aitkenhead and A.S. Neill. Wth Neill, in particular, he kept up a correspondence over many years. Neill was known best for founding earlier in the century, Summerhill, a small independent school in Suffolk which became one of the best-known schools of its kind in the way that it allowed complete freedom to its pupils to develop their lives without constraints of any kind and to run the school more or less as they wanted it to be run. The abiding influence that permeated the school was that of Neill himself who, like MacKenzie, was a sworn enemy of the Establishment and had an absolute belief in the goodness of children.

Even in his late 80s, Neill kept up his correspondence with the likes of MacKenzie, encouraging him and giving him the benefit of his astringent wit often delivered in his native Scots dialect, as in this extract from a letter he wrote to MacKenzie in December 1972 when MacKenzie's problems at Summerhill Academy had taken a turn for the worse:

Dear Bob,

Man, that's a hell of a picture you paint of Scots dominies. But English ones are similar...makes it difficult to be an optimist about education. In essence the Scots are where I was when I wrote my Log 1915, so it wasn't a surprise when the students of my own varsity, Edinburgh, recommended me for an Honorary degree and the Senatus turned it down...it disna bather me; it just maks me lach. I'm kinda oot o' things noo. Ower tired to see visitors and to lecture. Mike Duane looks in sometimes, but, not being able to go to London, I see few fowks...I'm past writing, but my life comes out in May,

'Neill, Neill, Orange Peel' the chant the kids greet me with, the wee ones...I hope I'll live to see it out. At 89 I canna have lang. Don't think I fear death since I think it is extinction...That is what annoys me, never to know what has happened to kids and freedom, to my grand-daughter of 5 months. So bugger old bastard Father Time, says I.

Rumour said you had been ill. I do hope it is wrong, for the world needs bonny fechters like you, there are so few about now...Duane, Aitkenhead, Holt, and others in USA. The so-called progressive schools are half-dead. St Christopher's advertises itself as having 'ordered freedom'.

You must feel very lonely amongst the local teachers who are so anti-life. I admire your sticking to the State system...I ran awa frae it.

Aweel, as guid a New Year as this lovely world of oors...Whitehouse, Nixon, Heath, etc. will allow.

Neill

MacKenzie, therefore, found great solace, throughout his life, in keeping in touch with fiery rebels such as Neill who appreciated more than most the lonely, hazardous path MacKenzie had chosen for himself as a radical reformer in the State sector compared with the degree of freedom to experiment enjoyed by Neill and Aitkenhead in the private sector. Yet all three shared a common vision of a child-centred education that was relevant to the needs of all children whatever their background. This common purpose, even though they met each other but rarely, brought the three men close together spiritually during the course of their lives. Thus it was fitting that MacKenzie should be asked to review a biography of Neill by Jonathon Croall that was published in 1983.

In this review MacKenzie says of Neill:

At times he had the intensity and pessimism of Ibsen and George Douglas Brown, but at other times poked fun at the famous. Once during dinner he asked Baden Powell if he had heard the story about himself in which at midnight he realised he hadn't done his good deed for the day, and so opened the cage of the canary and gave it to the cat. 'I have a vague memory that Powell's polite smile was not genuine', Neill later remarked.

Neill felt that the only abiding political revolution would depend on a change of values in our education system, on being rather than accounting. None of his pupils went into politics. In other words, parliamentary politics is not the best way of changing the world. Neill said that one of the most important discoveries of his life was that he had been allowing 'my petty ego to stand in the way of my progress'. Here we are in a world of losing your life so that we can save it; the world of being born again and taking no thought of the morrow.

MacKenzie concludes:

If the schools and Colleges of Education and University Departments of Education have the wisdom to put this book into their libraries, it would give the young a new understanding of what Neill of Summerhill (and Jesus of Nazareth)were on about.

CHAPTER TWELVE

A Search for Scotland

Following on the publication of *The Unbowed Head* in 1976, MacKenzie, as he had always done, continued to write vigorously on a whole range of educational topics, particularly for *The Times Educational Supplement* for which he did a series of articles between 1980 and 1982. For instance, he traces the journeys of St Paul, using his encyclopaedic knowledge of, and interest in, the history and culture of Western civilisation to show the relevance of these journeys (and what St Paul was on about) to the teenagers in our schools, taking up Paul's views on sex and circumcision, for instance and linking such issues to their preoccupation with their own developing sexuality:

> We don't take our 15 year olds into our confidence...we should confide in them about the dark side of human nature assuring them that it is normal and natural. We'd ask them to put into words, if they wanted to, their own dark unacknowledged feelings and we'd ask them why they thought the High Priests of the Jews proposed such a rite as circumcision.

His very individual interpretation of the truth that lies behind our perception of the past is seen in the following article he wrote for *The Times Educational Supplement* on the relevance of history for school pupils. In his article he advocates:

> A practical alternative to classroom history in a Scottish school. I'd like to take a class for one term to the town of Grenada in the south of Spain. They would be aged 16 and about to leave school. This would be the programme in which I'd invite them to participate.
>
> Daily we would climb a hill in the city and wander through the courts and under the arches and domes of the Moorish Alhambra whose romantic and exotic perfection has given its name to picture houses, I imagine,all over the world. The Alhambra was the last Spanish stronghold to be wrested from the Moors after their 900 years occupation. That done, in 1492, Isabella had time to spend on the supplicant on her doorstep, Christopher Columbus...
>
> The year 1492 marked the end of 900 years of Moorish rule in Spain, a turning point in human history. The Catholic kings replaced it with a different system of beliefs, a new legend. I'd like to show the pupils what goes into the making of a legend. For a while it buttresses men, shapes and interprets

for them the mysteries of life. It has its day of achievement and glory and then its insufficiency begins to appear...questions, easily submerged, begin to surface and find utterance.

One of the reasons for spending a term in Grenada would be to show to the young that nothing stays put, everything flows, as the Greek Heraclitus said long ago. In 1920 H.G. Wells in his *Outline of History* said that in spite of the siege of Grenada, living at that time, 'A man of foresight...might well have concluded that it was only a few generations before the whole world became Mongolian and possibly Moslem.' Just as today most people seem to take it for granted that a sort of liberal Christianity is destined to spread over the whole world, few people realise how recent and probably how temporary a thing is this European ascendancy.

Sixty years later our pupils are more accessible to the idea of the diminishing influence of Europe that Wells prophesied, and would be interested in probing the origins of that belief, how hidden persuaders of the 15th and the 16th centuries propagated it and helped the Catholic kings to establish their hold over men's minds.

I'd illustrate it from my own experience, I'd tell my pupils my father was a stationmaster on a Branch line of the Great North of Scotland Railway. I thought that the Iron Road, the Railway, would last forever. In a few brief years the Branch lines have gone The bridges have been dismantled; the station buildings changed into bungalows...I didn't know it could happen in so short a time. Everything changes.

The important question I'd put to our pupils in Grenada is this. Some changes happen quietly, imperceptibly. Others violently, with much suffering. We'd read to them the chapter on Grenada in Gerald Brenan's classic, *The Fall of Spain*. It's the story of how he went to look for the grave of the Grenada poet, Lorca, shot in the Civil War...'Here you have what was once the flower of Grenada', said the man. 'Look well and you'll see the bullet holes.' And, in fact, nearly every skull was shattered.

I'd explain to the pupils the purpose of the exercise. A change is overdue in our society. Can they help it into being, but without violence?

That MacKenzie saw himself as still continuing to play an active role in Scottish education is apparent in the overall tone and drift of what he writes about Spain. There is a clear consciousness on his part that his mission to change the face of Scottish education is incomplete and as such his stance should be uncompromising and consistent with his firmly-held views on combating the perverse and abiding influence of the Establishment. This sensitivity that he felt with regard to the role he perceived as needing to be maintained in the face of the reactionary forces around him, comes out in an odd difference of opinion that he had with the Open University in the 1980s over their intention to award him an honorary degree for his services to education.

Initially, MacKenzie had accepted the Honorary Degree of MA that had been conferred upon him. But he discovered that the Open University differentiated between those who received Doctorates and those who got honourary MA degrees. As a result, he wrote a letter to the Open University refusing the degree, criticising its non-egalitatian honorary degree structure and said that the acceptance of the offer of an honorary MA would let down those who had supported his ideals and beliefs over the years,

MacKenzie said in his letter to the Open University, 'The traditional Universities are ultimately propagandists, responsible, like the Church and the Secondary school exams, for the idealogical structure on which our society is based, and I do not wish to be associated with the philosophy.' He had thought the Open University was different because he had been impressed by the energetic questioning encouraged by Open University programmes, the powerful support it had given his work at Summerhill and its 'consistent' support at a dark time for me personally'. His letter went on,

> If I now accepted this honour you have proposed, it would puzzle some of the people who have been persuaded to reconsider the structure of ideas and feelings on which our society is maintained and especially our students. They would be likely to think I didn't mean it really, it was only a philosophical concept that was for discussion but not application. They might infer that, having spent many years in conflict with an educational system that regards the majority of its pupils as second class citizens, I had finally capitulated, resigning myself to an acceptance of the traditional graded structure I had been speaking against.

The letter ends, 'I realise, of course, that a psychiatrist might say I am rationalising hurt vanity and that he could be right. But at the end of the day, we have to make our decision, however difficult.'

The conclusion of the latter strikingly illustrates MacKenzie's dilemma. The inference of his last statement is that had he been offered an Honorary Doctorate instead of an Honorary MA, he might well have been tempted to accept it, being as it was from an institution he admire and had supported him in the past. However the realisation that an honorary MA was, in a sense inferior to an Honorary Doctorate and revealed a non-egalitarian approach to the awarding of such degrees soured MacKenzie's perception of conferring such honours, particularly on such as himself and so he felt compelled to turn the offer down.

What is striking about this key episode in MacKenzie's later life is the vigour and the passion of his mind, especially in the pursuit of the truth. It is in this restless search for truth that the idea for a book on Scotland seems to have germinated. No doubt he had read at some time or other Edwin Muir's pioneering work, *Scottish Journey*, written in the 1930s, but even if he had not, there seems to be an inevitability about the emergence of this last book. He had been in the habit over the years of recording his impressions of all of the countries he had visited, but no country was dearer to him than Scotland and its identity as a nation. Its future in terms of what it would mean to the lives of the people that were members of that nation, particularly the young, concerned him deeply in his final years. As he says in his opening chapter, 'The book is searching for clues about where we Scots are as we near the end of the century.' It was a search for intelligibility, in which he ransacked his recollection of encounters through the century and through the length and breadth of the country, trying to extort connections from myths and museums, the face of the countryside – 'the solutions that people clutched at in the hope of salvation.'

Thus *A Search for Scotland* is a book to be taken at different levels – as a travel book in its own right that speaks about different areas of Scotland, seeing them through the eyes of an acute observer of the countryside; and on another level it is a book that interprets the ebb and flow of human affairs in a historical setting as MacKenzie had the knowledge and the imaginative power to link the present day with the past and so invest a place or a scene with an immediacy that makes ordinary places come to life in the context of their past history. Lastly, it is a book that allows MacKenzie to reflect on his personal search for truth in the gathering twilight of his life which makes the final chapters of the book, where he reaches his sombre conclusions on the future directions he thinks we as Scots should aim for, particularly compelling.

Nowhere in the book does he reveal more of himself and his upbringing than in the chapter on Grampian which, of course, was where he was born and brought up in the part known as Aberdeenshire. His vivid evocation of the life of ordinary folk in areas such as Aberdeenshire in those relatively far-off days makes a remarkable contribution to our understanding of such places and of their inhabitants at that time. His vision of those days also opens up for us glimpses into our own past that we can relate to as part of that common heritage. For example, as one of the many folk whose grandfathers ground out a meagre living as farm servants on the 'fairm touns' that were a distinctive feature of the North-East of Scotland right up to the middle of the 20th century, I can readily identify with MacKenzie's account of how submissive these forebears of mine were – towing the line politically – and how as a reaction to their miserable working conditions, cultivated 'rochness' as a virtue.

> Many farm workers were numbed and desensitised by poverrty and wet clothes and the prospect of trudging along an endless furrow. They retaliated by 'rochness'. 'Roch' is the English 'rough' but it means much more than that. The 'roch' farm servant pretended to be indifferent to hygiene. His hero was an Aberdeenshire farm servant whose feats of rochness projected

> him into a legendary figure called 'Roch Tam'. His fellow workers vied with each other to impress him with their 'roch' initiatives. They lived in a farm bothy or chaumer and for breakfast they made brose and supped it with milk which had been poured into bowl the previous night. A thick layer of cream topped the milk when the farm worker sat down to his breakfast. One morning a farm servant, to impress Tam, having poured boiling water into a kaap of oat-meal, took it outside and pissed on the ground as he stirred it. Tam gave a snort of contempt and decided to teach the youngster a lesson in the real meaning of 'rochness'. The legend has it that he took up his bowl of milk and instead of a spoon he used his cock to ease the cream off the side of the bowl.

It is from our knowledge of 'weel-kent' places that make up our own backyard that we can proceed to an understanding of who we are and what we are about, MacKenzie argues. We all seek for a model which will encompass our higgledy-piggledy perception of life; something which will make sense of our experience and give direction to our lives. And he strongly urges us to start with the richness of our own heritage – which is precisely what educators should be doing if they are to let the children in their care have some sort of insight into how their own lives in a school setting are linked up with the past. This was a feature of the approach that we tried to put into practice at Whitfield High when we started there. We invented a school badge made up from the coats of arms of the ancient landed families who lived in the hinterland of the council housing estate where the school was situated. We came up with three specific images easily identifiable to children – an Eagle, a Key and a Rose that were used at Assembly to reinforce their sense of what we were trying to achieve on their behalf at the school. 'The Eagle stands for putting a lot of energy into everything that you do and aiming high.' I would explain at Assembly. 'The Key is about acquiring knowledge, you'll get plenty of that! But the Rose...Ah, that's about the poetry of life, music and painting and physical grace; and it's about conservation, looking after the bees on the roof of the school (where we kept an apiary) and the puckle hens and racing pigeons we keep in the school quadrangle.' And to round it off I would refer to a Standing Stone, a huge, seven-foot high stone gate-post that we had found in a dump and had 'planted' in a bed of concrete on the grassy slope leading up to the school (known to the staff as the Wullie Stane' because of its phallic overtones) and tell them that it stood for the rock upon which the school was built. The school was actually built on a mass of whinstone that had to be blasted out to establish a foundation. And I would conclude, 'And that is how your own personal life should be established – on a firm and sure understanding of right and wrong!'

Years later former pupils have confessed to me more than once that they couldn't remember much about the school Assemblies, but they do recall the Eagle and the Rose and roughly what they stood for – and even the 'Wullie Stane', but still remain a wee bit puzzled as to why I had mentioned it in the first place!

As MacKenzie journeys south from Grampian, leaving Aberdeen behind, he seems, as he does elsewhere in the book, to respond with an acute sensibility to the atmosphere of the countryside, especially in the Mearns and Angus coastal plain. He seems able to project an astonishingly primeval echo of what the land he is travelling through means to him and to us as creatures of the 20th century. This is particularly well sustained in this memorable evocation of what could be described as a mystical and visionary account of the Mearns and Angus countryside.

> By daytime the broad coastal plain of the Mearns and Angus is a cheerful place. James Patrick's pictures record the sunshine and the red soil and tall beeches and sycamores of great girth. In winter the well-found farms, their buildings and dykes and bridges all of the red sandstone, look comfortable and reassuring. Birds brooding on a snow-covered roof above a crow-stepped gable, a blue and red farm-cart, the earth puckered into hollows and rising into platforms, give the landscapes the richness of a Dutch painting...
>
> On the coming on of night it can feel different. In late afternoon in November I came through Angus. The ploughed land, the stubble and bracken and withered beech leaves and the red canes of willow and raspberry shone in glorious sunshine and the burnt stubble was inky black. The light thickened and the trees stood out black against the residual glow in the south-west and took on a clarity of silhouetted detail. People made for their lighted houses and closed the doors – 'Now spurs the lated traveller to gain the timely inn', wrote Shakespeare. Maybe it was all a phantasy, but he knew what the traveller meant, this eerie sense that came from the drawing on of night......maybe all of us have, for example, an awareness of the past which comes to a dog snuffling in the undergrowth, an elusive sense of kinship...it may be race memory or extra-sensory perception or only a will o' the wisp making fun of us...we should be encouraging the young to open their minds and spirits to other ways of looking at life and the universe, to loosen their attachments to the received doctrines...Maybe it's civilisation's turn to be driven back and contained...we begin to have a sense of the temporariness of the technological invasion of the landscape, a feeling that the pylons, the car-transporters, the electric headlights gashing the darkness, the metal sentries listening on the hill-tops are on their way out...

Among my personal memories of my early years at Whitfield High was an annual excursion that I undertook with a senior colleague to the site of the Roman camp at Inchtuthil near Coupar Angus. Both of us at that time taught Classical Studies to a group of second year pupils. The school mini-bus took us to the site of the camp where, apart from the ditch and ramparts, there was very little to see of the original. But we had the good fortune to have the services of the local minister who was an antiquarian and an expert on the Roman site. He took us and the dozen or so pupils to his manse after inspecting the site and made the whole visit come alive for us by showing us a Roman sword that had been fished out of the River Tay nearby and a bath-tile upon which was imprinted the thumb of the Roman slave who had fashioned it.

By coincidence MacKenzie visited the same spot on his travels and characteristically adds a further dimension to the inner excitement that such a place inspires:

> Ten miles north of Perth where Strathmore and Strathtay meet, the Romans built the HQ for Agricola's legion, the only legionary HQ in Scotland. The camp at Inchtuthil is a vast extent of level ground that makes the sky look an immense dome, and it was well sited to house a legion and provide a servicing and repair depot. It was hygienic and comfortable and the baths had glass windows. There were six thousand soldiers here and a large civilian population...In modern times nearly a million nails were dug up at Inchtuthil, twelve tons of them...Three years after the Romans crucified the defeated Caledonians, orders were given to dismantle and evacuate all the forts north of the Forth–Clyde line. They buried the nails under six feet of earth. The top layer of nails rusted and fused and kept oxygen away from the rest, and when a present generation dug them up they were like new. If the spirits of the legion's centurions are free to haunt the terrain they briefly controlled, they would see an obliterated camp beside the river they knew, the mellow western sun shining on golden stubble, a white house back from the river protected by a rampart of bluish firs, and then at night the lights of Perth ten miles away, tincturing the low clouds blood-red like a soaked bandage...nothing much to show for all that endeavour, the drills, the forced marches, the killings, the terror, the road building, the pep talks, the food transports. And all those nails.

The theme of the Roman occupation of Scotland and the tracing of Scotland's early history finds its way into a lot of MacKenzie's writing as he moves from one area of Scotland to another. This feeling is especially strong in his journey through the Borders with which he had a special rapport, arising out of the six years he spent there in the late 1960s as a teacher of English at Galashiels Academy. He digs deep in this Borders chapter into the primeval history of the area, seeing it almost as an independent kingdom that because of its strategic importance geographically was the crucible where much of the future destiny of Scotland as a nation was determined. He sees this in terms of its importance as a frontier both in Roman and in Medieval times and as an area where decisions were made about the shape and character of the religion that would hold sway both here and in the rest of Scotland. He appreciates the deeply-felt traditions of the Border area celebrated every year in the riding of the marches, as at Selkirk, and he weaves into his travelogue the influential Borders writers that gave the place a habitation and a name: James Hogg, Walter Scott and John Buchan. And yet it is the Borders that remains with him as the most potent symbol of this part of Scotland.

> In the Borders more than anywhere else in the world I've had this sense of the nearness and continuity of the past. At a fort on Hadrian's wall, quarter of a circle's circumference has been traced in the stone floor by a heavy door which had dropped on its hinges. I expected to hear a decurion rap out a question, 'Haven't you got those hinges repaired yet?'
>
> It was only yesterday that the Romans and the reivers and the monks were here, as large as life, 'Home they've gone and ta'en their wages', and now we've stepped into their shoes. The nearness of the past makes us long to snuggle up to it closer still to commune with previous tenants and ask them what wisdom they distilled from the welter of their experience which, filtered down through the centuries, we could benefit from. The trouble is, we Scots are sentimentalists, suckers for romance. When reality is too much for us, and often it was, particularly in the century after Mary Stuart, we hark back to the sustaining romance,, the charismatic hero or heroine, the whisky bottle...potions, opiates, charms have never been far from us as we sought to see life in a mellower light.. We do genuinely want to know the truth about our past, how it was then; but we subsidise minstrels who tell us what we want to hear.

Perhaps, in retrospect MacKenzie might have been reassured somewhat by the developments that have taken place since in universities and schools to resurrect Scottish history as a proper study of our roots with an increasing emphasis nowadays on social and economic change in a perspective that allows us to peer more closely at the events in the past that have shaped our lives. There is also some thing portentous in the passionate condemnation that MacKenzie makes of the closing down of the Borders railway, exemplifying it as a classic sign of the callousness of central government towards the needs of the people living in remote areas:

> It was a major Scottish asset, this scenic route from Edinburgh to Carlisle. It was called the Waverley route, where you can see its track it looks like another derelict Roman road, a line of communication withdrawn. It was for a century a unifying force, integrating the community. The decision to shut it down was initiated by experts ignorant of all save the economic consequences of their deeds and often even of these. The rape of the Waverley line is one more argument for taking power out of the hands of the élite and giving it to the people.

MacKenzie is particularly dismissive of Edinburgh which he sees as 'a city of museums and gowns and institutions, a place of checks and balances that slows down Scottish life, coldly formal, East-windy, unfeeling'...and he reserves some of his most scathing remarks for the New Town which he declares as being 'built to the specifications of apartheid, the patterns of upstairs, downstairs...designed to build social division into Scottish society...Scotland's intellectuals mounting the impressive front steps allowed their attention to be directed away from the basement windows below stairs behind which the ranked menials...ettled to get an eyeful of daylight while they performed their appointed duties...servicing the gentry.' He goes on to argue that the long-held Scottish tradition of reverencing intellectual ability and intellectuals as such is not well-founded. His own bitter experiences over the years at the hands of the Establishment convinces him of their vulnerability to 'praise and flattery and the temptation of titles and degrees and readier to be put on the waiting lists for honours' than he would have credited. And he puts this misapprehension that Scots suffer from down to the errors propagated by Scottish education and a Scottish upbringing. A lengthy analysis of the origins and character of Scottish education follows – and his verdict is chilling, 'It (Scottish education) lacks reverence for the young, the Scottish dominie quells his pupils. The Educational Institute of Scotland, participating in a book on World Education, illustrated its contribution with a drawing of a Scottish classroom in which the whole class had their hands up in answer to a question. No drones or rebels in this hive of busy bees!' He is equally critical of the universities which he perceives as being too hidebound by their own esoteric ceremonies and traditions to face up squarely to what their actual role should be in forging new directions to accommodate the aspirations of the Scottish people at the end of the 20th century, the vast majority of whom could neither comprehend nor be the beneficiaries of a university education.

In the end, MacKenzie, whilst paying due regard to the obvious attractions of the city of Edinburgh as a place of grace and beauty architecturally and with regard to its setting, nonetheless classifies it as 'a failed capital':

> From the ground on a late afternoon, every tuft and hook and feather of the sycamores and elms and birches is silhouetted clearly against the opalescent sky above the setting sun, and in that sky there is just a touch of pink like the inside of a mussel shell. In the East the full moon rising is like a Chinese lantern suspended against a pale-blue sky. Over at the Forth a prodigal eclipse of orange lights traces out the form of the Road Bridge...In spite of its richness of history, its beauty, its Festival, Edinburgh is a failed capital. It has never managed to assimilate the disparate forces that struggle within it, into a homogeneous whole...neither the Heart of Midlothian nor the

> Hibernian football ground gives the impression that the city is as concerned about the comfort and entertainment of its citizens as it is about its Festival patrons. This is what happens in modern times to a city that is hung up on a heraldic view of its past and capitalises on it by presenting to tourists a culture unrelated to the lives of its citizens...football crowds are beyond the Fringe!

Sixteen years of MacKenzie's life were spent as a school teacher in Fife, first as Principal Teacher of English at Templehall School in Kirkcaldy and then latterly as Headteacher of Braehead School in Buckhaven. It was here, of course, both as a teacher and as a writer that MacKenzie did his most significant work and it is in the chapter entitled 'The Kingdom of Fife' that much of his affection for the land he came to know intimately during his sojourn in Fife is most lovingly described. His eye for landscape and for detail within that landscape is informed by a lifetime of accumulated knowledge about wild flowers, birds, and marine life on the margins of the shore. Here, for instance, he paints for us an unforgettable picture, firstly, of a Fifeshire winter scene and then a waterscape in spring- and summer-time at Kilconquhar Loch.

> Like glimpses of sunshine, glints of beautiful landscape raise the spirits and give balm to hurt minds in the same way as music or poetry...Fife has a rich seam of such resources. When there is snow on the high ground between the Beinn Inn and the Eden valley the West Lomond stands out like the dome of St Peter's above the level white rampart of rock which is broken by an ancient lava-flow or a recent rock fall. From the Fife end of the Tay Road Bridge, Dundee's sky-scrapers at night are transmuted by random lightning into fairy towers. On the southern frontier of the Kingdom on a winter night, low black rocks stand out of the moonlit sea, a dense constellation of orange, primrose lights identifies Edinburgh and the moon-light is filtered on to the earth through soft mops of cotton wool cloud.. Where the cotton wool has come apart, the blue darkness of the night sky shows through. There are other scatters of light on the Lothian coast. There is a sharp east wind and, unceasingly, the low roar of the sea.
>
> In spring on Kilconquhar Loch are great-crested grebes, polchards, shelduck, swans, moorhens, reed bunting, teal, black-headed gulls, coot. Every spring, we waited for the return of a corn-bunting to utter his dry and jangling notes from the same section of the telephone wires on the Hatton Road near the wood above Keil's den. All these things and April sunshine, escaping fitfully from white clouds, sometimes blinkbonny, are like tunes and poems and familiar faces that beguile our pilgrimage. In the summer, oyster catchers bury their orange-red beaks in the sand where the lug-worms are...At night there is an incessant excited piping of sea-birds on the crags above the sands. The water thumps through the rock corridors like the thumping of ship pistons. Green-brown and dark brown seaweed, bladder wrack and fern-green entermorphia weed is thrown up on to the sands...In the shore pools there are dahlia anemones and periwinkles holding on to seaweed and star fish.

However, it is in the context of MacKenzie's travels in the Central Highlands that we get to the crux of his vision that encompasses much of what he sees as the way forward for Scottish education. It is a vision that has at its heart a realisation that the physical dimensions of a school can never fully accommodate the needs and aspirations of the young. A school in and by itself could not provide the range of educational values nor the quality of life experience that would transform their lives through the insights and understanding gained from living and learning in an environment such as the Highlands in the company of other young people. Guided and given leadership by teaching staff and project leaders, young people could be taught through hill-walking, orienteering and other outdoor skills to look after themselves and to find clues to their own identity and their own strengths and weaknesses which would supplement or even replace outworn dependence on education at 'second-hand' through classroom instruction and the examination system.

MacKenzie had much earlier (as far back as the early 1960s) outlined his ideas on how such a revolution could take place:

> Much of the present curriculum will disappear. There will be more activity, less listening. Schools will get a chain of huts and bothies throughout the Highlands and based on some house or shooting lodge, will explore their own country, learning its geology, natural history and historical background so that they can take a lively and understanding part in shaping its future. They will build boats and sail them. They will take part in gliding, the classroom providing them with the background of the theory of flight, map~reading and weather study which they will use in the air...The school will be much more part of the community...The boys will work for a week in local industry so that they can know about the job, and that would be an advantage for both those who might one day work there, and those who will go on to University...There will be far more travel abroad, not just to see the sights, but so they can understand how you look at life if your father is a Burgundy wine-grower or a Swedish lumber man. The prefect system will be replaced by an elected school council where pupils of all abilities will meet and solve the problems of how a large number of people can get on well together.

Twenty-five years later in the final sentences of his discourse on the Central Highlands, MacKenzie reaffirms his faith in nurturing the eternal human spirit of enquiry.

> The same spirit which lures the young into asking questions about geology and Thomas Telford spills into human biology, economics. They discover that economics is not a gauzy, impalpable philosophy. The decline and fall of an industry can be comprehended, grasped in concrete terms, like the fall in the level of the water in Glen Roy...The young cast around for clues.

> They begin to see the museums as resource centres from which they take what they want and ignore the rest. The Fort William museum offers tangible assistance to those who want to get Highland history into perspective. A burial cist dug up in Morar, contains the bones of a pre-Celtic, Iberian of the time of Confucius and Darius. The Aluminium works is on the site of Montrose's victory at Inverlochy. The railway goods yard is beside where the Hanoverian fort stood, and in the museum the governor's room is reproduced. When he was tired of looking at the dispositions of his occupying forces, his eyes could rest on the fine china.

MacKenzie's sojourn in the islands of Harris and Lewis and later in Skye invoke in him a characteristic concern for the past wrongs exercised against the crofting communities by the land-owners in the 19th century who forced so many families off their crofts to replace them with flocks of sheep. And he enlarges on the tragedy of the banishing of the crofting communities in his later journey through the North of Scotland following in the wake of John Prebble's great book *The Highland Clearances* and visiting three of the valleys that Prebble describes: Strathcarron, Strathnaver and Kildonan.

> In Strathcarron, in this remote valley, people lived under an ancient dispensation, helping themselves to a deer from the hill, salmon from the river or a tree from the wood...I doubt if it was all that different from the rural Aberdeenshire of my childhood eighty years later. They enjoyed the summer and tholed the winter as they tholed the political system. The keenest arguments were about rival interpretations of what the Nazareth joiner had really meant; for example, did he want ministers to be chosen by the lairds or by the people themselves? Life had gone on like this in the Ukraine and Switzerland and Wessex, seed-time and harvest, for centuries people felt safe. Subterranean economic rumblings like thunder, were no great cause for concern. Then came the cataclysm sudden, inexplicable, inexorable.

MacKenzie reminds us that it is only comparatively recently in historical terms that we as a nation have come to acknowledge the barbarity perpetrated by the authorities in conspiring to make the Clearances take place the way they did. MacKenzie claims that in a sense 'the middle classes of Scotland were accessories to the extirpation of a people. The *Inverness Courier* editorialised on the Clearances in the way that the London tabloids editorialised on the Miners' Strike in the 1980s.'

There is a story here, MacKenzie argues, that has not fully become part of the kind of history that needs to be taught to our children in the schools. The key to an understanding of the land that we live in, particularly the remoter parts of Scotland, the islands, the west and North-West and the far North of Scotland, remain a closed book to much of the Scottish people. Little is known also about the origins or purpose of great stone circles like that at Callanish in Lewis, and yet in such mysteries lie the wonder we can still feel (like that of a child) in the face of something we don't fully understand for all of our technological sophistication. An assessment of our tenure of our native land and its islands is part of our heritage that all of us as Scots people have to come to terms with.

> We drove along the twisting road round the Lochs Grosebay, Stockinish and Fiodabay towards Roal at the south point of Harris. Water lilies were in flower. The ubiquitous seaweed, orange-gold, ornamented the rocks at water level. Seals swam and climbed on the rocks...a plover endured our inspection for a long time unfrightened. I'd no idea that peewits were so richly coloured. It had metallic-green wings, blacks, whites, purples, chestnuts, orange, more in keeping with the peacock than I had thought. Sitting in a van at a Harris roadside close to an unconcerned peewit we achieved vaguely a feeling of community with the animate and the inanimate furniture of our parcel of earth...fitful glints of sunshine, the changing clouds, the standing stones, the shiny black coal-like mussels and other shells, yarrow, heather, seals and cormorants and curlews. We entered into the spirit of St Francis, acknowledging as brothers and sisters all these things that, happened to synchronise with our tenancy of the Scottish islands and mainland.

MacKenzie's quest ends, as it began it, in the familiar territory of his Aberdeenshire roots. His final journey is a night-time one from Inverness to Aberdeen and inspires in him, as it did in his chapter on the Mearns and Angus, sense of mystery as the car headlights illuminate the darkness and invest what would have been an ordinary daylight scene with a magic quality associated with our preoccupation with artificial light, 'In a night journey we realise more forcefully the amount of earth energy that is prodigally consumed by our desire not to go to bed with the sun but to remain 'waukrif' until the early hours'. For MacKenzie the last stages of his journey under cover of darkness are given the right setting – had it been in daylight he always felt it as a come-down to emerge from the poetry of the hills into the prose of the more profitable farm-lands,as he says,'to auld claes and parritch'.

The conclusion of *A Search for Scotland* is very much an opportunity for MacKenzie to release for the last time in public his pent-up anger and frustration at what he sees, since the 1980s, as the steady disintegration of a dream of better times ahead, especially in Britain, into a nightmare scenario that in the final years of the century had overtaken the whole globe.

> Ecological disasters were perturbing humanity. Rain forests were wiped out, the Sahara was extending, droughts became more frequent, Canadian lakes and German forests died, industrial and nuclear pollution increased, fish, sheep, reindeer and people were poisoned, our food was doctored...Reagan followed in the Nixon tradition. In the Stock Exchange and Lloyd's of London and Guinness the walls of integrity came tumbling down. The Theatre and Sport brazened out their dependence on their beer and tobacco patrons...Governments were unabashed when caught out telling lies. London was Babylon and the writing was on its Palace of Westminster walls... obscurantism was creeping back like a fog into education and religion. The USA stopped some of its students from learning Darwin and evolution. The Pope revived ancient references to the Devil as a rebelling angel...that he was quoting from the Gospels didn't make his speech less reactionary... mountains of food and lakes of milk accumulated. The earth itself was sick...

MacKenzie lays the blame for our ills squarely on the misconception long ago in western civilisation that those in our society who had power have always had our best interests at heart. Instead, MacKenzie claims, 'From history and literature I learned that the folk I belonged to were of little account, sacrificial pawns in the noble chess-game. They have been tortured, diddled, bribed, laying down their lives for causes not their own, lauded for being docile, execrated as "the mob" when briefly they rebelled.' And he then identifies the school system as one of the agencies through which the ruling élite continues to exercise its control over us and asks in terms of this appalling picture of pollution, political corruption, manipulation and regression, 'Where do we go from here?'

In trying to answer this question MacKenzie cites the example of how a small nation, the Boers of South Africa,(whom he met while serving in the RAF during the War) and were a small threatened group, identified with the Children of Israel and made the Jewish holy book their own. It was very much in the same spirit that the Scottish Covenanters 300 years ago, searching the Scriptures, were sustained by the same metaphor of life as that of the Jews in the Sinai desert who made bargains with their god which they called Covenants. So when the Voortrekkers came to a place in the Orange Free State where they got supplies of wheat, they called it 'Bethlehem', knowing that Bethlehem means 'the place of bread'. But just as the Boers drifted into a situation where they became a ruling minority and used their religion as a symbol of their distinctiveness and ultimately their superiority over the Blacks, so in Scotland, the impact of cultural values mainly derived from our English neighbours (a sort of élitism and imperialism cultivated by the English Public School tradition) has created an apartheid here – the privileged rulers and the majority who work for them. And he comes to a bitter conclusion, 'After all these years in Scottish education I have become aware that the schools are not on our side. They are the agencies of the rulers, they bring us up to do what we are told, and not to speak back, to learn our lessons and pass our exams. Above all, not to ask questions.'

MacKenzie now sees Capitalism as a spent force, 'unable to cope with our accumulating distresses.' And in an outpouring of righteous anger at what he sees as the scourge of failed Capitalist policies, he declares:

> We weren't born to cheat and be cheated, to be worried, to be unemployed, to be powerless to make changes in our society, to be catalogued in a computer, to be mugged by youngsters who are themselves drugged, to be alienated from our children, to be absorbed in the accumulating of material goods, to join a queue for a hospital bed, be stampeded down a steep place into extermination.

He doubts the ability of the recognised political parties to put our society to rights, for he sees it as inevitable that, despite the courage and idealism of the people in such movements, once they are established in power, they make of themselves an élite governed by an élite. So he falls back on the need to educate the critical understanding of every single person – which called for a revolution in child-rearing. He claims that our rejection of the majority of our young people in the schools has turned many to violence, drugs and suicide – 'we adults should confess out obtuseness and give them the most potent of cures, our affection.'

In the end, MacKenzie argues, we have to put our faith in young people. They have a tenderness towards all natural life and are closer than we are to understanding the terms on which we will be permitted to abide on the earth. MacKenzie is not optimistic; he senses in Scotland a feeling of powerlessness in the face of rampant money-making.

But MacKenzie, at the last, is unable to dispense with his own unshakeable belief in the emergence of truth, in the survival of enough residual gumption among ordinary people (not the politicians, businessmen, civil servants, lawyers, trade unionists, churchmen or academics) to start taking over the running of their own communities by themselves. By inference 'this chance' that we might avoid 'oblivion', would seem still to lie in our schools and in our education system being overhauled to accommodate the lesson that shines through all of MacKenzie's books and all that he stood for during his life.

> And indeed this will be the whole emphasis of the school...no longer on learning, but learning to live. In a civilisation which is being torn by new strains, one of the most important things we can do for our pupils is to help them to grow in understanding. It is an old, old idea that somehow we have strayed away from, 'Though I understand all mysteries, and all knowledge, and have not charity, am nothing.'

CHAPTER THIRTEEN

The Legacy of R.F. MacKenzie

The final years of MacKenzie's life centred as much as they ever did on his mission to communicate, as intensively and extensively as he could, his vision of the need for change in education. The knowledge that his health was failing during the course of 1986 when stomach cancer was diagnosed and had to be operated on, only acted as a spur for him to drive himself that bit more to complete the book *A Search for Scotland* that he had come to acknowledge as his last coherent attempt on a significant scale to pass on to posterity his deeply felt concerns for the future of his beloved native land. In the secluded setting of West Cults farmhouse, he feverishly put together during these last, two years of his life his final testament. This has as its central crux the fusion of his encyclopaedic knowledge and understanding of Scotland with his vision of what lay in store for it in the shadow of the new millennium. This urgency he felt all the more keenly, as he watched, with growing apprehension, the relentless drive towards unbridled materialism take hold of the country as a whole under the influence of the Thatcher government in London. The book, set as it is within Scotland, is as much a declaration of intent on his part in political and cultural terms that Scotland has to go its own way if it is to find its own salvation as it is a travelogue about Scotland in simple geographical terms. The emergence of a Scottish Parliament in the early years of the new millennium makes the reading of *A Search for Scotland* and the sentiments of its author of considerable significance in trying to assess what relevance MacKenzie's views and sense of vision still have for us as we near the turn-of the century.

Diana, in an interview for the Aberdeen *Leopard* magazine, not long after her husband's death said, 'He got more and more radical the older he got.' Evidence of this radicalism is clearly reflected in his final diatribe in *A Search for Scotland* against what he sees as the stifling materialism of the Thatcher government in the 1980s. It is also evident in his open support for the Miners' Strike in 1984–85 when he defended the strike in the correspondence columns of *The Scotsman* and spoke at meetings in Aberdeen in support of them. He is identified as one of a number of radicals in the Scottish tradition of radicalism In James D. Young's book *The Very Bastards of Creation* published in 1997, Young identifies A.S Neill along with Mackenzie as radicals who strove in their work to support the promulgation of what Young describes as the 'Democratic Intellect', as a way of combating the stultifying effects of traditional Scottish education. Young saw MacKenzie as being closely associated in spirit with the likes of John Maclean and Jimmy Maxton and members of the Scottish Teachers Socialist Society. Diana MacKenzie collaborated with Young in regard to providing him with information for the chapter in his book dealing with Neill and MacKenzie's place in the history of Scottish radicalism. MacKenzie had been a close friend of Young since the 1960s when Young had taught for a short time as an English and History teacher at Braehead. Young also makes reference in his chapter on Mackenzie to another manuscript for a book that MacKenzie intended for publication, called *Curriculum for a Cultural Revolution*. Although, according to Young, MacKenzie had completed the manuscript for publication by 1974, his publishers, Collins, refused it.

The last significant published work of MacKenzie that exists dates from 1987, the year of his death – an essay on education in Scotland that formed part of the programme for 'Jotters', a production by the Wildcat Theatre Company which came to Aberdeen Arts Centre in March 1987. In the concluding remarks of the essay, MacKenzie memorably puts the case for an enlightened view of the human personality:

The view insists on the worth and infinite potential of every human being.

> It's an ancient idea that survives in our minds in spite of Aristocrats' and capitalist control over our thoughts. Three thousand years ago in Jerusalem a temple singer expressed it in the speech pattern of his time, and more simply than I have done, 'ye are gods, and all of you are children of the most high.' He said, 'All of you, ye are gods: and all of you are children of the most high.'

The charismatic nature of MacKenzie's personality, the deep and lasting impact that he had upon the lives of many of the people he encountered during his life-time, pupils as well as teachers, should not be underestimated in trying to assess his importance as an inspirational figure. The central core of adherents that gave him support at Summerhill Academy during his battle with rebellious staff and the local authority still revere him as much as they did 25 years ago. They believe he has had a major impact not just on their lives and on how they have conducted their careers, but in regard to their innermost thoughts and beliefs. For instance, Jenny Kinnon, who is the Head teacher of a school for pupils with behavioural and emotional difficulties, says of MacKenzie with whom she was a Guidance teacher 25 years ago, 'Perhaps some of our decisions (about how we run the school) would have saddened R.F.; others, I know he would have encouraged. What I do know is that I have thought of him and he has influenced each and every one of the decisions I personally have had to make...Yes, he certainly was my mentor and still is.'

In a sense, this group of adherents that still keeps in touch with one another, has something about it of a band of disciples, sharing even after the passage of many years an inner feeling of spiritual well-being arising out of MacKenzie's visionary powers and his profound gentleness and humanity as a human being.

As a testament of the sort of impact he had on the lives of people he had encountered in the Summerhill years, a reunion of staff and pupils organised mainly by former pupil, Rosalie Martin, took place at an Aberdeen hotel on 1 November 1986. To this reunion there came about 200 former pupils and about 20 former staff with MacKenzie as the guest of honour. He was very ill at the time, and had to go into hospital not long afterwards for an operation. Nevertheless, Rosalie Martin and her friends made MacKenzie forget at least temporarily the pain he was suffering in the warmth of their reception for him. (Diana, who was also there, describes the feeling that met him as 'pure love'.) They spoke of how in bringing up their own children, they had been influenced by MacKenzie's concern that young children needed to be valued and cherished. He was presented with a writing set inscribed with his name and the words 'Lang may your lum reek!' It was the last time that Rosalie Martin saw him alive. She concludes in the letter she wrote to me recalling her memories of MacKenzie, 'When Bob died, I received a phone-call from the press telling me, and also asking if I would like to say a few words for the story in the paper. I had nothing to say to them, and asked if they would print one of Bob's favourite quotes. It was a Ghandi quote: "The thing I fear most is the hard heartedness of the educated." '

The operation that MacKenzie had to undergo towards the end of 1986 did enable him to recover some of his strength so that during the early part of 1987 he was able to resume where he had left off in his efforts to complete *A Search for Scotland* manuscript. In the wider world of politics he must have felt his worst fears confirmed at the growing strength in the country as a whole of the cult of consumerism manifested perhaps in its worst form in the 'yuppie' culture of the London Stock Market. Though never a paid-up member of a political party, the re-election in 1987 of yet another Conservative government led by Margaret Thatcher made him despair, as a life-long radical with strong socialist sympathies, of the ability of the Labour Party to carry out in practical terms the very things for which it was founded in the first place. Too often, Labour politicians had failed, when in power, to fulfil their obligations towards delivering a society that, in so far as education was concerned, provided opportunities for individual self-fulfilment which were espoused most cogently in the Advisory Report on Education in 1947.

During that last summer at Cults, as he put the finishing touches to the manuscript that was to become *A Search for Scotland*, he must have had conflicting emotions – there was the growing satisfaction that he would be able, despite his illness, to complete his book; against that, he was no longer physically able to cultivate the substantial area of ground that went along with his ownership of the farmhouse at West Cults. Since the late 1960s when he and the family had come to live in the farmhouse, he had taken enormous pleasure in making full use of the garden area to grow vegetables, utilising the vast quantities of pig dung that he and the boys had found in the outhouses to grow crops of exceptionally large potatoes. Nonetheless, he had the constant pleasure of welcoming close friends to the house. Bob Munro, who had taught at Summerhill in the early 1970s before going on to Stirling University and then to California where he eventually became a Headteacher, recalls going for a meal to Cults in August 1987 along with some other friends of MacKenzie. He remembers that MacKenzie was still working on *A Search for Scotland* and that at meal-time MacKenzie was on a special diet because of his illness. No mention, however, was made of MacKenzie's medical condition. Characteristically, he refused to accept it. To the end MacKenzie just got on with the work he had to do; which was what happened when he went into hospital for the last time in the autumn of 1987. The cancer was found to be inoperable and he and his family knew it was only a matter of time before the end would come. At his own request, he was brought back to the farmhouse in November of that year to be with his family. He died peacefully on 21 December just as the formal announcement was made that Summerhill Academy was to be phased out as a school.

MacKenzie's body was laid out in the front parlour in the traditional fashion before removal to the crematorium just outside Aberdeen. Douglas Lister, who had been his school chaplain at Braehead and who was a friend of the family, phoned to ask if he could come and be in attendance at the funeral which Diana and the family had agreed should be private – family members only. Douglas Lister's request was agreed to, but on the understanding that there was to be no sermonising at the crematorium service. Neil, his elder son, however read some extracts from his father's book, *State School*, relating to his school trip to the island of Rhum with pupils from Braehead. Here is part of what Neil read out to the small gathering as a way of commemorating his Dad's memory in a setting that his Dad would have thoroughly enjoyed:

> We strolled along the wide Kinloch Glen, slaking our thirst from time to time in an ice-cold burn. Then a zoologist in a Land Rover stopped and we piled in and he ran us three miles north through the terminal moraines of Kilmory Glen till we reached the north coast of Kilmory. From the wonderful silver sands we bathed and came near to an inquisitive seal swimming inshore. Then I strolled along the east shore of the bay and looking over the western shoulder of Rhum saw, close at hand, the islands of Canna and Sanday. When I look back on it now I remember it as one of the most peaceful, happy days of my life. There were just the sea and the sky and the islands, and the much contorted red rock enclosing the sands, and the inquisitive seal. No pressures.

Neil recalls that it was a fine, crisp, sunny, December day when the funeral cortège moved off from the farmhouse and MacKenzie made his last journey up the narrow twisting path from the banks of the River Dee on to the North Deeside Road and from there to the crematorium just outside Aberdeen on the road to Alford, almost within sighting distance of Bennachie, the hill that he had often contemplated from afar as a child in his native Garioch. It was a quiet and dignified end.

As Vivienne Forrest remarks in her tribute to MacKenzie in the Aberdeen *Leopard* magazine in February 1998, although his death was terribly mourned by his friends, his passing was 'unremarked by all save the more discerning of the press.' Indeed, apart from a temporary revival of interest two years later in 1989 when *A Search for Scotland*, was published, MacKenzie very quickly drifted out of the public consciousness. When, five years later, I contacted Alasdair, his younger son, with a view to writing a biography about him, he told me that the family had the impression that his father had been all but forgotten about as a public figure.

My own interest in MacKenzie stemmed not just from my fond memories of the three dramatic years I had spent with him as his Principal Teacher of English at Summerhill, but with my own career as Headteacher newly over, the debt I recognised I now owed him for much of the success I had as a teacher. The realisation that no-one had written an official biography of a man I considered to be one of the most influential educationists of our time led to my getting in touch, through

Alasdair, with Diana, his widow, who readily gave me access to his papers. Once I had seen the wealth of material he had left, including diaries and journals covering much of his earlier life, I realised that there was a task needing to be done – not just by way of repaying a debt but to restore to a great man a measure of the esteem he is due for a life spent in the service of humanity.

Published articles on MacKenzie in the ten years since his death have been few and far between. However, David Gordon did a valuable paper for the *Scottish Educational Review* in 1988 that, under the title of 'The Legacy of R.F. MacKenzie', argues that MacKenzie's critique of the Scottish educational system was the most coherent and valuable aspect of his work that has relevance for the educationist of today.

In coming to this conclusion, Gordon rightly emphasises the degree to which MacKenzie can be defined as much a social reformer as an educational one, though, in Gordon's view, MacKenzie expected too much of schools by exaggerating their potential as agents of social reform. However, he goes on to argue that MacKenzie's lasting relevance has at its core his criticism that in educational and political terms the way we educate our children is inimical to the welfare of the children for whom it is designed. Within that overall criticism, Gordon identifies four strands in MacKenzie's critique of Scottish education that have direct relevance to any assessment we are to make of MacKenzie's stature as an educational thinker.

The first of these strands can be taken under the heading of 'Education for Docility'. This means, in effect, that in his view the Establishment through the agency of the school system creates a climate in a school which stultifies the imagination of children, makes them unwilling and unlikely to question the *status quo* and leads inevitably to a perpetuation of all of the values that the Establishment wants to nurture in order to preserve the interests of the few, (the élite) at the expense of the many (the population at large). As Gordon puts it, 'An Establishment regenerates itself through the educational system, and the few are chosen by certification – the reward for conforming.'

Secondly, MacKenzie identifies what may be called 'The Loveless School' as having a traumatic effect on the emotional development of children. Even though corporal punishment has gone, nevertheless, in MacKenzie's view, schools still continue to place a premium upon control and in doing so, do not permit the flowering of the individual pupil's unique gift. Streaming, for example, brings about an insidious labelling of children. He deplores such élitism and the criteria upon which it is based. Not to treat each child as equal and unique is to lack love and respect, and to lack love and respect is to be brutal. Guidance systems may have gone some way towards ameliorating the brutality of the system, MacKenzie would argue, but he would view the introduction of guidance systems as largely cosmetic because they are there because of deficiencies in the system; and the deficiencies in the system have not disappeared because they are there.

The third strand relates to his criticism of the school curriculum. Although the curriculum has become more relevant and more skills-based, MacKenzie would still argue strongly that teachers too often refer to subjects as though they were the ends and not the means. As Gordon puts it, 'Resistance to whole-school activities and developments is strong and defending the subject has long become a conditioned reflex...Despite Social and Vocational Skills and other new, multi-disciplinary "subjects", the old barriers seem depressingly intact.'

MacKenzie's most radical proposal, of course, was to scrap the exam system. Schools are élitist, MacKenzie argues, because they are judged by their exam results. With the introduction of Exam League Tables in the early 1990s it is hard to deny that MacKenzie's assertion still holds good. Nowadays, more than ever, a 'good' school is one with high academic success. But MacKenzie also objects to exams because they measure only what is easily measured and the real values of education, since they are difficult to assess, are not subscribed importance in the curriculum. As MacKenzie puts it, 'You cannot put a percentage on human beings, or evaluate how much they got out of a Rachmaninov concerto, or building or sailing a boat.' Although MacKenzie does not examine the implications for other institutions of scrapping the exam system, he does clearly see it as the most powerful tool in the hands of the establishment. Not only does it inhibit enquiry, it inspires boredom; it impedes experiment and progress; it enslaves the curriculum; it ignores real values; it measures useless information; it ignores character.

Much of Gordon's analysis of what is of lasting value in MacKenzie's critique of the Scottish Education system can, therefore, still be seen as applicable to education now and as it might develop into the next century. Clearly, MacKenzie expected too much of the schools that they could provide the degree of social and educational reform that he was looking for. He is right to suggest that in the past schools have never been the agents of social reform; they have acted instead as agencies which have inhibited change. However, in the light of the emergence of a Scottish Parliament, MacKenzie's more extravagant claims for a new Scottish society and a vast regeneration of Scottish culture (something less than credible in 1988 when Gordon wrote his article), now seems far from impossible. On the other hand, I would agree with Gordon in his conclusion that MacKenzie 'does not sufficiently stress the fact that it is his fellow teachers who provide the main obstacle to the advance of the kind of education he advocates.' The evidence of my own experience as a Headteacher would lead me to concur with the view that the teaching profession needs to look at itself as perhaps one of the greatest stumbling blocks to a more enlightened overview of what sort of education we need to aim for in the future that enshrines the ideals MacKenzie was advocating for our children.

MacKenzie's legacy has been reflected most potently in the astonishing debate that has surrounded the whole direction that education has been taking in the late 1990s under the pressures exercised upon it by the demands of what Neil Postman, Professor of Communication Arts and Sciences at New York University, calls 'the god of economic utility'. This tells the young what they are to do for a living and that therefore the main purpose of learning is to prepare them for entry into economic life. This is closely related to the 'great god of technology' which has led to both the President of the USA, and the new UK Prime Minister, announcing that the goal of education in the 21st century is to have a lap-top computer on every student's desk. Postman argues, and MacKenzie would agree with him, that for education to have any meaning to those for whom it is intended, it must have 'significant gods to serve', and he suggests 'narratives' that would give point to education.

One he entitles 'the Good Space-ship Earth' which makes clear the inter-dependence of human beings and their need for solidarity. 'This is an idea whose time has come', Postman continues. 'It is a story of interdependence and global co-operation...a story that depicts waste and indifference as evil, that requires a vision of the future and a commitment to the present.' In the same way, Postman and MacKenzie seem to be on the same wavelength in another possible narrative that he postulates, 'The Story of the Fallen Angel'. This would operate on the principle that human beings make mistakes. We would have a curriculum that does not see knowledge as a fixed commodity, but as an on-going struggle to overcome human error. Such a curriculum would have as its purpose to cure ourselves of the belief in absolute knowledge, and to promote the idea that we are dangerous to ourselves and others when we aspire to the knowledge of gods.

The general sweep of Postman's ideas seems to chime in with one of MacKenzie's main criticisms of conventional education that it lacked coherence in being too subject-based and had no rationale that linked it into a grand design that would fire the imagination (like the philosophy that that underpinned the Inverlair project) and free children from the rigidity of a curriculum dominated by the need for exams. As Postman puts it, 'We need to begin and to sustain a conversation about the metaphysical basis of schooling, and we must, in the end, find narratives that are worthy of such an expensive and time-consuming enterprise.'

The strange alchemy that was brought about by the fact that both A.S. Neill and MacKenzie were the Heads of two schools that bore the same name – Summerhill – each school strongly associated with the radicalism that both men stood for, has continued to the present day. Mackenzie's Summerhill became the victim of the market philosophy of the Thatcher government when it was phased out in the late 1980s. More recently (in October 1997) a similar fate seemed about to befall Neill's Summerhill because, in its case, of its standards of literacy not being high enough.

The threat of closure of an institution that MacKenzie himself had great reverence for because of its founder's unstinting support for child-centred education, enraged what appears to be a growing force of liberally-minded people who are becoming more and more alarmed by the government's obsession of promoting conformity at the expense of experiment and innovation. Linda Grant, a columnist in the Guardian, took up the case for the threat of closure to Neill's Summerhill in a breath-taking exposé of the more sinister aspects of the new Labour government's preoccupation with a mechanistic approach to education:

> The threatened closure of Summerhill exposes the dark heart of current education policy...Labour has unquestionably inherited and propelled forward a Thatcherite model of education which is essentially Stalinist and mechanistic, in which children exist only to service the labour market. It is absolutely correct that parents in all classes are desperate to secure their children's place in the future and know that without qualifications they are unlikely to have that place. But the insistence on grades and academic measurements and League Tables as the only indication of effectiveness of teaching – the language of hit-squads and failure – have created an ethos in which children as individuals are lost.
>
> If David Blunkett's (the Education Secretary) men and women from the Ministry succeed in closing down Summerhill, what will have triumphed is the homogenisation of education. It would be melodramatic to describe a Metropolis-style factory nightmare of children poured into a funnel and emerging at the other end in neat identical rows on a conveyer belt, but something is badly wrong if in a small corner of the system, Summerhill can't be allowed to exist. Just as important is what the Summerhill ethos represents. More and more parents are finding out that League Tables aren't everything and are beginning to demand schools which offer something more rounded. How do you measure the means by which an unhappy, lonely child makes friends or a nervous one finds confidence?

> When it is a beautiful day, the younger children won't be in class, Zoe Redhead, (the late A.S. Neill's wife who now runs Summerhill) says: 'We can't compete if something exciting is happening in the woods.' Summerhill won't do for most children, but all of us grow up into adults for whom there is more to life than work and whose thoughts are often turned to that excitement beyond the office or the shop or factory; the place where we neither struggle, nor learn, but play. Beyond League Tables there will always be something unknown and exciting in the woods and no humane system will try to pretend there isn't.

MacKenzie would have subscribed enthusiastically to that article by Linda Grant in its condemnation of the present government's drive towards arid testing as the sole criterion of educational success and in its passionate defence of alternative approaches to education. That there should be a reaction to the present-day obsession for an educational policy driven only by economic and technological necessity, is certainly desirable, but by no means inevitable. A reconsideration of the life and work of R.F. MacKenzie might be a big step in the right direction as would research into the sort of 'narratives' that Professor Postman advocates, towards transforming the way we formulate our education policies into more positive directions or that is precisely the sort of thing MacKenzie would be advocating if he were alive today – the rejection of what has become a remorselessly mechanistic system of education for one that is humane and child-centred and not distorted by the need to pass exams. Figures other than MacKenzie need to make their voices heard – particularly in the teaching profession – if the present stalemate and feeling of malaise that surrounds education like a black cloud is to be dispersed.

It was very much along the same lines that Peter Preston, former Editor of *The Guardian* wrote movingly about MacKenzie in November 1996, reflecting sadly at the commotion that was taking place in the UK at the time about the Ridings School in Halifax which had been condemned publicly for its poor standards of achievement and discipline. Preston rightly sees Mackenzie as the sort of man who would not have allowed children to be publicly condemned in this way. The heading of Preston's article says as much: 'Teacher who never failed his children.'

> MacKenzie started from the children, not the system. He gathered round him a staff of like minds which fizzed with purpose, which sought – from a grey, impoverished town of a catchment area – to turn out thinking, rounded human beings. They didn't stream or categorise at Braehead. They put uncounted hours into finding where a kid came from and what he or she could do that would build self-esteem and wider horizons. It was avowedly experimental. That's why it was shut down. The state sector couldn't abide experiment...It was mission impossible.

> And yet, in the deepest sense, Braehead School was a moral school. It didn't stick a mission statement on the wall hailing 'Loyalty, Trust and Confidence' or 'Respect for the Dignity of People'. It lived these things, seeking to replace the decline of Christian underpinning (then as now)...by the community of pupils and teachers together. Old Labour lowered the boom. New Labour would probably not raise it in the first place.
>
> We ought, I think, to be clear about current panic. Bob MacKenzie would manage a melancholy smile. Schools in his bitter experience didn't mould society. The expectations of society moulded schools...To remember MacKenzie now, to pluck him from the mists of forgetfulness, is really to establish the basic conundrum. His way – his separate way – was no panacea for a country short of technologists or mathematicians. But in his life, he showed that there was also a choice and a balance. Authority, even then invoking past modes, decreed that there could be no choice, no deviation...he was always more interested in the future of society than in ignorant reconstruction of fusty memories.
>
> He was a modern, moral man.

And it is as a man that MacKenzie will be remembered; a man who had the vision to see beyond the everyday problems that assail us during our earthly pilgrimage; and in so far as he was also a prophet, he had that special capacity to inspire us mentally and spiritually and let us have rare glimpses of a world where human beings would at last begin to use education as a means of enriching the lives of children, making them truly valued and cherished.

He was indeed a 'man before his time'; but his time, as Peter Preston suggests, is as much about now as it is do with the past or the future; and, in the same way, his message is timeless in its truth and in its wisdom.

Bibliography

Outline of History, by H.G. Wells.

Road Fortune, by Hunter Diack and R.F. MacKenzie. MacMillan, 1935.

Secondary Education: A Report of the Advisory Council on Education in Scotland. HMSO, 1947.

A Question of Living, by R.F. MacKenzie. Collins, 1963.

Escape from the Classroom, by R.F. MacKenzie. Collins 1965.

The Sins of the Children, by R.F. MacKenzie. Collins, 1967.

State School, by R.F. MacKenzie. Penguin, 1970.

The Unbowed Head, by R.F. MacKenzie. Edinburgh University Press, 1976.

A Search for Scotland, by R.F. MacKenzie. Collins,1989.

The Life and Times of Logie School, edited by Peter A. Murphy. Danscot Print Ltd, Perth, 1976.

Scottish Educational Review, May 1988 edition. Scottish Academic Press.

The Last Hundred, by Hamish Brown. Mainstream, 1995.

The Very Bastards of Creation, by James D. Young. Clydeside Press, 1997.

Index